SHAYKH HUSAYN ANSARIAN

The Islamic Family Structure

AL-BURĀQ
Heighten The Mind

First edition

This book was professionally typeset by al-Burāq.
Find out more at al-Buraq.org

Contents

One

Introduction

Introduction by the theologian, great researcher and commentator on Nahj ul-Balaghah: the erudite Professor Muhammad Taqy Jafary:

m, 2In the Name of Allah the Exalted

"Praise be to Allah" and Peace be upon our Master and Prophet Muhammad and pious, pure and infallible huosehold. It is obvious that the importance of establishing a family and its related means and essentials in the sacred religion of Islam is evident enough with no need of proofs. It is this very important status of the family that Allah (Great be His glory) in the Qur'an; the Impeccable Imams or Muslim leaders in their practices and policies; and the sages, authoritative as well as unbiased commentators have all presented the final comments and most constructive subjects on the matter of THE ISLAMIC FAMILY STRUCTURE.

Today what has destroyed the fundamental pillars of life itself is emergence of disorder in the sacred family system ignoring its necessary principles and values. Thus the present era deserves to be named "THE ERA OF MAN'S ALIENATION FROM MAN" which has resulted in the incurable disease of "MAN'S ESTRANGEMENT FROM HIMSELF". Without having the family structure reformed, it is quite irrelevant and inappropriate to expect a healthy society and a community capable of enjoying a reasonable social life. This book entitled "THE ISLAMIC FAMILY STRUCTURE" authored by Mr. Hujjatul-Islam Wal-Muslimeen Hajj Sheik Ansarian (May God support him) is one of the few helpful and remarkable books I have seen about the Islamic family structure. I have read a reasonable portion of the book and must state that this work reflects research and arrangement of materials presented in such a way that it proves to be a beneficial publication for all social strata.

Among the characteristics one may mention is its diligent researching of sources; proper interpretation of the matter; accurate reference and source citation; the adequate, aesthetic expressions used to attain what the author has had in mind; and the author's faith and sincerity regarding his various researches. Therefore, the study of this book and research on its various subjects will be very helpful and instructive for those seeking the truth concerning the rules and matters of the Islamic family structure. I beg God the Almighty for the ever-increasing success of the book's honorable author Mr. Hujjatul-Islam Wal-Muslimeen Ansarian.

Muhammad Taqy Jafary Farvardin 21, 1376 (Iranian calendar)
April 1997 A.D.

Two

Author's Preface

⁓ ✦◉✦ ⁓

"In the Name of Allah, the Beneficent, the Merciful."

I started a series of lectures on the subject of the Islamic family structure in 1984, since a need for this topic was felt in the society. I conducted these lectures on various occasions such as Muharram, Safar and the Holy month of Ramazan and my lectures were based on the verses from the Holy Qur'an and traditions from authentic sources of traditions (Hadith).

These lectures were warmly welcomed by the people, especially by the youth, and this unprecedented attendance was due to nothing but a display of God's blessing and kindness Who is always supporting the Islamic religious orders. The video and cassette tapes of those lectures which are about thirty in number were soon distributed all over the country, and the contents of the lectures were published in one of Tehran's evening papers and were distributed for the public. As expected, the lectures had a reasonable effect upon families since they reflected the contents of the Holy

Qur'an and the knowledge of the Household of the Prophet (pbuh)[1] which are in line with man's nature and fulfill all his spiritual and material needs.

Concerned friends and religious brothers suggested several times that I convert these lectures into a book so that they could be better used by the heroic people of Iran. However, the writing of a twelve-volume series on the Islamic Mysticism taking seven years; and the interpretation as well as description of Sahifeh-e-Sajjadiyeh taking five years and other notes together with journal articles left me no time to undertake the task.

Another portion of my time was devoted to traveling to various parts of the country for preaching, but my friends still kept on insisting.

Mr. Reza Kalhur owns a publishing house. His brother is a young, enthusiastic and virtuous believer and is working in the religious schools in Qum where I am a student.. He came to Tehran on the anniversary of the martyrdom of Fatimah Zahra (Pbuh)Islam's highly respectable Lady who is herself the best model for a wife and a mother in Islam and asked me for permission to note down the lectures from tape and to have them published[2]. Since I found that offer to be the same as my own long old wish and that of my friends, I asked him to do so because I still was confronted with a shortage of time. Thirty tapes were taken down by Mr. Kalhur. Thanks to his careful attention, all the traditions in the lectures were carefully documented with proper reference citations. They gave me their notes which were taken down right from the tapes. While reviewing the tapes I realized it was necessary to eliminate, rewrite or change some of the sentences. The book in hand is the result of more than two months of rewriting. It would have been easier to write a book from scratch than to rewrite notes taken down from lecture tapes. The beauties of this book lie in the verses of the Holy Qur'an, the traditions and accounts of the lives of God's saints; and its ugliness is due to my pen.

---

[1] Pbuh is used throughout the book to denote peace be upon him or her or them. When used for the prophet, his Household is included. When used for others, it only refers to that person.

[2] Translation note: This is mentioned by the respectable author as an act of humbleness.

Please inform me of any errors by writing to Um-Abiha Publishers at P.O.Box 37185-913, Qum, I.R.I. It is hoped that this book will be helpful for families, especially for young men and women who have just married or intend to marry, and it can be instrumental in aligning their family structure with God's will so that they can succeed in this life and in the Hereafter. These lectures were conducted in a way which included life from its beginning to the end. Thirty of these lectures were selected whose titles appear in the table of contents. You could present this book as a gift to a newly-wed couple instead of flowers, which will fade away in a few hours, resulting in God's blessings in their life and possibly a source of great heavenly rewards for you.

Mr. Husayn Ansarian

Three

Translators' Forward

"In the Name of Allah, the Beneficent, the Merciful."

First of all we thank God for granting us the opportunity to undertake and complete such a tremendous task. Next we wish to express our most sincere gratitude of Mr. A. Namaee for editing parts of the book and providing us with many useful suggestions, and for his efforts to get this work through the many phases it must. We also wish to thank Mr. A. Tavakoli for reviewing some of the book, and for giving us many useful suggestions. We also like to thank Mr. Mehdi Peiravi and H. Motakef for their help in preparing parts of the typed manuscript.

Ms. Morgan and Dr. Peiravi

Four

Part 1: Principle of Marriage in the Cosmos

"And of everything We have created pairs: That ye may receive instruction." [Holy Qur'an: Zariyat 51:49]

The System of Joining and Coupling in Inanimate Objects

Allah (God) wisely and fairly willed to create pairs of everything in the firmly-founded and extensive order of Creation. In the expansive scene of Creation the pairing of everything is an absolute truth with no exception. Even before man came to know this fact through his knowledge and perform scientific research on it, the Glorious Qur'an had made this truth known in numerous verses, including verse 49 of the Blessed Surah (Chapter) entitled "The Winds That Scatter (Al-Zariyat)". This scientific fact covers everything in Creation, including inanimate objects, plants, animals and humankind.

This great statement which is a scientific fact and an explicit expression regarding everything which is in the cosmos, implies one of the miracles of the Glorious Qur'an being mentioned centuries before the scientific Renaissance came about; and in a city like Mecca or Medina with few who could read or write and lack of books or schools. This Qur'anic statement (51:49) is also a strong reason proving the originality of this scripture, its being scientific and the justification of the Prophethood of the Last of the Prophets Muhammad (Pbuh).

The Glorious Qur'an has other verses about other aspects of Creation which have surprised and perplexed today's scientists and leave no room for doubt about its rightfulness to anyone in any rank or position and the fact that it is the guiding light in man's life.

"This is the Book: In it is guidance sure, without doubt." [Holy Qur'an: Baqara 2:2]

God's divine favor and mercy has set in the inner nature of all couples of any type the inclination, attraction, loving relationship and strong affinity for one another that will lead to marriage, consummation, birth and increase in the population. Thus, the magnificent order of Creation continues on and on and all creatures, of any sex or type, will attain happiness and pleasure in life and will benefit from their own existence and from the company of other beings.

The relationship of generation in the world of inanimate objects, in whatever form it takes, is manifested in the inclination for the combining of one element with another resulting in the creation of a third one. Consider the combination of oxygen and hydrogen, which are both flammable elements. The result of the combination of these combustible gases is cold water that is the essential liquid for living and cheerfulness. All of the following are wonders of Creation and a result of the will and mercy of the Lord of the two worlds. For instance, mutual attraction along with its numerous results or the case of positive and negative currents in a form with countless benefits can be mentioned here. It is this relationship between two elements and their affinity for each other, and briefly speaking the attraction existing between inanimate objects which is the cause of the generation and continuation of their existence; and the perpetuity of the excellent order of Creation as well as the beautiful expanse of existence.

Indeed, what an amazing power and what a great will is displayed when such a relationship of intimacy between two combustible elements can be established. The combination of these two elements creates cold water, pleasant abundance of springs, roaring rivers, great seas, endless oceans and fine rain. What a wonderful power it is which results in the production of diamonds from the combination of elements in the deep of the dark earth and in the heart of granite and in a place where there is a pitch-black bed of rock darker than night!

What a mighty will exists that can form red agate from the combination of several materials in the dark mines of Yemen and from the deep earth of Nayshabur sky blue turquoise is produced! Also from the combination of earth with animal fossils, thousands of useful things for man are created and obtained. What mercy and favor exists that through the combination of earth and stone or other materials with earth and stone such useful metals like gold, silver, copper and iron are produced! What a strong will and great wisdom exists that grants to His creatures so many blessings from the combination of elements with one another! What a strong will and great wisdom that has created such close affinity between the sun and the earthbetween the collection of elements in this fiery ball and the earth's elements! Many blessings result from the combination of the sun's and the earth's elements. As Allah states in the Glorious Qur'an, no one has the ability to count these blessings.

It is God who created the skies and the Earth, sent down water from the sky and by means of rain gave you fruits to eat. He put ships under your control so that you could make them sail on the seas, and He gave you control of the rivers all over the Earth. And gave you power over the sun and the moon which are in constant motion and let you benefit from the day and the night. Whatever you asked of Him, He granted to you. If you try to count God's blessings, you will not be able to do so !

> *"It is God Who hath created the heavens and the earth and sendeth down rain from the skies, and with it bringeth out fruits wherewith to feed you; it is He Who hath made the ships subject to you, that they may sail through the sea by His command; and the rivers (also) hath He made subject to you.*
>
> *And He hath made subject to you the sun and the moon, both diligently pursuing their courses; and the night and the day hath He (also) made subject to you.*
>
> *And He giveth you of all that ye ask for. But if ye count the favors of God, never will ye be able to number them. Verily man is given up to injustice and ingratitude." [Holy Qur'an: Abraham 14:32-34].*

The degree of affinity and attraction of the elements and their being negative or positive and the loving relationship between them for generations is based on an orderly system, special laws, efficiency and just regulations. There are no excesses to be found in these inclinations (or attractions) and these relationships and this sincerity never turn cold. In this beautiful, broad and loving scene there exists no rage or fighting, no discord and opposition.

Divorce and separation have no meaning in these amorous unions. If in this great extent of Creation divorce, rage, opposition, separation and hatred existed, then undoubtedly corruption would completely cover the earth making a mess and destroying everything.

All the elements in the world of inanimate objects have a certain size and weight. All these inanimate bodies have appropriate distances and develop and circulate according to their own position. Their combination with one another is based on their match. Elements do not break out of their own pre-determined order and do not become enemies fighting with one another. Wherever they exist in this better system, they observe their own lawful existence limits.

> *"It is not permitted to the sun to catch up with the moon, nor can the night outstrip the day: each (just) swims along in (its own) orbit (according to Law)." [Holy Qur'an: Ya-Sin 36:40]*

There will happen no change in the weight, size, length, width, depth, color, and properties of the celestial bodies; and their distance from one another is always constant. For instance, the distance between the Sun and the Earth, being approximately 150 million kilometers, never increases or decreases.

If the distance increases, all the earthly creatures freeze; and if the distance decreases, all the elements of the terrestrial globe will be burnt up. Nothing can be seen except for knowledge, justice and unfathomable wisdom which are all based on God's will being manifested in all creatures. That is why whenever those having conscience and being fair, who think and understand, and those who are pure and innocent, look at the system of Creation wholeheartedly, and humbly remember the Creator the great organizer of this order. They sincerely say:

> *"Our Lord! not for naught Hast Thou created (all) this!" [Holy Qur'an: Al-iImran:3:191]*

O' yes, orderliness, laws, limits, rights and facts are inwardly and externally manifested in all of the elements of Creation. And the names and attributes of Allah are displayed in all the creatures so clearly that even the illiterate can read and understand them.

The strangest thing is that all these creatures with their own especial systems are heading straight for their beloved and their goal that is God the Almighty.

"That to thy Lord is the final Goal;" [Holy Qur'an: Najm 53:42]

The System of Plant Symbiosis

The system of combining or in other words; pollination and reproduction in the vegetable and plant kingdoms is carried out in such a way that any onlooker would get thoroughly astonished. It is impossible here to explain all the aspects of this important matter, since it would take up too much time. In a few sentences, a brief look at this wonderful scientific fact accompanied by its especial conditions and surprising laws as well as its extremely accurately arranged plans, will be presented to my dear readers.

If one has paid especial attention to the various flowers, one may see some delicate bars and stamens in the middle of the flowers called styles. The number of them varies from flower to flower, there being a certain reason for this anyway. At the top of them there is a small, yellow projection called an anther. There exists a small bag with four cavities in which pollens are placed in the anther.

The fine powder called pollen consists of microscopic grains which are actually very similar to animals' sperm. After the process of pollination is performed between the anther and the female parts, the flower seeds are produced. The pollen particles being very tiny have within themselves a very complex structure and amazingly as well as elaborately-done work. Large amounts of protoplasm, fat, sugar, starch and nitric materials are found in them, and in the middle there exist two nuclei one of which is smaller than the other. The larger one is called the growing seed and the smaller one is the reproductive seed. The functions of both will soon be explained.

The Pistil

This is the part located on the axis of the flower and on the top part there is a raised section called the stigma. Its surface is covered with a sticky material which is supposed to hold the pollen and help its growth.

On the bottom of the pistil which is attached to the flat portion of the flower, there is a raised section called the ovary. It holds small seeds attached to the ovarian wall by tiny stem-like structures through which they absorb water and the necessary materials. The ovary also has an outstanding structure.

Reproduction

After the seed capsules are torn open and the pollen reaches the female stigma, it immediately starts to grow. It must be stated there are different means by which the pollen can reach the stigma. The observation of this very fact greatly surprises those who study Creation.

There are various insects that instinctively perform this important function. They are attracted to the flowers due to their color, smell and the specially sugary material inside them. Landing on the flower, they transfer the pollen attached to their furred legs, this being especially essential in flowers having separate male and female styles set on different bases. As mentioned before, once the pollen lands on the stigma it starts to grow. The larger nucleus being the growing one starts to grow with the pollen and moves towards the ovary near which it is totally demolished. However, the smaller nucleus which is reproductive passes through a tiny tube entering the ovary and compounds with the ovules. Reproduction takes place in that dark secret space thus a new flower will be born. Man, water and air are some other means by which plants and vegetables are reproduced. In the plant's world, just as that of inanimate objects, certain laws for combination and reproduction are at work through God's will. These laws are carried out without any difficulties, arguments or divorce. Thus man and other living creatures obtain their food.

The System of Animal Copulation and Reproduction

The attraction of the male animal for the female one and the mutual attraction existing between these two living beings, expressly for getting pleasure out of life, reproduction and survival of the species, is one of the biological wonders. Anyone who ponders over the desire and attention paid by animals to this vital issue; and the order and discipline governing coupling and copulation, will be greatly surprised.

All of the following issues are actually the manifestation of God's will and are considered to be wonders of Creation: the couple's cooperation in building their nest; the nest structure; guarding their secrets; choosing the site and time; and more important than all this is copulation. Other wonders are paying attention to the chicks' condition and providing them with food; teaching them what they must be taught and protecting them from danger and unexpected events, etc.

Man is really surprised by the egg-layers' and mammals' world of secrets: copulation, attention paid to guarding the eggs, fetuses and the newly-born ones. The conditions and regulations governing coupling, copulation and reproduction are appropriate and based on the divine laws. There is not a moving creature, but He hath grasp of its fore-lock. Verily it is my Lord that is on a straight Path. [Holy Qur'an: Hud 11:56] No animal tries to attract another species of animal. The male animal does not deviate from its straight, divine path and there is no deviation found in the sexual instincts of animals. The male sperm is intended for females of the same species and no other species is taken into consideration.

Animals do not attack females belonging to another male of the same species and they do not pursue other female animals. Oviparous animals and mammals are not any different in this regard.

Those who ponder over the order and discipline of all affairs, especially copulation and reproduction of birds, reptiles, herbivores and water creatures will really get astonished. The animals' life styles and the rules that govern them are good lessons for those people who have not taken God's guidance and live a life lacking spirituality. Animals are similar to inanimate objects, elements, the moon, sky, Earth and vegetation in regard to order and discipline.

Man and Marriage

Coupling, copulation and reproductiossn in the world of inanimate objects, plants and animals are based on the rules of Creation and the correct order of the instincts. This vital issue and magnificent, natural program, however, must be carried out and be based on divine regulations; those heavenly rules pointed in the Glorious Qur'an and in celestial maxims of the Prophets and Imams [3].

The basic ingredients of this fact (marriage) have been placed in man and woman in the form of instincts, attraction, friendship, love, and kindness and are arranged according to God's wise will.

> *"And among His signs is this, that He created for you mates from among yourselves, that ye may dwell in tranquillity with them, and He has put love and mercy between your (hearts): verily in that are Signs for those who reflect." [Holy Qur'an: Rum 30:21]*
>
> *"It is He Who has created man from water: then has He established relationships of lineage and marriage: for thy Lord Has power (over all things)." [Holy Qur'an: Furqan 25:54]*

In the Islamic immaculate culture, the action of choosing a spouse is recommended and greatly admired as an excellent program. If being

---

[3] Divine leaders

unmarried might lead one to commit sins, it is absolutely obligatory to become united in marriage.

At this point, one must wholeheartedly put into action God's decree concerning marriage and not be afraid of the expenses involved, since worrying about future living expenses is a Satanic thought resulting from the mental weakness and not relying upon God's grace.

Now let's consider the following Qur'anic verse from the Chapter Nur regarding marriage and God's guarantee to provide for living expenses:

> *"Marry those among you who are single, or the virtuous ones among your slaves, male or female: If they are in poverty, God will give them means out of His grace:For God encompasseth all, and He knoweth all things." [Holy Qur'an: Nur 24:32]*

Literally speaking, "marry" in this verse is an order addressing all men and women in the society. One can conclude from this verse that marriage is necessary for those who need to get married or else their health and chastity would be endangered. The verse may also be used to instruct parents and those who can pay for the wedding expenses, to marry off young men and women.

Let's Be Lenient in Making Preparations for Marriage

It is a natural, human and vital affair for men to be attracted to women and vice versa, especially when the buds of the instincts bloom and the flower of lust with its intense degree and power appears at the time when one is marriageable. Marriage is an undeniable affair for anyone. The just desire of the youth, whether they be young women or men, concerning the future of establishing a married life is an obvious truth. This truth is as clear as the sun shining in the middle of the day for anyone, especially parents who have offspring of marriageable age.

The most important and the best way to prevent sinning and protect the society from falling into the whirlpool of corruption is to marry off young women and men when they need to be married. This is undeniable except by fools and the ignorant.

Based on the above discussion, during the first stage of this union, parents, other relations and anyone else concerned with the couple's marriage must be lenient in preparing facilities for this divine affair. They must make the wedding arrangements in the simplest way possible. At the next stage, it is necessary for the young man and woman planning to marry to avoid having inappropriate expectations from each other. And they should avoid creating strict conditions for marriage so that inclinations, instincts, lust and desires may easily follow their own natural path and the foundations of life would be laid on with prosperity. Thus, the building of success will be erected in this world and in the Hereafter.

According to the Qur'anic verses and the traditions, undoubtedly God the Benevolent will be lenient in this world and especially in the Hereafter regarding the deeds of those who are lenient about their own affairs; especially the ones concerning the marriage of their sons and daughters. On the other hand, men and women who are too strict will cause their offspring to suffer from nervous and psychic diseases; and become ill-tempered due to the pressure of instincts and lust. These innocent ones may commit sins and their hopes and desires be gone with the wind. In this world and especially in the Hereafter God will be strict and angry with them and they will burn in the fire of God's Wrath.

Being too cautious about marriage will cause one to become too strict. The copulation of a couple in nature takes place extremely easily. This superior system undoubtedly could not exist now if the process of combining and copulation was difficult in nature.

O' you parents and offspring do not be too strict about the preparations for this divine and humane union; in determining the nuptial gift; in determining the marriage conditions; and in arranging the engagement party, the religious ceremony and the wedding party. Don't be too strict about performing local customs and do not propose plans which are beyond the financial abilities of the two families. Let the marriage take place easily as God the Benevolent will ease your affairs in this world and in the Hereafter.

17

Therefore, put into practice the ways of the pious ones and learn some lessons from this source of benefits and blessings. And establish your life based upon the characteristics of the pious ones, since happiness and the good of this world and the Hereafter are subject to following the example of the lovers of God the Eternal.

The Commander of the Faithful[4] introduces the pious ones as follows:

"They are continually subject to self-control from any involvement in corruption. They require little and every good deed is expected from them. People feel safe and secure in their company."[Hedayat ul-Elm, p.651]

At any rate, those who are involved in the wedding preparations must avoid the following: inappropriate expectations; imposing various unbearable matters on those making preparations; following one's own carnal desires; getting entrapped in incorrect customs; being extremely envious of what others have; and finally being too strict in all of the wedding affairs.

From the very beginning, the foundation of the marriage must be founded upon piety, goodness, leniency, and only for the sake of acquiring God's satisfaction.

After the contract of marriage, the man who had seen the woman before the union and had approved of her, must start a new life with her and guarantee the continuance of the divine love and mercy established between the couple. And the woman, who had seen her husband before marriage and had accepted him, must be a complaisant wife easy to live with and respect his rights in all areas.

The following instances are not signs of dignity: excessively expensive nuptial gifts; expensive ceremonies; entertaining lots of guests; following illogical and inappropriate customs and traditions and imposing strict conditions. But the following are dignified acts: the couple must match each other in rank; both families should obey the Islamic ethics; both husband and wife must observe divine and human rights; both partners must continue to be loving and kind for the continuation of the marriage and to avoid arguments.

---

4   Imam Ali (a.s)

The life of a couple, such as that of the Commander of the Faithful4. and Fatimah (Pbuh), is the best model for each Muslim man and woman. Fatimah was the source of peace for her husband making a peaceful home environment, and Ali (Pbuh) was an excellent model and teacher for the children and a sympathetic assistant in the house and family affairs. He would not hesitate to help in simple matters around the house such as: cleaning; preparing the bread dough and helping to take care of the children. He would not let his wife have a hard time in doing household duties and would not make her do everything around the house.

It is obligatory for a husband and wife to respect each other's rights and be each other's helper in all aspects of life. They should not think that oppression is limited to Pharaohs, the King Nimrood and other oppressors throughout history. Any unjust act that harms others is oppression and God does not like oppression and the oppressor. He dislikes any violation of other's rights no matter how insignificant.

God willing, all issues regarding the Islamic Family Structure will be discussed little by little in the following chapters. Here some important traditions concerning the value and significance of marriage and its benefits have been cited from authentic sources. It is hoped that you will realize the strength of divine issues and that no other culture has Islam's wise and fine plans.

Traditions on the Value and Importance of Marriage

The Prophet (Pbuh) said: God's Mercy and attention will be bestowed upon man in four situations: when it rains; when a child kindly looks at his/her father; when the door of the Ka'aba (House of God) is opened and when a marriage contract is drawn up and two join each other in a new life.[Marriage in Islam, p.17]

The Prophet (Pbuh) said: You must marry and marry off your single sons and daughters. The sign of a Muslim's prosperity is to pay the expenses for a woman to get married. And nothing is better approved by God than a Muslim home enriched by marriage. [Marriage in Islam, p.7]

The Prophet (Pbuh) said: Marry off your single men until God will make them good-tempered and increase their daily bread as well as generosity. [Marriage in Islam, p.8]

The Holy Prophet of God (Pbuh) said: Marriage is my practice and whoever turns away from it does not belong to my nation. [Bihar al-Anwar, v.103, p.222.]

The Prophet (Pbuh) said:Whoever gets married has actually attained half of his/her religion and for the other half he/she should be pious. [Bihar al-Anwar, v.103, p.219.]

6-Imam Sadiq (Pbuh) said: A man came to my father, the Imam Baqir. My father asked him if he was married, but the man said no. Then my father told him that he would not like to own the world with everything in it and live one night without his wife. Then my father continued by saying that two units (rakaats) of prayer of a married man is better than a single man's night of worship and day of fasting. Then my father gave the man seven Durhams and told him to buy the necessities for marriage with this money since the Prophet (Pbuh) has said: Choose a spouse and this will cause an increase in your daily bread. [Vasa'il al-Shiia, v.14, p.7]

The Prophet (Pbuh) said: O' young ones; Whoever of you has the means to get married, then marry so that you seldom look at other women and remain sinless. [Marriage in Islam, p.14]

The Prophet (Pbuh) said: No contract in Islam is more approved by God than marriage. [Bihar alAnwar, v.103, p.222]

The Prophet (Pbuh) said: Whoever gets married has obtained half of prosperity. [Mustadrak alVasa'il, Introductory Chapters, Ch.1]

The Prophet (Pbuh) said: Whoever marries at an early age will cause Satan to scream and say that the one who married saved two-thirds of his religion from my access. God's servant must remain virtuous to maintain the other third. [Bihar al-Anwar, v.103, p.221]

In fact, marriage is highly valued in Islam and it benefits man and woman greatly. Hopefully, families will ease this humane, divine and important issue and abstain from making conditions difficult to meet and be more lenient. And it is hoped they will perform these ceremonies according to their own social status being satisfied with what is available. Thus the youth's desires would be naturally met and their instincts, being God-given blessings not turn into sin.

What are the roots of nervous and psychic diseases, inattentiveness to educational matters, being lazy in practicing prayer, rape, prostitution, lust and of lustful deviations? This question must be asked from parents who are too strict and entrapped in wrong traditions and habits being extremely envious of what others have. And also this question must be asked from those youngsters who are not pious and those who have the financial ability to provide for the youths' marriage but do not spend their wealth in the way of God. Whatever logical and acceptable answer they may have in this world, they shall have the same answer in God's just court in the Hereafter.

Five

Part 2: Divine Virtues in the Family and Society

❧

But the raiment of the righteousness That is the best. [Holy Qur'an: A'raf 7:26]

True Concept of Piety

The literal infinitive and root of the abstract Arabic noun TAQWA, which has the most beautiful and original meaning, is "WQY". WAQAYA means self-control, being fearful and protecting one's self from all divinely prohibited actions. Actually the word WAQAYA means the spirit, power and ability attained by the practice of giving up sinning, by practicing abstinence and by self-restraint against committing sins. keeping the soul's control over sin and forbidden pleasures.

Trying to be pious and acquire the spirit of self-control in the face of sin is the best step to be taken in life; and amongst all actions is the action most approved of. Trying to acquire piety is actually the practice of worshipping God: the worship which God has instructed humankind to perform. This kind of worship includes a program which will undoubtedly please God.[5]

The philosophy behind physical, financial and moral worship is the cognition of piety by a true believer. Any type of worship, movement or action which does not result in piety is not to be considered worshipping at all.

A society is a combination of thousands of families and one family consists of one wife, one husband and a number of offspring. Actually the building blocks of the family and society are individuals. If each and every individual has developed the spirit of piety, we shall have healthy families and a superior society. The family will be an environment in which internal peace and safety from the external world govern. In this type of family there is room enough for the individuals to fully develop. As a result we shall have a society in which all individuals are sources of benefit for each other and everyone is safe from others' mischief and harm.

The pious people are loved by God and are divinely favored by the Prophets and religious leaders (the Imams): they are practically generous and productive Allah beings. The pious ones are people of fine character and heavenly morality having angel-like faces, and lack evil spirits.

The individual's, the family's and the society's reputations depend on the existence of saintly piety, and no individual, family or society is more worthy to God than the pious one. The harm caused by wives, husbands, fathers, mothers, children and society's individuals to each other is the direct result of irreligiousness. The terrible fear that people in families and societies have of each other is the bitter fruit of ungodliness. The ample damage done to the affairs of people's lives results from the lack of piety.Actually, it is a divine necessity for husbands and wives to be beautified with piety so as to have a healthy society. And it is also necessary that the parents pass on this beneficial, divine desire to their offspring. From the very beginning of training their children, parents must make sure to develop the basic environment for piety.

How praiseworthy it is to pay attention to the abundant benefits of the

---

[5] Allah

Qur'anic verses and religious traditions on piety; and then begin to evaluate their benefits! Look at the truth of the matter in this way: if all young women and men were God-fearing, and made arrangements of marriage with an angelic capital of piety, what wonderful families and societies would be established!

Piety and Its Praiseworthy Degrees

The enlightened ones and those who according to the Qur'an show insight and have made spiritual journeys mention three degrees of piety.

I Outstanding Piety II Especial Piety

III Ordinary Piety

In a very notable tradition Imam Sadiq (Pbuh) explained these three degrees in the following manner:

I Outstanding Piety The first degree of piety is being completely absorbed by Allah and consists of the individual abstaining from religiously lawful things and actions, much more the religiously doubtful things and actions.

II Especial Piety (In Awe of Allah) The second degree of piety is "In Awe of Allah" meaning the individual abstains from all religiously doubtful things and actions, much more the prohibited ones.

III Ordinary Piety The third degree of piety results from fear of Hell's punishment and God's painful Wrath. This degree consists of abstaining from all sins and forbidden things and actions. [Mava'ez al-'Addadiyi, p.180].

Of course, the meaning of abstaining from religiously lawful things and actions expressed in Imam Sadiq's statement has the following meaning: those having this type of piety do not pursue many of the religiously lawful affairs since they feel they do not require them. And concerning the lawful necessities they require for subsistence, they observe the utmost frugality.

The power to be contented is practicable for everyone, and if anyone denies it, the excuse will not be accepted. Being contented with what is religiously lawful and limiting the materialistic affairs of life are moral actions and approved of programs providing the environment for the realization of angelic piety in all affairs.

Hajji Sabzevary and Moderation

In order to preach Islam I traveled to the town of Sabzevar (Iran) in 1983 where I inquired about whereabouts of the family of the Great Sage and Noble mystic Hajji Mulla-Hady Sabzevary. I was told that one of his great grandchildren lives in this town. He was wise, knowledgeable, knew philosophy and had interpreted the Qur'an twice for the people of the mosque of which he is the Imam.[6]

I rushed to visit him and his appearance, morality, style of living and his encounters with others displayed a perspective of Hajji 's pure life. I asked him about his noble great-grandfather. He described amazing issues about his plans and life conditions and said that Hajji was respected by all scholarly, political personages. He said people would rush to him from far away places to benefit from his knowledge, but he lived in real moderation concerning his food, clothing and housing. Sometimes, observing cleanliness, he would wear his clothes for nearly ten years patching them when necessary as this is the practice of the Prophet Muhammad (Pbuh) and that of God's Saints.

Luxury-Loving and Wastefulness

According to Allah, these two acts are satanic and due to one's selfish and carnal desires. What prohibits man from abiding by God's limits for life? More specifically, if man were more content he would have an easier life, less stress and insecurity. Once man's physical needs can be met with a reasonable house, a normal vehicle and sufficient food and clothing, we should avoid keeping up with the Joneses. We should get used to normal expenditures, and avoid extra expenditures and obtaining what is considered luxurious and fashionable. We should not use the West as a model for our life-style. They themselves are plagued with many errors.

---

[6] Leader of congregational prayer

Industry and technology should not make us think that whatever they say and write is correct and that their lifestyle is in accordance with reality.

What is important in the Islamic religion is the well-being of the soul and body, the neighborhoods, towns, cities and regions. What is paid attention to in this culture considering material, spiritual and personal affairs, and social faith and ethics is for the good of man in this world and the Hereafter.

The pure Islamic culture and school for refining human beings scorns wastefulness, luxury-loving, making heavy expenditures, ornamenting the outward appearance of one's life without considering moderation and economizing on expenses. This even applies to the matter of building a mosque being the Muslims' place of worship. Mosques must be adorned with the utmost spirituality inwardly, and be ornamented outwardly in the simplest way so that hearts may not be tempted and souls not be separated from Allah.

Provide yourself with simple clothing, however, observe the etiquette for wearing it. Attain your essential foodstuffs but observe the good manners of eating. One may buy an appropriate vehicle of transportation according to his/her social status but the driving regulations should not be ignored. Purchase a house for yourself, but not one which will enslave your soul. All of the above are the results of piety, abstinence and paying attention to God. The Jewish and Christian lifestyles considering housing and furnishings, transportation vehicles, clothing, foodstuffs and other luxuries are entangled in wastefulness. The Christian churches and Jewish synagogues are adorned with gold, jewels and other ornaments as well as devices, instruments, statues, antiques, tableaux and couches costing millions of dollars. The lifestyles of the Jewish rabbis and Christian clergymen, even that of their leader the Pope is entangled in wastefulness and extravagant expenditures causing one's eyes to pop out. If the personal hat and clothing of the Pope were sold, millions of starving people could be saved from hunger.

Amassing great amounts of wealth, usury, great robberies even in broad daylight and a thousand other notoriously disgraceful plans are the deeds of God's enemies. God's friends must accustom themselves to God's consent and protect themselves from extravagant expenditures and wastefulness. All these facts are generated and maintained by piety. A home decorated with piety and a pious couple could actually possess a divine treasure and heavenly capital. Their life is richly blessed with happiness, peace and friendliness as well as comfort, security, health, righteousness, justice, nobility, benevolence and truth. One's home and place of worship must be such that one can feel at peace and be secure; and it should be a place to get closer to God. In short, we must establish our lives based on piety and moderation considering God and the Hereafter so as to please God and obtain the good of the Hereafter.

Even today one can live on a meager income if one is pious and content.

Of course, in case a problem should arise and the believer could not handle it on his low income, it is the duty of the believers to assist their brother immediately and save him from suffering any hardships.

Let's Invite Each Other to Piety

Considering that not all men and women can attain the first two degrees of piety being (1) outstanding and (2) especial piety, we should not invite the general public to these two stages of piety as these degrees of piety belong only to the Prophets, the Imams and God's especial Saints. However, it is feasible for all men and women to attain ordinary or the general type of piety; that is to abstain from the religiously forbidden ethical, carnal and financial affairs.

Therefore, it is everyone's duty to politely invite others to piety and to encourage each other to abstain from various forbidden acts, so that divine virtues may encompass man's life including individuals and families and thus the society can benefit from it.

It is divinely obligatory for all people in all ranks to attain piety, especially a husband and wife who should teach piety to their children. The righteous say children are God-given responsibilities and their hearts, and souls are pure and void of any corruption like blank tableaux. This blank tableau can accept any design. If a child is taught good deeds, words and ethics at home and if he/she is guided to learn the truth, he/ she will attain the prosperity of this world and the Hereafter. The parents who cause this to happen shall share in the reward as do the teachers who have participated in his/her training.

If, however, the parents be corrupted and ungodly drawing satanic designs on the child's heart, life and soul, then the child will become corrupted and be raised like an animal just following his lusts and carnal desires. The child will be spoiled and the responsibility will undoubtedly lie with his parents or teacher.

"Save yourselves and your families from a Fire."[Holy Qur'an: Tahrim 66:6]

Why do parents usually protect their children from fire and prevent them from approaching danger? Should they not also protect their children from the flames of God's Wrath in the Hereafter resulting from lack of piety, evil acts, no morality, faith and good deeds. The practical approach to protect children from punishment in the Hereafter is for the parents to be pious and to teach them piety. To train their children parents must be benevolent teachers, persuasive preachers and sympathetic inviters to good deeds. They must first ornament themselves with piety, faith and good deeds. Then they must train their children, teach them principles of morality and protect them from bad friends and wicked teachers.

They must try to raise the child in such a way that he/she does not become deeply fond of wealth, luxury and wastefulness as well as excessive ornaments. Thus, he/she would not turn into a wasteful, greedy, looting, lustful and stubborn individual in the future. If the society consists of ungodly individuals, it will be like a building constructed from low grade materials. It will collapse and living in it will become difficult for everyone.

There would be no need for prisons, police, courts and the extensive judicial system, if all homes were based on piety and couples were virtuous and taught their children piety. If so, large amounts of money spent on preventing robbery, corruption and looting would be saved and could be spent for the public's well-being.

Signs of the Pious

Using the Qur'anic verses and religious traditions, religious authorities consider the following to be signs of the pious:

- Learning enough of the religious sciences necessary for his actions, morality, business deals and relations with family members and the society
- Protecting his body's health by using hygienic measures and observing good etiquette while eating and drinking
- Resorting to one's intellect in daily affairs and being honest in all aspects of life
- Having modesty, not lying as well as maintaining good temper and not being wicked
- Not being a hypocrite and hating extra material goods
- Not being deceitful, making excuses or committing treason
- Honoring the virtuous and the wise
- Carrying out one's religious duties, including the obligatory and supererogatory acts.
- Following divine scholars since they teach man what is forbidden and what is allowed in God's religion, and only except man's progress

Imam Sadiq (Pbuh) stated the following concerning the fact that one must follow the divine scholars: A sign of a liar is that he informs you of issues in the Heavens and the Earth, but when asked about the religiously lawful and forbidden, he has no answer to give. [Usul al-Kafi, v.2. p.340; Muhjat ul-Biyza, v.5, p.140] Some other signs of the pious ones are:

1. Patience in the face of terrible events

2. Observing the Islamic customs and principles of morality in all affairs
3. Diligence in making supplications
4. Perseverance in intellectual affairs

The pious should have sincere intentions and be pure in soul. They should progress to the stage of knowledge of certainty, then to the stage of reality of certainty, and then to the truth of certainty.

A Pious Man and Wife

A pious man never uses any means, except the lawful ones, and never accepts any unlawfully made money, in order to earn his living.

Thus, he respects the rights of all with whom he deals, and no one is harmed by his activities outside the home. He does not get involved in what is religiously unlawful due to his piety and does not lose the treasure of purity of his soul and contentment. When a pious man has finished working and returns home, he leaves all his tiredness at the doorstep and enters the house in a cheerful, delightful state. He smiles kindly at his wife and tells her to relax after working all day at cleaning, cooking and caring for the children. He praises her and faces her with kindness, paying respect to each one according to his/her position in the family.

Once in a while, a pious man reminds his family members about the religiously lawful and forbidden, virtue and vice, good and evil deeds and does not let them forget religious issues.

A pious man does not spend all his time outside of home, and does not limit his happiness and laughter just to his circle of friends. Also he does not excessively attend the mosque and religious ceremonies.

A pious man notes that Islam has instructed us to be moderate and consider economy in all aspects of life, even in worship. Islam has even prohibited us from usurping the rights of our wife and children under the pretext of visiting our friends or attending ceremonies. At this point, I must remind my respectable colleagues who are in charge of mosques and religious ceremonies to shorten the duration of religious programs. A congregation prayer and an hour of preaching should suffice, as this was the practice of the Prophet (Pbuh) and the Noble Imams. They raised great men and women in a short time and with brief sermons.

Worshipping in excess, especially in regards to the supererogatory acts, and drawing on and on the meetings, will bore the listeners. Gradually this will cause a psychological complex in the listener concerning religious programs. The only result of this is the harm done to the mosque and religious clubs as well as to the people, especially those with a low tolerance. Anyway, a pious man will observe the proper etiquette in all aspects of life. In this way, he will help to establish a fine family and attract his family's kindness to himself.

The pious wife protects her chastity, innocence and purity and eagerly does the housework. She prepares the means for her husband's comfort and helps him to relax as he is tired from work outside the home. She cares for her children in the most honorable way and behaves with her husband and children within the limits of Islamic morality. She does not forget to worship God daily and makes the home the center of love, kindness, eagerness and delight.

The pious woman, by relying on the divine Islamic principles, follows her husband's orders. She avoids getting angry and encounters her husband's kinsmen with kindness and Islamic morality. When her husband comes from his work, she is at the door to welcome him. When he leaves for work, she sees him off and requests him to bring home only the lawful goods. She says that she will be content with the lawful goods, even if they are meager, and will not accept the responsibility of unlawful goods. Do not exceed the limits set by God to obtain unlawful wealth under the pretext of being married or having children and a lot of expenses.

The pious woman does not try to keep up with the Joneses causing her husband to be embarrassed because she wants the same things his kin have or hers does. Such a pious couple are approved of by God, are a source of goodness and a good example of divine human beings. In the shade of this couple, the kind of family which God likes, is created. In any case, the husband and wife take care of each other in all of life affairs based on the

Islamic wisdom and laws, just as God's Saints did.

Exemplary Shopkeeper

My maternal grandfather told me that once he and his friends traveled from the Khansar region near Isfahan to visit the holy shrine of Imam Reza (Pbuh). This happened in the old days when people used to travel on quadrupeds.

He was in charge of shopping in Damghan city. Early in the morning, he entered a shop to buy some goods. Since he was a pilgrim, the shopkeeper invited him in and started serving him. At the same time someone entered the shop to purchase goods and intended to buy a lot.

The shopkeeper asked him to cross the street and purchase from the store opposite his shop, so the man left the store. My grandfather said he got surprised and asked the shopkeeper the reason. He replied that earlier that morning he had seen the other shopkeeper in a sad mood. When questioned why he was so sad, he stated that he had a debt to be repaid on that day, but business was bad. The shopkeeper said he could not remain indifferent, so he sent his customer to shop from that poor man's store. Possibly in this way he could pay back his debt.

Believers should support each other. Everyone should support his/her friends. Especially, a husband should support his wife and a wife should support her husband so that their life is established on the basis of divine and humane principles yielding noble children. spray scent in your house at the time of morning prayer by reading the Qur'an. Your heavenly recital of the Holy Qur'an will affect your wife and children, and they will become better acquainted with worship services and God willing the true message of the Qur'an and will become benevolent and pious.

Six

Part 3: The Lofty Goals Behind Marriage in Islam

━━━⟡⟡⟡━━━

"God doth wish to lighten your (difficulties)." [Holy Qur'an: Nisaa 4:28]

An Honorable Household

If a young adult or an adult man or woman does not marry, it seems to be rather impossible to remain chaste and free of corruption. It is a difficult problem to find a young adult out of millions, not married, yet be chaste and sinless. If we find a youth who is truly chaste and not married, then we may say she/he is one of God's Saints. Avoiding commitment of sins, remaining immune from corruption, being safe from the outburst of the instincts, and not being married at the same time is something only the Prophet Joseph could do.

A house in which an unmarried man and a woman live is not safe from corruption. If the man has no wife and the woman no husband, and their sexual instincts are alive with the pressure of lust, then those two have various mental, family and social problems and live in corruption. Marriage is a natural and divine law. It makes some problems easier to solve which are concerned with keeping the youth chaste and pious.

The establishment of a household in society must be founded on a healthy and peaceful basis. The couple live together by marrying and respecting each other's rights. Wherever a Muslim household is established it must be based on God's revelation and in the remembrance of Him day and night.

> *"(Lit is such a Light) In houses, which God Hath permitted to be raised to honor; for the celebration, In them, of His name: in them is He glorified in the mornings and In the evenings, (again and again)." [Holy Qur'an: Nur 24:36]*

In such a house, with such attributes, one finds a household of believers in which worshipping God flourishes. God has ordered a marriage to take place there and the couple obeys all divine, humane laws. The Glorious Qur'an orders that marriage should take place so that a man and a woman's problems are solved through the realization of this tradition and they being the future teachers of some children will remain incorruptible.

A man and his wife establish a mutual life. Being in harmony with each other they make a home for God's remembrance. In such a house, the couple are real servants of God and their offspring are the fruits of virtue. Their behavior and morality are signs of divine etiquette and the traditions of the Prophets. When a believing couple get married, they both feel responsible to follow the divine laws. They find each other to be a helper to the other. They are two loving friends, two intimate companions, two sources of faith and two pillars of love and kindness. Thus they protect life from difficulties. If a difficulty should arise, they solve it easily and confront it with the arms of patience and fortitude.

The Worst People

Living in seclusion and not having a companion leads to many difficulties. It causes depression, despondency, nervous disorders and all types of mental and physical disorders. Being alone causes one to enter the world of imagination and vain thoughts and succumb to mental and moral illnesses. The Prophet (Pbuh) said:

Most of the People of the Fire on the Day of Judgment are those who refused to marry and start a family."[Marriage in Islam, p.26]

Also the Prophet (Pbuh) said:

The worst of your dead ones are the celibates. [Bihar al-Anwar, v.100, pp.220-221]

In another tradition he mentioned: The most ignoble of your dead ones are the celibates. [Ibid]

In a wise speech he said:

The most Satanic ones amongst you are the celibates. Celibacy is the brother of Satan.[Ibid]

In some heavenly words he said: The best of my nation are the married ones and the worst are the celibates.[Ibid]

The Prophet (Pbuh) also said:

If the dead celibates return to this world, they will surely marry. [Marriage in Islam, p.27]

And in another tradition the Prophet (Pbuh) said: God curses the man who refuses to take a wife. [Ibid]

Why does the Noble Prophet of Islam interpret the celibates to be dwellers of the Fire, ignoble ones, brothers of Satan, the wicked, the seditious, and the cursed? This is because those who do not marry are forced into corruption, sedition, sin and make problems for their society and the family. In all aspects of life, they cause a lot of trouble.

According to the Qur'anic verses and Prophetic traditions, marriage endows humans with nobleness and respectfulness. Marriage keeps man safe from wickedness and God's punishment. It protects him from falling into the clutches of Satan. Marriage protects man from becoming a source of vice and corruption and he will be safe from God's Wrath. All of this results in his comfort, peace and safety, righteousness and piety making life easier. This is why in the Holy Qur'an the lawful, Islamic marriage has been pointed out.

> **"God doth wish to lighten your (difficulties)."** **[Holy Qur'an: Nisaa 4:28]**

The Blooming of Talents

If a young man and woman marry based upon their nature and follow God's commandment and the divine Prophets' ways, undoubtedly the way for the blossoming of hidden talents will be opened up and the tree of life will bear excellent fruits. They will be saved from the peak of God's Wrath, a seditious nature, the dangerous clutches of Satan and God's curse all being the consequences of being celibate. Marrying results in the following: peace of mind; an inner feeling of security; overcoming the problems of celibacy; arriving at a heavenly, angelic environment; the proper background for correct ways of thinking; and control of the outburst of the instincts and lust.

Many of the distinguished men of letters, Islamic scholars whose names have been recorded in the history of the world, have practically made progress of 100 years in only one night. In general, these individuals have attained lofty positions in science and knowledge in the shade of marriage which brings peace of mind. Their names are on the tip of everyone's tongue due to their knowledge, piety, chastity, nobleness, service to others and servitude to God.

In the book entitled "Zendegany Ayatullah Boroojerdy"[7], we read: " In 1935 at the age of twenty-two, he received a letter from his father asking him to return to Boroojerd. He thought that his father wanted to send him to Najaf the largest Shiite seminary existedto continue his education.

---

[7] AYATULLAH BOROOJERDY'S BIOGRAPHY, P. 95

However, upon his return and after visiting his father and other relatives contrary to his expectations, he observed that they had arranged for his marriage. However, he became sad. In reply to his father who noticed his sadness and asked him about the reason for it, he answered that he had been studiously acquiring knowledge with peace of mind. But now he noted that marriage would hold him up.

So his father told him that if he followed his orders, there would be hope that God would grant him an opportunity to reach his lofty goals. His father told him to beware of not marrying, because it was probable he would not get anywhere no matter how studious he was. This removed all his doubts. After marrying and staying there a while, he returned to Isfahan where he continued his studies and tutorials for another five years.

In Isfahan his loyal and well-matched spouse provided the means for his peace, progress, comfort and security, as she was a kind friend, a sympathetic assistant and a calm servant. He was so busy studying that sometimes he would study until dawn. He had stated several times he would attempt to memorize the Holy Qur'an when not busy at other tasks. And during this period in Isfahan he memorized Chapter 9 entitled Baraat (Immunity) which he remembered his whole life and continued to recite.

The late scholar Tabataba-ey, the author of the Holy Qur'an's interpretation named Al-Mizan acknowledges that part of his scientific and spiritual progress was due to his noble wife. Marriage is a source of peace and security and it provides a background for the development of talents and the realization of perfection.

Striving for the Well-Being of the Household and Home

In addition to positive worldly gains, marriage and maintaining a spouse and attending to the children have serious spiritual benefits. Working and striving to provide sustenance for the wife and children are considered to be a wonderful form of worship being equal to engaging in war in the way of God. The following has been narrated from the Immaculate Imams:

One who works really hard to provide for his family's sustenance from what is lawful is similar to one who fights in a war in the way of God. [Bihar al-Anwar, v.101, p.72]

It is very difficult to obey God's order instructing the mother to respect her children's rights, the wife to respect her husband's rights, or the husband to respect those of his family and provide for their spiritual needs. This too is considered to be worship and deserves the rewards of the Hereafter. Raising a good generation with children who are good-doers and excellent offspring is essential and satisfies God. It is of utmost importance to keep the household safe from corruption and to provide the means for growth, education and development of the family. This is the best type of worship of God.

The Fourth Imam (Pbuh) has wisely stated:

Whoever provides the best means for the spiritual and material needs of his wife and children is closer than others to attaining God's gratitude.[Bihar al-Anwar, v.101, p.73]

Anyhow, the society is the product of the family. All people who serve a nation, whether it be the president, minister, or a Member of Parliament have their roots in the house and the family. The home and those who manage it are the main factors in their education and development. Home is like a piece of land which if separated from the truth will be like a salt desert with no flowers blossoming. And if connected to the truth, it is logical to expect flowers in bloom.

Man's success or failure is primarily originated from parent's conduct. If they strive for their children's success, they have performed a major act of worship and will eternally benefit from marriage. If, however, they are the cause of their offspring's failure, they have not only benefited from the holy tree of marriage but they have practically prepared the means for their own loss. It is for this reason that the Prophet (Pbuh) stated the following in different Islamic traditions:

The roots of anyone's failure exist within their mother, and so does their blessed fortune. [Bihar al-Anwar, v.5, p.157.]

And as the great poet Kalim Kashany said: The only thing that comes out of the jug is what's inside it.

Now it is up to the parents to fill the hearts, the minds and the brains of their children with whatever they have.

Establish the Loftiest Goal for Marriage

One's goal for marriage should be spiritual, holy and pure. One must marry in order to obey God's order and the Prophets' manner and to provide for the prosperity of his/her spouse as well as divinely raising children.

Both men and women should prepare themselves for engaging in a great act of worship when they marry. They should consider God's approval of their union and they should realize that through their loin and uterus, they carry God's loan. They must know that the child is only God's trust which is the guest of the father's loin for a short time and then is the guest of the mother's uterus for nearly six to nine months. During this time, the child with no option absorbs his/her father's characteristics and traits through a God-given property. It has been narrated that the Prophet (Pbuh) would sometimes let pregnant women come and watch the wars against God's enemies. They would witness the glorious scenes of the Holy War and sword-fighting in God's way, and hear the warriors shouting divine slogans.

All this was for the development of the fetus in the uterus through what he/she heard and saw, and thus a well-bred, brave, ambitious child hearing divine sounds in the womb would develop.

Have you not heard that God ordered forty days of fasting for the Prophet (Pbuh) before the formation of the existence of his daughter Fatimah (Pbuh) in his loin. Then he ate heavenly foods for the meal on the last night of fasting. The sperm was then transferred to the mother's womb.

Do not let your eyes be the judge for marriage. Do not let lust be the matchmaker for marriage. Do not let the goal for marriage be getting wealthy by either family. Do not let the goal of marriage be seeing a beautiful face or a deceiving look. It has been proven that if these are the goals for marriage, such marriages do not have a good ending and bear little or no fruit.

Let spirituality, God and worshipping Him, striving to respect your spouse's rights, raising good children and attaining God's pleasure be your goals in marriage so that it bears eternal fruits. Let lawful lust, consent and leisure be subject to these lofty and divine goals so that you can gain complete pleasure and rewards of the Hereafter, too. If two individuals are divinely joined, their marriage will last forever since divine marriage never ends in divorce. One who marries for God's sake, wholeheartedly respects his/her spouse's rights and does not impose the least harm upon the spouse.

It is a religiously lawful requirement to protect the spouse's honor in front of the children and their relatives. And it is divinely forbidden to belittle one's spouse. Muslim men and women must consider the marriage of the Commander of the Faithful (Imam Ali) and Hazrat Fatimah Zahrah (Pbuh) as their model. This lofty marriage, which was contracted for God's sake, was based on heavenly goals and resulted in immaculate and divine offspring. The following verses have been interpreted to refer to this marriage in Shiite traditions:

*"He combined the two seas between which there is a distance. **They do not exceed each other's limits (mingle) and pearls and coral come from these two seas.**" [Holy Qur'an: Rahman 55:19-23]*

What is meant by the two seas is the Commander of the Faithful and Hazrat Fatimah Zahrah being two seas of wisdom, patience, faith and insight. What is meant by distance is the Noble Prophet of Islam Muhammad (Pbuh); and what is meant by pearls and coral are their offspring the Imams Hassan and

Husayn (Pbuh). [Nur al-Thaqalayn, v.5, p.191, tradition 19]

The family structure must be purely divine and Islamic so that it can attract and absorb God's benevolence. If undesirable and ungodly customs, Satanic conditions or that part of the culture of the Age of Ignorance which the Prophet (Pbuh) had ordered to be abolished be not avoided in marriage, then evil will appear in the marriage and this tree will bear sour fruits. The Prophet (Pbuh) ordered: Everything should be abolished from the Age of Ignorance except the Islamic traditions. [Bihar al-Anwar, v.77, ch.6, p.128, tradition 32.]

The Family Structure in the West

The family structure in Europe and America lacks any foundation or content and is a faulty structure. Following the example of the family structure in the West is incorrect and it paves the way to ruin one's life.

The Westerners do not have pure and holy goals in marriage. Lust and satisfaction of the instincts is the reason why they marry. Noble and pure men and women are few in number there, so that is why corruption is overwhelming in Europe and America.

Most men and many women in the West marry after periods of unlawful sexual relationships and usually put their offspring in day care centers. Then they take them from the nursery school void of paternal and maternal love and pure emotions and they let them join in any type of corruption. They send them to the schools so that they apparently learn good behavior and become familiar with a few words. Then at the age of eighteen, they force them out of the home and leave them up to the environment and the society.

The ethics that they teach at home or school is how to be a gentleman, how to earn money and know about economics. They pay no attention to the inner facts and inner roots. Westerners are unable to raise human beings.

Is this not obvious from the fact that when they establish a society or a government, the society is a source of corruption and the government is the primary means of exploitation and colonization of the oppressed people on earth. The crimes committed by the graduates from Western schools and universities cannot be compensated for until the Day of Judgment.

If they are polite and calm for a while, it is because they have not yet found anything to capture. Their story is like that of the man who told his friend about his polite cat which held a lit candle and guided guests to their seats at a table full of delicious foods. The friend said one cannot trust the cat's politeness. He added that he is ready to prove it. When in practice, the cat was seen with a candle light guiding the guests and not greedy for the food on the table, the friend took a mouse out of his pocket and freed it in the middle of the table. The cat dropped the candle and jumped on the table on a wild mouse chase destroying all the food and ruining the party. The policy of the Westerners is similar to that of the cat. As long as they do not see their desired food, they are calm and polite. But once they see the oil, gold or other mines of the weaker nations, they drop the torch of politeness and jump like voracious animals to devour all material and spiritual goods and start a blood bath for material gain.

The abundance of corruption, unlawful lust, murder and looting, prostitution and other evil deeds in the West is a direct result of the loose family structure there. If the houses in Europe or in the United States were filled with knowledge and God's remembrance and worship, then their products would have been noble humans with heavenly principles of morality. But since these homes are void of truth and God, their fruits are sour, stinking or tasteless. One cannot use such a system as a model, and those who do so will become even worse than the Westerners.

Seven

Part 4: Woman's Position in Human History and Islam

❦

Imam Sadiq (Pbuh) said: Most benefits come from women.[Vasa'il-al-Shia, v.14, p.11]

Mental Deviation of Corrupt Men Regarding Women

Haughty tribes and nations which lived without following God's teachings preached by the Prophets and mentioned in the scriptures all suffered from mental deviation regarding humankind and all world affairs. They made wrong judgments about Creation and nearly all creatures. They stated incorrect things based on their wrong impressions and unjust judgments; thus they lived a life full of oppression both to themselves and others. The pages of life history were hideously portrayed by them.

Among these judgments were the wrong ones concerning women they were against morality and humanity and facts. After studying books on this issue written in the West and the East, I came to the conclusion that the nations which lived without fear of God and revelations, thought incorrectly and were drowning in carnal desires, making ten oppressive judgments which were illogical and inhumane.

1.) A woman is completely weak and helpless, thus she must obey her husband in all affairs without any questions. She does not have the right to interfere in daily affairs, even in the home matters.
2.) Woman is a creature with a satanic soul. Thus she is not human or if any attention is to be paid to her, she must be treated as something between human and animal. Therefore, she is worthless, deserves no respect and lacks a personality.
3.) She cannot own any positions but can only own a few things, if the man wishes so.
4.) She receives no inheritance but she is to be inherited after the death of her father or husband.
5.) She does not have the right to worship or enter the spiritual domain. Her worshipping is worthless because she is weak in mind and is whimsical.
6.) She does not deserve legal attachment to her father and son, and the only link between them is blood.
7.) Once married, her children are not the grandchildren of her father. Alienation of her children and her father is certain since the family relations continue through the male children.
8.) On death, she is quite different from the man, since the man is immortal upon death. Woman, however, terminates once dead.
9.) She is an object to be used by the man just as his material property. He can loan her, rent her, donate her, sell her, dismiss her or even murder her.
10.) She is a tool to satisfy man's lust. There is no legal limit in the way men exploit women. Europe and America which are far from God's revelations, have gone so far that woman is considered to be a commodity to be used to attract more customers for the cinemas, television, video, satellite and various journals. Among these the pornographic ones have the most income.

Islam's Response to the Corrupt Men's Mental Deviations Regarding Women

Islam is a divine religion and a way of life. The Islamic culture is in harmony with all human values and humanity. Islamic laws are decreed by God who has created man and knows all about man's nature. God has decreed laws based on man's nature and has guided him to facts he must realize.

Islam's responses to the above ten absurd statements regarding women which have been made during the past ages are as follows:

1.) Woman's creation and her existence is exactly similar to man's; and she is exactly the same as God has willed. She is truly human as stated in the following verses of the Glorious Qur'an:

> *"We have indeed created man in the best of moulds."[Holy Qur'an: Tin 95:4]*
>
> *"(Such is) the artistry of God, Who disposes of all things in perfect order: for He is well acquainted with all that ye do." [Holy Qur'an: Naml 27:88]*
>
> *"He Who has made everything which He has created." [Holy Qur'an: Sajda 32:7]*

2.) She has a purely divine and human soul which God has breathed into her. She has especial privileges due to this soul and she is the source of perfection. Her soul is no different from that of man. Her identity is the same as man's identity and her essence is similar to man's.

> *"O mankind ! reverence your Guardian-Lord, Who created you from a single person, created, of like nature, his mate, and from them twain scattered (like seeds) countless men and women."[Holy Qur'an: Nisaa 4:1]*
>
> *"And among His Signs is this, that He created for you mates from among yourselves, that ye may dwell in tranquillity with*

45

them." [Holy Qur'an: Rum 30:21]

Imam Baqir (Pbuh) has been quoted as saying that God created Eve from the remaining clay from which He created Adam [Tafsir-i-Ayashy].

The above-mentioned verses indicate that the creation of man and woman is in no way different. She has nothing less than man. Her soul is the soul that God breathed into her. She is a perfect creature who can use God's guidance and her talents, soul, mind and nature to reach the highest spiritual position. She may also ignore all facts and degrade to the lowest point.

3.) She has the right to ownership, and whatever she righteously earns is hers. Her rights to ownership are exactly similar to those of man's.

> *"That man can have nothing but what he strives for." [Holy Qur'an: Najm 53:39]*

Truly an individual owns what he earns by his/her own hard work and diligent efforts. This is a God-given right for both man and woman in this world and in the Hereafter.

> *"It is not lawful for you, (Men), to take back any of your gifts (from your wives)." [Holy Qur'an: Baqara 2:229]*

Imam Sadiq has been quoted as saying: "Three acts are considered to be robbery: being too jealous to pay the alms tax; not paying the wife's nuptial gift and borrowing money with the intention of not paying it back. [Bihar al-Anwar, v.100, p.349.]

> *"Those of you who die and leave widows should bequeath for their widows a year's maintenance and residence. "[Holy Qur'an: Baqara 2:240]*

Apart from the nuptial gift and the expenses in a man's will due to the widow after his death, God in His decree to men after divorcing their wives states:

"For divorced women maintenance (should be provided) on a reasonable (scale). This is a duty on the righteous." [Holy Qur'an: Baqara 2:241]

4.) *"A woman has the right to inherit from her father, her mother, her husband and her offspring. It is prescribed, when death approaches any of you, if he leave any goods, that he make a bequest to parents and next of kin, according to reasonable usage." [Holy Qur'an: Baqara 2:180]*

"From what is left by parents and those nearest related there is a share for men and a share for women, whether the property be small or large, a determinate share." [Holy Qur'an: Nisaa 4:7]

This noble verse is opposed to the erroneous habits and customs which deprive women and children of the most certain right of inheritance. This oppressive custom was practiced by the Arabs. The magnificent verse canceled the Arab's treasonous custom.

5.) A woman's worship of God is precisely the same as man's in God's sight. It is praiseworthy and dear. Men do not have especial rights to Heaven and divine rewards. It is stated in the Glorious Qur'an:

"Whoever works righteousness, man or woman, and has Faith, verily, to him will We give a new life, a life that is good and pure, and We will bestow on such their reward according to the best of their actions." [Holy Qur'an: Nahl 16:97]

It is clearly understood from this noble verse that the only criteria approved by God is the faith and good deeds of man being the product of his faith. There are no other conditions such as sex, age, race, tribe or social status for attaining a pure life and the reward of the Hereafter. The Prophet (Pbuh) said:

Four ladies are the noblest in Paradise: Khadijah, the daughter of Khovayled, Fatimah the daughter of the Prophet Muhammad (Pbuh), Mary the daughter of Omran, and Asia the daughter of Muzahim.

It is certain that should a woman be a servant of God, and a worshipper, she will have God's reward and a pure life near God; and if she tends to corruption and becomes agnostic like some corrupt men, then her abode will be Eternal Torture. As the Glorious Qur'an states in the following verse, the wives of Noah and Lot are to be tortured forever and abide in Hell.

God sets forth, for an example to the unbelievers, the wife of Noah and the wife of Lot:

> *"They were (respectively) under two of our righteous servants, but they were false to their (husbands), and they profited nothing before God on their account, but were told: Enter ye the fire along with (others) that enter! "[Holy Qur'an: Tahrim 66:10]*

The Chapter Mary and the Chapter Dahr and the verses about the believing wife of Pharaoh in the Holy Qur'an, all show that women possess a noble position in regards to worship, and can benefit from a great reward in the Hereafter. This all strongly defeats those who have repeatedly claimed during the past ages that woman's worship has no value in any religion and for God.

6.) Women are the offspring of their own parents and the mothers of their own children and no one can deprive them of this right, as this is oppressive. The Holy Qur'an considers girls to be similar to boys in being their parents' offspring. Once women marry and have children, they are considered as the mothers of their children.

The Qur'an expresses God's anger about the Arabs' crime of burying their daughters alive and considered it to be an oppressive act:

> *"Kill not your children on a plea of want." [Holy Qur'an: An'am*

6:151]

The Qur'an has clearly stated that daughters are your offspring and in the verse related to inheritance it states:

"God (thus) directs you as regards your children's (inheritance): to the male a portion equal to that of two females."[Holy Qur'an: Nisaa 4:11]

It has clearly referred to daughters as offspring and has provided an undeniable answer to the idle talkers of history. Women are the mothers of their own children and it is stated in the Glorious Qur'an:

"The mothers shall give suck to their offspring for two whole years." [Holy Qur'an: Baqara 2:233]

The Holy Qur'an has stated about the story of Moses:

"So we sent this inspiration to the mother of Moses." [Holy Qur'an: Qasas 28:7]

The Prophet (Pbuh) stated the following about his daughter Hazrat Fatimah Zahra (Pbuh):

Fatimah is a chip off the old block. [Bihar al-Anwar, v.43, p.23] And in another tradition he said:

Our children, whether they be boys or girls, are in our bloodline. [Safinat ul-Bihar, v.8, p.580.]

7.) Without any doubt a woman's children are the grandchildren of her father. The noteworthy attention paid by Muhammad, the Prophet (Pbuh) to Hassan and Husayn, being his two dearest grandchildren, is a clear rejection of the statement of the ignorant idle talkers of history stating that a daughter's children are not the grandchildren of her father. According to

49

the Islamic jurisprudence, the one whose mother is a Sayyedeh[8]. is certainly related to His Holiness.[9] And the noble Shiite scholar Sayyid Murteza has decreed that one can pay the one-fifth levy to people who are related to the Prophet (Pbuh) on their mother's side.

8.) A woman does not terminate after death, but rather she has an eternal life just like men. If she is a good servant of God, she will abide in Heaven forever and if she does not worship God, she will abide in Hell forever. Over one thousand Qur'anic verses related to the Hereafter clearly prove this matter.

9.) Woman is not a commodity, but rather as the verses of God's Book have clearly expressed she is an intelligent, strong-willed creature who is exactly the same as man in terms of nature and creation. She benefits from all human and divine privileges and characteristics.

10.) Woman is not an object to be consumed and satisfy man's lust, but rather she is man's partner who establishes half of their life together. She is the critical element in the continuance of the human race. If a man marries a woman with pure intentions, it is considered to be a type of worship. And if he treats her properly, he can earn the reward of the Hereafter as it is stated in the Glorious Qur'an:

> *"Your wives are as a tilth unto you; So approach your tilth when or how ye will; but do some good act for your souls beforehand; and fear God, and know that ye are to meet Him (in the Hereafter) and give (these) good tidings to those who believe."[Holy Qur'an: Baqara 2:3]*

Using the expression "tilth" in the above-mentioned verse, God wants to show the necessity of the existence of women in human society and show that they are not means to satisfy lust, but rather are the pure means to

---

8   In the Prophet Muhammad's bloodline.

9   The Prophet Muhammad (pbuh)

maintain the human race. This is a serious warning to those who consider women to be sensual means. By "doing some good act for your souls beforehand" it is meant to send some supplies ahead for the Hereafter by making love to your wives.

This points to the fact that the ultimate objective of sexual intercourse is not self-fulfillment, and the believers should use this act to bear and raise good children. They should consider this holy act to be a spiritual supply for the Hereafter. So the Qur'an admonishes us to choose our spouse in such a way that will result in raising well-behaved children which will be a great social and human reserve.

Since the subject up for discussion in the beginning of the verse is sexual intercourse, being man's most attractive instinct, God has admonished man with the phrase "and fear God" so that he pays attention to God's decrees in regards to sexual intercourse. And at the end of the verse God warns us that on the Day of Judgment we will rush to meet God and see the results of our own actions. By using the phrase "and give these good tidings to the believers" God gives encouragement to the believers who submit to these decrees, thereby benefiting in their worldly and spiritual lives.[Tafsir i-Nimuneh, v.1, p.97]

The glory and value of this center of love is expressed in an extremely important tradition from Imam Sadiq (Pbuh) saying:

When Eve was created, Adam said to God " Who is this gorgeous creature whose proximity and gazing at her saves me from loneliness and makes me get used to her. He was answered, " She is my slave girl. Would you like her to stay with you, to be your companion and your friend? And would you like her to satisfy your rightful desires? " Adam answered in the positive. He was told, "then thank me for the companion I gave you as long as you live." [Vasa'il-al-Shia, v.14, p.2]

Therefore a righteous woman and a loyal wife is one of God's blessings which requires praise and gratitude throughout life. Imam Sadiq (Pbuh) said:

Most benefits come from women. [Vasa'il-al-Shia, v.14, p.11]

This is a wonderful tradition which considers women as the source of most benefits. Upon marrying a woman, a man fulfills the conditions of half of his religion. Respecting her rights is considered to be worshipping God. Being kind to her is considered to be obeying God. Having well-behaved children from her is considered to be as a supply for the Hereafter.

Serving her is a means of satisfying God. According to Muhammad the Prophet, a woman who is a mother has Heaven under her feet. These are all part of the benefits that Imam Sadiq (Pbuh) said come from women.

I admonish young men who intend to get married, those who have married and believing men to pay attention to these divine facts and to seriously avoid denying a woman her rights. They should realize the highly valuable jewel[10] they have married. I also admonish young women who intend to get married, those who have married, and all the distinguished women to realize their worth considering these facts. They should praise and thank God the Benevolent for their being women. They should be good and righteous spouses for their husbands based on the guidance from the Holy Qur'an, the statements of the Prophet (Pbuh) and the Noble Imams. They ought to use their pure sensations and feelings in being women, wives and mothers, and should obey divine decrees in all of life affairs so as to have a healthy home and family, pure and well-behaved children and a happy and secure life. Thus, they can attain God's pleasure and fill their lives with pleasure, happiness, beauty and sweetness by means of their actions, principles of morality and behavior.

Another Look at History Regarding Women's Life and Status

The men of the Age of Ignorance were terribly brutal to women. They lived in ignorance of God's logic, illumination and revelation and condemned women to be a means for man's life of capricious desires. They viewed women as being the main factor for supplying all of their lustful pleasures. These men thought reading and writing to be dangerous for women and

---

[10] Woman.

would not let them leave the house to carry out daily affairs or visit relatives. Men restricted the woman's place for living to the four walls of her home, and considered her to be a creature lacking any will as opposed to men who could do anything they wanted.

In the Christian neighborhood where the people were completely deviated from God's religion, it was said:

The mouth of a woman should be muffled just as that of a dog.

Those Christians doubted whether the woman had the spirit of a human or of an animal.

In Africa woman was considered to be goods and wealth and the Africans did not consider her any better in worth than a cow or sheep. Whoever had more numbers of women was known to be the wealthiest. It was a normal affair to buy and sell women and use them in ploughing the land.

In Chaldea and Babylon women were sold just as all other goods were. Every year a bazaar was set up so as to sell the young girls who had reached the age of marriage.

In India, girls were married off at the age of five and no rights were due to them. They considered a woman's life subject to the man's. Woman was thought to be woman an uninvited guest for the man. When her husband died, she was incinerated with him. No creature was thought to be inferior to a widow.

Nowadays as it is written in the newspapers, many Indians kill their daughters in childhood since they are afraid they cannot buy their trousseaux.

In China and Tibet women had no other right except to do housework at home. So as to keep a woman from walking normally, her feet were bound in a metal frame after birth. Upon reaching fifteen years of age the frame was removed.

In Greece the center of knowledge and philosophy, it was thought to be a crime for a woman to bear a female baby. The second time she bore a girl she was prosecuted in court and condemned to pay a fine and the third time she was sentenced to death.

As the Glorious Qur'an states, burying girls alive in Arabia was a normal case:

"When news is brought to one of them, of (the birth of) a female (child), his face darkens, and he is filled with inward grief! With shame does he hide himself from his people, because of the bad news he has had! Shall he retain it on (sufferance and) in contempt, or bury it in the dust? Ah! What an evil (choice) they decide on!" [Holy Qur'an: Nahl 16:58-59]

The above descriptions are only some of the crimes which ignorant and stupid men allowed to commit in regards to women. Details of these matters have been registered in books on the subject of women's lives and you may refer to these sources.

Also you have read about the opinion of the Divine Religion Islam about women in the ten points mentioned above. Let's take a look at how the Qur'an and religious traditions treat the subject of woman in the following categories:

*MOTHER (Umm): **"The source of everything mother."*** [Holy Qur'an: Qasas 28:7]

*TILTH (Harath): **"The means by which the human race survives."*** [Holy Qur'an: Baqara 2:23] *"**Garments (Lebas): the garment for life.***" [Holy Qur'an: Baqara 2:187] "**Pacifier (Taskeen): the cause for peace of mind.***" [Holy Qur'an: Rum 30:21] Sweet Basil (Rayhaneh): an elegant sweet-smelling flower* [Traditions quoted in Vasa'il-al-Shia, chapter on offspring]

Blessing (Ne'mat): God's favor [Ibid]

Men and youth, whether they be married or intend to get married, must pay more attention to the spiritual status and benefits of the existence of this beautiful and beneficial creation of God. They must know that chaste women have borne the Prophets, the Imams, the Saints, the sages, the mystics, the judges, the writers, the great jurisprudents and the gooddoers among God's servants. Women are the source of all goodness and blessings in people's lives.

Dear fathers and mothers must be very careful to polish the characters of their daughters and devotedly train their children divinely and humanly as much as possible. Husbands must respect all the rights of their spouses with dignity and manners. Thus, women become ready to raise the next generation properly after being raised properly by their parents and their rights being observed by their husbands. Thus, human society will be spiritually fed in the best way.

Is it not true that a young Christian woman who was captured in war finally arrived at Imam Hady's house? Did she not give birth to the 12th Imam (who shall spread universal justice), after receiving divine training by the 10th Imam and Hazrat Hakimeh Khatoon?

Women are the source of all perfection and potential truths which will be realized upon receiving the light of guidance, revelations and having a good instructor. And they will become the source of everlasting feats and eternal resources.

Belittling a woman, attacking her personality, enforcing limits upon her beyond the wise religious decrees and torturing her are all disapproved of by the religion: these deeds are considered to be some sort of disgusting and terrible oppression. The same is true for not allowing her to visit her parents and relations, facing with her with a sour face, bringing home the husband's daily tiredness and work problems and not fulfilling her instincts, especially her sexual ones.

If you want to base your lives upon love and kindness, respect the woman's personality, tell her you love her, ask her about herself, assist her in house duties, avoid bothering her and forgive some of her actions which result from her tiresome housework and her physical limitations. This way you can experience the sweetness of life and you have really worshipped God the Benevolent in the best way.

Woman is the source of all goodness and the field for cultivating humanity. She is your garment in life, the source of peace of mind, the delicate flower in the rose garden of Creation. You have beside you one of God's blessings. The Noble Prophet of Islam (Pbuh) compared the love for women to the love for sweet smells and prayer:

What I love in the world is woman and sweet smells. And the apple of my eye is prayer. [Bihar al-Anwar, v.103, p.218]

If one observes the rights of woman, respects her personality and brings forth praiseworthy offspring, then his file of good deeds does not come to an end even after his death. He will benefit from the good deeds of his well-behaved children after his death.

The Prophet (Pbuh) stated:

When an individual dies, his/her actions come to an end unless three things take place:

He/she has committed some beneficial actions which will last forever.

He/she has taught others some knowledge which they would benefit from.

He/she has raised exemplary children who pray for him/her.

Therefore, mothers and fathers must realize the worth of their daughters. Men must appreciate their pure and praiseworthy spouses. Taking care of female children and wives is a source of benefit in this world and in the Hereafter for men.

Eight

Part 5: Man's and Woman's Independence in Islam

Don't be anyone's slave since God created you to be free." [Bihar al-Anwar, v.77, p.214]

Human Freedom and Independence

Mankind's creation is based upon his freedom in life, independence in carrying out daily affairs and in control over choices. No one has the right to make another his slave imprisoning that individual to serve his own needs. To deprive others of freedom and free will is a mortal sin, capital treason and a great crime.

Liberty and the control over one's affairs are ingrained in man's essence, whose nature was created with this truth in mind. Freedom and independence are the greatest blessings God has bestowed upon mankind. These are is the most excellent sources of growth, perfection and attaining higher worldly and spiritual positions. The field of freedom is the best area. The condition of having control over one's affairs and being free is the most wonderful condition for an individual.

One very important case of Islam's struggle against oppression concerns that of man's liberty. Islam fights like a tiger against those whose philosophy is based on colonization and exploitation and want to enslave men who have been created to be independent. Islam emphatically decrees that an all-out holy war (Jihad) must be made against oppression and the oppressors who have attacked freedom.

All of the damages imposed upon mankind's life throughout history are the direct result of depriving people of liberty and attacking their freedom. Listening to and putting up with bullying, accepting to be oppressed, and selling one's freedom are the greatest sins and will be the cause of being deprived of God's Mercy. Also one's worldly and spiritual interests will be endangered.

It is absolutely necessary to protect one's freedom, the ability to make choices and one's free will; all of which God the Almighty has bestowed upon man so that he may develop, reach a state of perfection and his talents would blossom.

Whenever these benefits are endangered, you must defend them even if it costs your very life.

A Strange Story About Freedom

In history it has been recorded that the Caliph Yazeed or one of his agents was on his way to make the pilgrimage to Mecca, when he entered the town of Medina, he sent for a Koreyshite citizen and when the man came, Yazeed (or his agent) asked him: "Confess that you are my slave! If I wish I will sell you as a slave and if not I will keep you as a slave."

The Koreyshite responded: "I swear to God that you are not any nobler than I am regarding family roots. Your father was not any better than my father in the Age of Ignorance and in the era of Islam. You are not at all superior to me regarding faith and religion. You are not any better than I am. Given that I possess all these characteristics, how do you expect me to confess to be your slave?"

The oppressor told him: "If you do not confess to this, I will order your execution."

The man responded: "Killing me is not any worse than killing Imam Husayn."

At this point, the order of execution was issued and he became a martyr for the sake of freedom and free will. [Ruzih i-Kafy, p.313]

The Commander of the Faithful[11] stated:

O people! People were not born slaves. Verily all people are free."[Mizan al-Hikmat, v.2, p.351]

And he also stated:

Do not be anyone's slave since God created you to be free." [Bihar al-Anwar, v.77, p.214]

Then we must note that what is meant by freedom is freedom from slavery and worship of other men, freedom from lust, erroneous instincts and moral corruption. Man is born pure and innocent as a superior creature free from slavery with nobility and honor. In short, man is free from all vices and has free will. He is then guided by God, his own wisdom and nature, the Prophets, the Imams, the Holy Qur'an and the sages to use this freedom and free will in order to make the best choices and become prosperous in this world and in the Hereafter.

If an individual pays no attention to the above-mentioned explanations and turns his back on God's guidance, undoubtedly one will lose the pearl of freedom, free will and control when dealing with the tyrants and the Satans of the time. One will get involved in greediness, haughtiness, jealousy, instincts and lust. That person will be a slave to the world and other people. He/she will be a slave to lust and instincts, a prisoner of greediness and will not benefit from nobility, prosperity and the blessings of this world and of the Hereafter.

There are some who commit any crime and pollute themselves with any

---

[11] Imam Ali

sort of lust and sin: They obey anybody and call this roguery "freedom." They are ignorant slaves, vile servants, contemptible bondsmen and poor creatures.

The Commander of the Faithful (Pbuh) stated:

Those who give up their unlawful desires are really free men. He also said:

The world is simply a highway and the people on it are of two groups: The first have sold themselves to lust, materialism and dirty tricks. They are in danger of perishing. The second group have freed themselves from all those disgusting acts: They are free of any sort of evil in this world and punishment in the Hereafter."

Imam Sadiq (Pbuh) stated:

There are five characteristics which if a man does not have one, there would remain not much in him to benefit from:

1) Faithfulness; 2) Thinking about the future; 3) Modesty; 4) Being goodtempered; 5) Freedom, which is what causes all these characteristics to come together in an individual. [Mawa'ez Al-Adadieh, p.268.]

Imam Ali (Pbuh) said:

Do not let greediness enslave you since God has created you to be free. [Mizan al-Hikmat, v.2, pp.351-2]

He also stated:

One of the divine favors granted to the free individual is to legally earn his living. [Ibid]

An Important Matter

A person must pay strict attention to the truth and meaning of freedom, the worth of free will and control, and the fact that when man remains in the shade of God's guidance he will benefit from independence, free will and control. Then he shall attain lofty positions, efficient ranks, and truths which he thought he could never understand.

Let's try to preserve our independence throughout our whole lifetime, even in the face of all events and catastrophes. Doing so will make us happy and satisfy our Lord.

You know that the atom is made up of neutrons, protons and one or several electrons. By God's will the electrons are attracted to their own central axis orbiting at the specified speed and in the specified order. As long as this speed and rotation continue based on that especial order and the forces of attraction and repulsion, the atom is beneficial wherever it may be and whatever it may do.

However, when the forces of attraction and repulsion are removed, the electrons lose their special order and separate from the central nucleus, the result will be nothing but destruction.

We can compare man to the atom. His nature, his search for God and his monotheistic belief are like the atom's nucleus. And the continuation of his existence is dependent upon all his body parts and his internal states being attracted to God and his actions being based on God's decrees.

His actions should never be void of submission to God. Separation from God and leaving the domain of attraction of His Love and Knowledge or in other words leaving God's orbit, will result in corruption in man's physical parts and his inner being.

The Holy Qur'an states:

> *"As to those who reject faith, I will punish them with terrible agony in this world and in the Hereafter, nor will there be anyone to help them." [Holy Qur'an: Al-i-Imran 3:56]*

One of the factors in controlling man from indulging in some types of corruption is the very important program of marriage. When man has the required worthiness meaning that he benefits from faith, morality and action to the extent of his capabilities and also finds a good match in life, his appearance and internal states are controlled. His independence will be preserved and he will be safe from being enslaved by unlawful lust, corrupt programs and unsuitable friends.

There are so many men who having faith, good dispositions and nobleness helped their spouses to attain divine status, positions and humane nobleness.

Also there are so many women, who being aware and insightful, have helped their husbands to attain lofty human status and magnificent, heavenly positions.

A Dignified and Worthy Spouse

In the year 60 A.H. (681 A.D.), Zuhayr Ibn Qayn Bijali went on the pilgrimage to Mecca with a few of his attendants and performed the necessary ceremonies there. He was the head of this small caravan which had set out from his house to the House of God (Ka'aba) in Mecca and would then return home. Zuhayr thought he would return home, but this was not to be his fate. Zuhayr was traveling from the House of God to God, but he himself was not aware of the fact. Zuhayr's small caravan did not wish to stay at the same way-station as the caravan of Imam Husayn (Pbuh). He did not want to join up with Husayn (Pbuh).

If Husayn's caravan stopped at that way-station, then Zuhayr's would pass by it and stop at the next way-station. And if Husayn did not stop at that way-station, then Zuhayr would stop and rest there. Zuhayr would do his best not to come face to face with Husayn (Pbuh). Why was this so?

Zuhayr's social status necessitated that he would do so since he was not one of the companions of Ali (Pbuh) and his household[12]. He had nothing to do with Ali's household. Zuhayr was one of Uthman's supporters, a strong backer of Yazeed's government and an ally to the existing governmental system. On one hand, he knew Imam Husayn (Pbuh) and held especial respect for Ali's household. He did not want to be partner in the assassination of Ali's son Husayn (Pbuh). He wanted to remain impartial in the matter: he wanted to preserve his friendship with the Ummayyad clan [Uthman's clan] while at the same time not fight with Husayn (Pbuh). Therefore he could not come face to face with Husayn (Pbuh), since such an occurrence would be reported to Yazeed. If Husayn (Pbuh) requested Zuhayr to help him, what would Zuhayr do? If he helped Husayn (Pbuh), he must cut off

---

[12] Translator's note: Imam Ali is the father of Imam Husayn.

relations with his allies and fellowmen. And if he did not help Husayn (Pbuh), disobeying Husayn (Pbuh) was not allowed.

Husayn is the son of Ali (Pbuh) and Fatimah (Pbuh): He is eminent and the only remembrance of the Prophet of Islam. How could Zuhayr not obey Husayn's order? What would he have to say to God? How could he handle the fire of Hell? Remaining impartial was the best way out, so Zuhayr's caravan should stop at a way-stop in which there was the least possibility of Zuhayr meeting Husayn (Pbuh). Zuhayr wanted to do one thing, but fate determined something else.

The way-stations in the dry, hot wilderness of Arabia are very far apart, so the caravans must stop at the closest way-station whether they want to or not. Zuhayr's caravan had to stop at the same one as Husayn's caravan did: The place which converted the followers of the Caliph Uthman into the followers of Ali (Pbuh), and the followers of Yazeed became the followers of Husayn (Pbuh). The tents of Zuhayr and his companions were set up in one place and the harem curtains of Husayn's caravan were hung up beside those tents. Husayn (Pbuh) knew that Zuhayr was brave, generous, well-known, an eloquent speaker and an able person. What a waste it was that he had all these worthy qualities, but was far away from true human beings and was subject to animals like the Umayyad clan! What a waste for an enlightened man not to benefit from freedom! This worthy pearl did not deserve to be amongst ruins and not be an outstanding human being.

At this way-station, Zuhayr also took the necessary precautions not to confront Husayn (Pbuh). Husayn (Pbuh) had revolted against Yazeed's government and Zuhayr was one of the government's supporters. The government expected its supporters to be enemies with its enemies and to subdue any rebels. Coming into contact with those mutinous fellows was considered to be the greatest offense.

Zuhayr was sitting in his tent busy eating a meal with his relatives when suddenly the tall figure of Imam Husayn's representative appeared, greeted Zuhayr and said: "Zuhayr Abu 'Abdullah! Husayn (Pbuh) born of Ali (Pbuh) requests you to come to him!"

Zuhayr had come face-to-face with exactly what he was afraid of. Being terribly frightened, he could not utter a single word and could not think of what was suitable to do. He had not thought that such a situation would come up and was perplexed about what to do. Should he ignore Husayn's message and disobey his command, or should he turn his back on Yazeed and go over to Husayn's side. Both actions would not be considered to be impartial which was his goal. Now the situation does not allow him to be impartial.

A heavy silence fell upon those present. Eating and talking were forgotten. Husayn's messenger stood looking at the scene. He was confused and asked himself why they were so quiet. Why didn't Zuhayr come with him and why didn't he say he wouldn't come? Husayn (Pbuh) had not put any pressure on Zuhayr and Zuhayr was free to answer as he liked.

A few minutes passed in silence and Zuhayr couldn't make a decision. Should he say yes or no? The light of guidance was needed to free Zuhayr from his dark state of doubt and wondering and help him make up his mind. That was the most important moment in Zuhayr's life: the moment to choose between life and death. He was aware of the government's power. Zuhayr was familiar with Husayn's companions and knew that Husayn (Pbuh) and everyone with him would be killed. He knew that Husayn's family would be captured. He knew why Husayn (Pbuh) had sent for him and that Husayn's path led towards Heaven and Yazeed's to Hell: the former ends in prosperity and the latter in destruction.

Suddenly a lady's voice broke the silence and enabled him to make a decision. She was Zuhayr's wife, Delham who said: "O' Zuhayr! The son of the Prophet (Pbuh) is calling you and you do not go? Glory be to God! Go and see what he has to say. Listen to him and return." How wonderful is a good wife.

Zuhayr got up to go to Husayn (Pbuh). A short time later he returned smiling with no signs of sorrow on his visage. No one knew what Husayn (Pbuh) had told him in that short period of time.

When Zuhayr returned to his own tent, he said: "Take down my tent and set it up next to Husayn's (Pbuh)." A river joined the sea. Zuhayr who followed Yazeed became a follower of Husayn (Pbuh). He was released from oppression and reached the domain of justice. The follower of the Caliph Uthman went and the follower of Ali (Pbuh) came back. See how prosperity envelopes man. Zuhayr faced his companions and said: "Whoever is my follower shall join me or else, farewell!"

Zuhayr's cousin, Salman Bajly joined Zuhayr and became a follower of Imam Husayn (Pbuh). And after saying the noon prayer with Imam Husayn (Pbuh), he was martyred on the Day of Martyrdom. Zuhayr rejected this world and whatever was in it, so he joined Husayn (Pbuh) and died with him. Just now Zuhayr is with Husayn (Pbuh) in the other world. Zuhayr said good-bye to his dear wife and stated: "You must go back to your family so that you will not be harmed because of me."

He returned her property to her and sent her back to her clan with her cousin. Delham cried and said good-bye to her worthy husband stating: God be your helper and want the best for you! In this last moment of ours, I have a request for you. On the Day of Judgment when you are admitted to the presence of Husayn's grandfather the Prophet (Pbuh), remember me and don't forget me! [Pishvaye Shahidan, p.328]

O' yes, freedom, thinking freely, choosing Husayn (Pbuh), and Zuhayr's free will had all been looted from him by the Ummayad clan, but his wife caused all these things to be returned to him. In the shade of freedom, Zuhayr was freed from the bonds of the ungodly and was embraced by ever-lasting prosperity. Therefore, it would not be an exaggeration to say that marriage guarantees freedom and free-will, and returns freedom to man.

Protect the spirit of Allah in you by getting married. Safeguard your position as God's representative on Earth (Caliph) from the looting of lust and corruption. Increase your faith and your own good deeds by marrying, thereby receive half of your religion. Protect the other half of your religion with piety and abstaining from the divinely forbidden acts. Men share in the blossoming of women's talents and women help men to rise in status.

Woman is a wise, deserving and able creature, so much so that the great sages have decreed she causes truth to appear in man's being. And man is honorable, of noble birth and a dignified creature, so much so that it has been said on his behalf that he causes woman to reach lofty ranks.

Ali (Pbuh) stated that the first woman from amongst the women of this world who steps into Heaven is Khadijah[13]. This implies woman has a divine spirit and she is in the position of being God's representative on Earth. And she possesses an excellent essence and human, moral and religious resources.

O' yes, a woman free of temptations, free of being a prisoner of the ungodly, free of lust and tendencies towards forbidden acts; together with a free man are two precious pearls and two lofty truths in this magnificent expanse of Creation.

Imam Husayn (Pbuh) has attributed Hurr ibn Yazeed's free personality to the noble mother of that martyr. And the Commander of the Faithful Ali (Pbuh) thought the greatness of Malik Ashtar to be the very reflection of his mother's chastity and godliness.

At home, the man must be the example of all good acts for woman and vice versa. And both should be excellent models and a good example for their children.

One's Independence in Marriage

Mothers and fathers must pay attention to the fact that the right to choose a spouse with important conditions that dear Islam has stated belongs to the offspring themselves. Parents do not have the right to force their son to marry a girl whom he does not approve of. Also parents do not have the right to force their daughters to marry the ones she does not want to. The offspring have the God-given right of freedom to choose their spouse. A very important tradition has commented upon the right to choose in

---

[13] The Prophet Muhammad's wife.

marriage: Ibn Aby Ya'fur said that he had the following request direction from Imam Sadiq (Pbuh):

I had chosen a certain woman to marry but my mother and father have chosen another. What should I do?" The Imam said: "Marry the one whom you like to and forget about the other one whom your father and mother have approved of." [Bihar al-Anwar, v.103, p.235]

In the practical treatises of great Shiite authorities regarding marriage we read:

If a suitable spouse is found for a young girl and is religiously according to custom a good match for her, and her father and grandfather are too strict and do not approve, then their permission is not required. [Risalehi-Tuwzih Al-Ma'sael, Ayatullah Fazel Lankarany , p.418, Matter 2236] Therefore, if a young man has found his best match and a young girl has also found her best match, the approval or lack of approval of the father and mother does not work as a condition. The young couple may marry with the permission of Islam and the approval of God.

Mothers and fathers should not force their own wishes and selfish desires of their clan upon young men and women who want to marry. It is forbidden in Islam to force others to do things. To undergo force is also prohibited by Islam.

Men and women are free to choose legitimate work and the wages they earn belong to them: Their ownership of the income is legitimate. The wife does not have any rights to man's property except with his permission and vice versa. We must note that men and women's independence must be respected in all aspects of life.

Nine

Part 6: Woman's Status in the Logic of Revelation

~❦~

"O Mary! God hath chosen thee and purified thee above the women of all nations." [Holy Qur'an: Al-i-Imran 3:42]

God's Pure Religion

The revered religion of Islam fundamentally differs from other religions and schools of thought in all areas. The Shiite school of thought is actually Islam interpreted by the Household of the Prophet (Pbuh) and the rightful successors to the Noble Prophet Muhammad (Pbuh). The Orthodox Islam has been expressed in the words of the Impeccable Imams. It differs greatly from all other schools of thought, cultures and religions in regards to its views on and description of monotheism, the Day of Judgment, the

68

angels, the Prophethood, the religious leadership (Imamat), the Qur'an, the individual, the family, the society, materialistic and spiritual affairs, moral and practical matters, woman, man, offspring, business affairs, training and education, governmental issues, etc.

What Islam states in this regard is pure fact and measures which are in accord with the physical world and our inner being. In short, Islam's viewpoints are in line with the facts which exist in God's Knowledge and the real world. What is expressed by the interpreters of truth in the religion of Islam is the product of their pure knowledge and divine insight, and is extracted from the depth of the Qur'anic verses.

The issues existing in this religion originate in the Glorious Qur'an. The Holy Qur'an starts with the description of Mercifulness, Beneficence and Sovereignty of God. The interpretation of these facts originates in the angelic, divine heart of the Prophet of Islam (Pbuh); and continues in the statements of the Immaculate Imams starting with Ali (Pbuh), the son of Abu Talib: It ends with the twelfth Imam's statements.

"Merciful" (Ar-Rahman) is one of God's especial names, and is not meant to be used for others; however, "Benevolent" (Ar-Rahim) can also be applied to others. Both adjectives have the same root in Arabic "rahmat" implies when translated that God is Merciful. Some interpreters of the Qur'anic verses hold the view that "Merciful" refers to God's general Mercy for all people, whether they are good or bad; while "Beneficent" refers to God's especial Mercy for his obedient, pious servants. His "Mercifulness" is to be manifested in this world, but His "Beneficence" will be granted in the Hereafter.

One cannot, however, see any difference between the two in the Holy Qur'an:

> *"But My Mercy extendeth to all things." [Holy Qur'an: A'raf 7:156]*

It is noteworthy that this divine attribute can be realized in the creation of all creatures, in provisions for their sustenance and their security against catastrophes.

Man's supplication, using these two attributes, results in a mystic state and an especial spirit and joy. This will in turn result in God's attention and favor to his servant. It has been noted in the Islamic literature that God said:

I am ashamed of not responding positively to man's request should he invoke me through my Mercifulness and Beneficence.

The creation of people and providing for their sustenance is the realization of His Mercifulness, and their guidance and prosperity is the product of His Beneficence. God has commended His Mercifulness in other forms in the Glorious Qur'an in phrases such as "the Best of the mercifuls", "the Most Merciful of the mercifuls" and "Possessing Mercy." Even though figures cannot be used to express God's Mercifulness, the Prophet (Pbuh) has tangibly explained the matter to help people understand it:

There exist one hundred of God's Mercies. God distributed one of these over the seven Heavens and the Earth. He grants all people whatever they deserve with just that one mercy; and the people are loving and merciful to each other with what they gain from that one mercy. He has kept the other ninety-nine with Him so that on the Day of Judgment He add them to that one and distribute them amongst the obedient believers.

Sovereignty implies ownership since God's Ownership spans over all creatures and worlds and is irrevocable. He is an Owner who has full power over the growth and development of all creatures. The connection between His Ownership and plans for all existing particles is real, eternal and intrinsic. Therefore, it is not reasonable for man to choose another Lord or Owner, or accept any plans or laws other than His.

Real monotheism can be really demonstrated in all aspects of life if man wholeheartedly submits to His Ownership and Plans and rejects any other ownership or claims thereof. He must reject any culture or school of thought which oppressively intends to grasp a hold on man's life. The delightful phrase "There is no God but God" carries exactly the same meaning in all aspects of life.

Verily Gods' Mercy and His Light of Sovereignty encompass man's whole physical and spiritual needs, and God's Plans, Benevolence and Favor guarantee man's prosperity in this world and the Hereafter.

The Supplication of the Divine Prophets for God's Sover-eignty and Mercy

All divine Prophets rejected all lords and owners, plans, mercy and favor other than God's. They considered themselves to belong to Him and be the objects of His Lordship and worshippers of the Worshipped at all times. They carried out an all-out war against undue claimants to Sovereignty. Some of them lost their lives to safeguard this monotheistic culture and God's Sovereignty and Mercy forever. They would always implore God's Sovereignty and Mercy at times of hardship and need. Adam (Pbuh) stated:

> *"Our Lord ! We have wronged our own souls: If Thou forgive us not and bestow not upon us thy Mercy, we shall certainly be lost."* *[Holy Qur'an: A'raf 7:23]*

Noah in his prayers to free the believers and himself and to uproot oppression, said:

> *"O my Lord! Leave not of the unbelievers, a single one on earth!"* *[Holy Qur'an: Nuh 71:26]*

Abraham (Pbuh) used to pray like this:

> *"O our Lord! I have made some of my offspring to dwell in a valley without cultivation, by Thy Sacred House; In order, O our Lord, that they may establish regular prayer." [Holy Qur'an: Abraham 14:37]*

Moses implored God during a time of hardship at the town gates of Madin and said:

> *"O my Lord ! truly am I in (desperate) need of any good that Thou dost send me!"[Holy Qur'an: Qasas 28:24]*

The Prophet Joseph (Pbuh) said:

> *"O my Lord ! Thou hast indeed bestowed on me some power, and taught me something of the interpretation of dreams and events-O Thou creator of the heavens and the earth! Thou art my protector in this world and in the Hereafter. Take Thou my soul (at death) as one submitting to Thy Will (as a Muslim), and unite me with the righteous." [Holy Qur'an: Yusuf 12:101]*

Zacharias stated:

> *"O my Lord ! leave me not without offspring, though Thou art the best of inheritors." [Holy Qur'an: Anbiyaa 21:89]*

God taught His Noble Prophet to pray like this:

> *"O my Lord! grant Thou forgiveness and mercy! For Thou art the Best of those who show mercy!" [Holy Qur'an: Mu-minun 23:118]*

God narrates that His Saints and Lovers stand in prayer in the darkness of the night saying:

> *"Our Lord! not for naught Hast Thou created (all) this!" [Holy Qur'an: AlImran 3:191]*

The word "Lord" (Rabb) has repeatedly been uttered in the prayers of the Immaculate Imams: namely; Dua i-Kumail, Abu-Hamzeh, Arafeh and the fifteen supplications of Imam Sajjad (Pbuh). The supplication of the Prophets to their Lord and the repeated occurrence of the word "Lord" in these prayers is a clear manifestation of the importance of this issue and its influence on all aspects of man's life. Those who prayed not only implored God's sovereignty and Mercy in words, but also this encompassed their entire life, all their beliefs, actions and morality both theoretically and practically.

The Grand Status of Worshipping God

Men and women are essentially similar to each other. They are not any different in the way they develop towards perfection, show signs of humanity, and attain spiritual status. They will be saved from being entrapped in selfish desires and being slaves to false deities, if they accept God's Sovereignty. They can do this by following their inherent inclinations; and by benefiting from wisdom, Prophethood, religious Leadership (Imamat), sympathetic teachers and qualified trainers. Thus, they will accept God's Sovereignty, Plans and Guidance in all aspects of life and remain secure from satanic cultures and wrong schools of thought. In this way they will benefit from belonging to the True Owner and will attain a lofty angelic status.

In their outward appearance and natural disposition, men and women are an example of God's Mercifulness, Beneficence and Sovereignty. This fact is expressed in the verses of the Holy Scripture[14] and there is no room for doubt. Woman is human possessing spiritual talents and aptitude. In the logic of divine revelations, woman has the same identity and essence as man. She is divine Mercy and a sign of God's Sovereignty.

The following are all evil results left over from oppressive cultures, Pharaohs of the past and claimants to man's ownership: belittling and attacking her; not respecting her rights; not satisfying her legitimate wants; considering her to be a weak human; unjustly divorcing her and

---

14 The Holy Quran

73

discrimination between the two sexes. In the old days when some fathers had a daughter in Italy, they became really happy.

They thought that they had received new property which they could sell as an aid thirteen or fourteen years later meeting their household expenses. At times, they burned women in a big pan of frying olive oil when they got angry with them. Women were used as maids or sex objects and are still deprived of many of their due rights. But in the logic of revelations and in God's religion, women are considered as having a high status with spiritual essence and are full of divine powers and lots of talents.

If women recognized their own position and protected their human status and if they benefited from the excellent Islamic teachings for their training and the Holy Qur'an development, then they would be able to reach the position of holy Mary, the noble Khadijah and the esteemed Zaynab. Thus, they can reach a status which ensures their nearness to God. Otherwise they will earn nothing but eternal damnation and worldly degradation, if they do not appreciate God's blessings just as some men do.

Woman in the Logic of Revelation

We read in the great commentary called Majma ul-Bayana [v.8, p.358] Esma, the daughter of Amis, and wife of Jafar, the son of Abi Talib, went to visit the Prophet's wives upon returning from their divine emigration to Ethiopia which was done to safeguard the religion. She asked them if there existed any verses in the Holy Qur'an regarding women. They answered no. Then she rushed to see the Prophet (Pbuh) and told him that women were in despair and at a loss. The Prophet (Pbuh) asked the reason. She answered men have been favorably mentioned in the Holy Qur'an.

God the Benevolent revealed:

> *"For Muslim men and women, for believing men and women, for devout men and women, for true men and women, for men and women who are patient and constant, for men and women who humble themselves, for men and women who give in charity,*

for men and women who fast (and deny themselves), for men and women who guard their chastity, and for men and women who engage much in God's praise, for them God has prepared forgiveness and great reward." [Holy Qur'an: Ahzab 33:35]

It is clearly stated in this verse that women, just like men, can attain ten angelic spiritual positions and attain God's forgiveness and a great reward in the Hereafter: 1) Islam (submission to God); 2) Faith; 3) Obedience; 4) Truthfulness; 5) Patience and perseverance; 6) Humbleness and fear of God's Glory and Punishment; 7) Benevolence and charity; 8) Fasting; 9) Self-control of carnal desires and 10) Remembrance of God.

Esma, the daughter of Yazid Ansary went to see the Prophet Muhammad (Pbuh) when he was with his companions. She said: "May my parents bestow their lives upon you. I am a representative of other women. No woman in the East or the West disagrees with me. You are appointed to men and women by God. We have faith in you and God. However, women are really restricted to the house. They submit to their husbands to satisfy their lust and will be pregnant for a long time. However, men can freely attend the congregation and Friday prayers; visit the sick; attend burial ceremonies; go on pilgrimage several times; and most important of all, fight in the way of God. While men go on pilgrimage or to guard the country borders, women guard their property, sew their clothes and raise children. What do we earn from this partnership?"

The Prophet (Pbuh) asked his companions if they had ever heard of anything better than what she had said in regards to her religion. They said they did not think she had discovered such realities so properly. The Prophet (Pbuh) addressed her and said: "Go and admonish all other women that if they are good wives for their husbands, and if they seek to please their husbands, and if they are complaisant with their husbands regarding daily affairs, then their reward equals all that their husbands can earn through all the acts you mentioned." The woman departed happily chanting:

"There is no god but God. He is the Greatest". [Mizan al-Hikmat, v.9, p.96]

The eighth Imam has narrated his forefathers quoting the Prophet (Pbuh):

In the presence of God the believer is similar to the nearest angels. Verily a believer has a higher status than angels. Nothing is better liked by God than a repenting believing man or woman.

Intellect and Lust as Measures for Prosperity or Misery

Intellect is the force that aids in understanding and accepting facts, planning for health and prosperity and designing beneficial affairs in man's life. This precious pearl has been interpreted as the inner Prophet in traditions from the Holy Household of the Prophet Muhammad (Pbuh). [Usul al-Kafy, Chapter on the Intellect]

Lust is a natural God-given instinct which can be used to derive pleasure from life, and provides for a motivation to strive for the life of this world and also, at times for the Hereafter. If it is bound using one's intellect, life will be good, and God's Mercy will be bestowed upon it. Man's existence would then exemplify human traits and his worth would be higher than that of the angels.

But if our intellect is enslaved by lust, it will not be able to guide us. Then unbounded lust and numerous desires will govern our lives. Once man follows lust he will not be able to see anything but material affairs. His criteria in life will be based on food and lust. All signs of humanity will vanish in him, and he will become worse than the beasts.

It is narrated that Abdullah, the son of Sanan, asked Imam Sadiq (Pbuh) whether men or angels were superior to each other. He responded that the Commander of the Faithful Ali (Pbuh) said:

God the Glorious and the Almighty has given angels intellect with no lust; the animals have lust without intellect; and man has both intellect and lust. Whoever can govern his lust with his intellect is superior to the angels, and whoever loses control of his intellect or his lust is inferior to the animals. [Bihar al-Anwar, v.57, p.299]

This is true for both men and women. A women can also be nobler than the angels should this be manifested in her. But if she ignores intellectual foresight, the inner light and the prophet within, and strives for jewelry and ornaments for lustful seduction of others, then she will be worse than animals, just like infidels, and corrupt men.

Ten

Part 7: Obstacles to Marriage

"God intends every facility for you ; He does not want to put you to difficulties." [Holy Qur'an: Baqara 2:185]

Strictness in Marriage

Young men and women's need to marry is natural and intrinsic. It seems hard for them to resist sexual instincts for a very long time. Delaying marriage has at times led to corruption and sin. Preventing marriage has at times made young men and women ill. The need to marry and obstacles to marriage have at times led to a love affair which not only causes corruption, but may also leads to suicide attempts. When they reach the age of marriage and suggest they want to get married, some parents call them kids. They consider the need to get married as being rude. They attack their children and belittle them. Such a confrontation may lead children with a weak belief to deviation. Some parents propose such strict conditions for marriage which are either too hard or impossible for the parents of the other party to fulfill. Such insistence delays the marriage and the young human flowers will wither.

Sometimes when a young man goes to propose marriage, he encounters the sour faces of the girl's family and gives up. The girl will then remain in her father's home with her feelings hurt, and she might get too old to marry. This may also happen with the boy's family.

At times, young men or women have limitations placed on their decision-making due to paternal or maternal domination. They do not marry and thus are hurt. There are also occasions when the young man or woman place such strict restrictions on marriage which prevent it. Such strictness is considered unjust, immoral, inhumane, ungodly and illegitimate in Islam. Those who are too strict are admonished about the consequences of their actions in this world and in the Hereafter. It is said that God the Benevolent is lenient with lenient people, and is strict with strict ones.

Being strict in marriage is similar to opposing the sexual urges and the natural human instincts of young men and women. God will be strict with those who are too strict and will deprive them of His Mercy and Favor. Himad, the son of Uthman said:

A man complained of someone to Imam Sadiq (Pbuh). A short time later another man arrived. When the first was asked the reason why he had complained he said, "This owes me money and I want to get my money back to the last penny." Imam Sadiq became angry, turned around and said to the creditor: "Have you not read God's statement in the Holy Qur'an?":

"Fear the terrible reckoning;"[Holy Qur'an: Ra'd 13:21]

Do you think that this "terrible reckoning" refers to God's oppression of man. No, verily by God: "They fear not but the deep investigation." Know that: "One who is so strict in investigating is committing evil." O' parents, young men and women, beware of strictness especially in marriage . Avoid this inhumane act. Take it easy and provide the means for the marriage of your daughters and sons. This will prevent the spread of corruption and sin.

Use Your Own Case to Judge for Others

The parents should remember that they themselves were once young and were very eager to get married. They wished their parents would provide the means for their marriage. They hoped their parents would let them marry in an environment full of love and kindness without imposing hard conditions. If they observed that their parents raised issues or set up obstacles that might delay this divine cause, they would get upset with their parents and would even hate them.

Now that they are in the past position of their parents and want to marry off their sons or daughters, they should put themselves in their child's shoes. They should consider their hopes and aspirations, the pressure of their carnal desires and their strong will to establish a new life. This could lead to leniency and can simplify the marriage of their offspring.

The Commander of the Faithful Ali (Pbuh) has pointed this out in an important tradition:

To better understand the facts of life and human issues, use your own case to judge for others. Prefer for others what you prefer for yourself. Dislike for others what you dislike for yourself. Just as you do not like anyone to oppress you, do not oppress others. Just as you like to be treated well, treat others well. Consider bad for others what you consider bad for yourself. Be happy with people in cases in which you expect them to be happy with you.

Imam Hassan Mujtaba (Pbuh) said:

"Live with people the way you like them to live with you." [Mizan alHikmat, v.6, p.316]

This is what Islam duly expects of all. This is the beneficial decree of the religion. This is the way that makes it easy to live with others, and prevents sins from corrupting our lives. It fills life with love and loyalty, health and friendship, and simplicity and sweet affection.

Parents should remember what they preferred when they were young themselves. They wished to marry with someone from a family of an equal rank. They wished that both families would avoid undergoing excessive, unbearable expenses. So they should prefer the same things for their children. By putting aside undue expectations and avoiding heavy expenses, they should provide the means for the marriage of their children.

God grants a great reward to those who provide the means for marriage. Parents should be the first ones to provide the means for the marriage of their children, and follow it all the way through with love, nobility and kindness.

The Prophet (Pbuh) said:

Whoever strives to provide the means for the marriage of believing men and women to the point that God will join them in marriage, will receive a thousand companions with big, beautiful and lustrous eyes in Heaven as a reward. His reward is equal to one year of worship for each step taken or word uttered. [Marriage in Islam, p.18]

How can parents who are too strict about the marriage of their children deprive themselves of such a great reward from God, while they could easily provide the means for the marriage? How can they respond to their children in God's Just Court on the Day of Judgment if the children become corrupted, suffer from physical or mental shock or get psychologically distressed?

Imam Musa, the son of Jafa (Pbuh), requested his noble aunt by mail to send some property put aside for contributing to the nuptial gift of the spouse of Muhammad, the son of Jafar. She immediately did so as soon as she received the letter. The letter stated:

There exists in the Hereafter a divine shelter. Only the Prophet, the guardian appointed by his will, those who free a slave or provide for the payment of a believer's debt, or marry off a believing unmarried man can benefit from this shelter. [Marriage in Islam, p.18-19]

The Commander of the Faithful Ali (Pbuh) stated:

The greatest sin is stealing a Muslim's property, and the best form of intervention is intervening in marriage. [Ibid]

Imam Sadiq (Pbuh) said:

Whoever marries off an unmarried man, will be amongst those who will

81

receive God's Favor and Mercy in the Hereafter. [Ibid, pp.20-21]

He also said:

God will favorably look at four groups of people in the Hereafter: salesmen who accept returned goods; those who relieve one's sorrow; those who free a slave; and those who marry off an unmarried man. [Ibid, pp.20-21]

The Prophet (Pbuh) said:

Whoever breaks up an arranged marriage or a couple will be damned by God in this world and in the Hereafter, and God has decreed that he be stoned with a thousand fiery rocks. Whoever tries to break up a couple but fails to do so, will be damned by God in this world and in the Hereafter and will be forbidden to see God's Mercy. [Ibid, pp.20-21]

I wish all parents were aware of these concepts and could benefit from great divine rewards by following these facts. I also wish that those who are aware of these concepts, but are too haughty to follow them would stop it and avoid God's eternal damnation, anger and torture.

Haughtiness is a Satanic Attribute

Today we suffer from early maturity. This is due to the cultural invasion of the minds and spirits of our youth by the voices and images of the atheist global media. Pornography is an international catastrophe causing sexual arousal. Therefore, it is both religiously ordained and morally expected of the Islamic government and people, the rich, the relatives and the parents to do all they can to ease the marriage of the youth. They should eliminate the wrong customs and traditions, discard western traditions, and forget imposing strict conditions so that the young men and women's beliefs, principles of belief and human behavior remain partially intact. Thus, they may be saved from falling into sin.

Do not be too haughty. Let the divine decrees, the orders of the Noble Prophet Muhammad and the Immaculate Imams be put into practice. It has unfortunately been observed that some parents make such gestures during marriage proposal meetings that one might think they are powerful beings.

They think that their child is a prince or princess and their marriage ceremonies should be conducted like those at the time of Pharaoh. They make such lavish proposals that the other family is astonished and is forced to forget about the marriage. Then the children are forced to find illegitimate friends and commit various sexual sins to satisfy their instincts. The Holy Qur'an has considered haughtiness as one of Satan's attributes:

"... and they bowed down not so Satan: he refused and was haughty: he was of those who reject faith." [Holy Qur'an: Baqara 2:34]

(God) said:

"Get thee down from this: it is not for thee to be arrogant here: get out, for thou art of the meanest (of creatures)." [Holy Qur'an: A'raf 7:13]

Ali (Pbuh) said:

You should not be haughty with people and God regarding daily matters, since verily haughtiness is one of the greatest sins and worst defects, and it is the facade, appearance and attribute of Satan. [Mizan al-Hikmat, v.8, p.298]

He also said:

Avoid haughtiness since this attribute is the start of rebellion and transgression against God. [Mizan al-Hikmat, v.8, pp.300-302]

That noble man also said:

Haughtiness is the worst disposition. [Ibid] The Prophet (Pbuh) said:

Avoid haughtiness since verily man continues to live in haughtiness, so much so that God the Almighty and Glorious says:

O' you who record the deeds, record the name of my servant as one of the worst oppressors. [Ibid]

He also said to Abuzar:

O' Abuzar, whoever dies with the slightest bit of haughtiness in his heart will not smell the sweet scent of Heaven, unless he repents before he dies and gives up haughtiness. [Ibid]

How come a creature formed from sperm and powerless in the face of disasters is haughty with people and God? How come he considers himself to be superior to others while nothing in this world works according to his will?

Imam Sadiq (Pbuh) narrated his ancestors as having said a fight started between Salman. The man rudely asked: "Who are you to confront me?" Salman answered: "I am the first, and you were at first an unclean sperm. I am the last, and at last you will be a stinking corpse in the grave. When the Hereafter comes and the balance is set up, then whoever has done more good will be nobler, and whoever has done little will be inferior." [Bihar al-Anwar, v.73, p.231]

Allameh Majlesi has proposed the following treatment and remedy for this dangerous disease:

There are two ways to treat haughtiness and attain modesty, one being scientific and the other practical. The scientific approach is to get to know oneself and one's Creator. This cognizance is enough to purify one's inner being from haughtiness. The reason for this is that with this real knowledge of one's self and one's existence, one will realize that he is inferior to anything else and he has no right but to be humble and down to earth. Once he gets to know God through the signs of the universe and the soul, and delving into the verses of the Holy Qur'an, then he would realize that no one but God deserves Sovereignty, Grandeur and Haughtiness. The practical approach to cure haughtiness is to be humble before God and people in all actions, deeds and behavior; to observe the morality of the humble people and use the pious ones as his model. He should note that the Prophet (Pbuh), who is the best of all people used to sit down on the ground to eat food and said a servant eats food like other servants.[Bihar al-Anwar, v.73, pp.201-205]

Therefore you should be humble before your son or daughter regarding marriage. This means that you should consider your child who is at the peak of his/her natural instincts, hopes and aspirations and not consider your own customs, traditions, and conditions. You should be lenient in your conditions, and minimize your expectations from the other family. Thus a happy, blessed and secure marriage will take place and the couple can conveniently live together.

An Amazing Story about Leniency in Marriage

The late Mulla Muhammad Taqi Majlesi, who was a wise jurisprudent and an outstanding scholar, had three learned sons and four noble daughters. His first daughter was named Amineh Beigom. Her marriage to the commentator of the twelve-volume book Usul-al-Kafi, Mulla Salih Mazandarani, was a divine, amazing and pleasant one.

Mulla Salih Mazandarani who is a renowned Shiite scholar had an adventurous life, which is briefly described here. His father, Mulla Ahmad, was so poor that he could not provide for his son's living expenses.

Muhammad, who was then a young adult, went to Isfahan to study in one of the schools there. The school had an endowed property. The income was used to pay some money to each student based on his rank. Muhammad who had just started studying received very little which was insufficient for his daily needs. He suffered so much that he had to study at night under the light of one of the school's lamps.

However, he was so studious that he overcame all deprivations and difficulties and attained a high scholarly status. He managed to attend Mulla Muhammad Taqi Allameh Majlesi's class. A short time later he surpassed all other students and received his wise professor's especial attention.

The author of Mirat al-Ahwal wrote: Mulla Salih who was then a young scholar was considering choosing a spouse to marry. Allameh Majlesi became informed of that and one day after his class asked Salih if he would permit him to find him a spouse. He lowered his head and after a moment said yes. Allameh Majlesi got up and went home. He called his learned daughter Amineh Beigom, who had mastered all the sciences perfectly. He said to her: My dear daughter. I have found you a spouse who is extremely poor, but absolutely wise, pious and mature. But it is up to you to decide.

The holy noble learned daughter shyly said: "Dear father, being poor is not a defect for men." Thus she expressed her approval of this marriage. At a felicitous hour they held the marriage ceremony and prepared the bride for the groom.

On the wedding night, the groom unveiled her face and found her very beautiful. He went to a corner and started praising God and studying. He ran into a difficult academic issue which he was unable to resolve. Amineh Beigom realized the problem. When he left home the next day, she wrote the answer in full detail and put it in its place. When the man came home that night and saw that his unresolved issue was solved by that knowledgeable woman, he thanked God by placing his forehead on the ground, and prayed all night long. Thus three days passed. When Allameh Majlesi was informed, he told him: "If this wife is not suitable for you, let me know. I will get you another one." Mullah Salih replied: "No, that is not the issue. I keep away from her because no matter how much I praise God for this blessing that He has bestowed on me, I cannot be grateful enough." When Allameh Majlesi heard his answer, he said: "Confessing that one cannot be grateful enough to God is itself the utmost form of being grateful to Him." [Ayatollah Boroojerdy's Biography, Davani, p.79]

Note that first Majlesi kindly provided the means for his daughter's higher education so she could attain a high scientific status. He brought her up with purity, chastity, morality, humbleness and contentment. He chose the easiest way for her marriage, and married her off to one matching her in faith, morality and responsibility. He did not force her to accept Mulla Salih as a husband. He was not haughty, therefore he let her decide whether or not to marry him. When three days passed and the marriage had not been consummated, since Mulla Salih was praising God, he thought the man did not want his daughter. He was so humble that he proposed to get him a different wife if she was not good enough for him.

This is the morality of God's saints, lovers of truth, righteous men, chaste and faithful women, and pure families. These marriages are filled with divine blessing and God's Mercy and Favor. Mulla Salih and that knowledgeable lady had six sons who became scientists, jurisprudents, learned and eloquent, and two learned daughters. One of their daughters married the great Abu-al Ma'Ali and is the mother of Mir AbuTalib, both of whom are renowned scholars. Mir AbuTalib's son-in-law was Sayyid Muhammad Boroojerdy who is the fifth ancestor of the great Ayatullah Boroojerdy. The great Ayatullah Boroojerdy is also a maternal descendant of Majlesi. This is how they are related to the Majlesi family. Their second daughter married Sayyid Abdulkarim Tabatabaee, the sixth grandfather of Ayatullah Boroojerdy. She is the mother of Sayyid Muhammad Tabatabaee.

The Immaculate Imams (Pbuh) have been narrated as saying: God has taught his Prophets whatever man needs to know. One day the Prophet (Pbuh) climbed the mosque pulpit and after praising God he said to the people that the angel entrusted with revelations descended to me from the All-knowledgeable and said: "Young girls are like fruits which must be picked off the branch as soon as they ripen, or else they will be decayed by sun-shine and wind. When they reach adolescence, the outburst of their instincts cannot be cured except by marriage, or else they may be corrupted as they are humans, too." [Mustadrak al-Vasa'il, Introductory Chapters on Marriage, Ch.23.]

Parents should provide the means to marry off their daughters as soon as they develop enough to have a husband and carry out a joint life with a suitable man. This way they abide by God's decree and attain an infinitely great reward.

Perils of Keeping up With the Joneses

Keeping up with the Joneses is a bad behavior observed in some people. By considering the much higher financial status of either their neighbors or friends, they try desperately to attain a similar status. The unmarried girl who looks at the financial status of other girls in the family or among friends, wishes that her future husband, and her wedding ceremony be exactly similar to theirs. Thus she insists on rejecting the marriage proposals of those who are not that well-off. She puts off the marriage so long that she feels obliged either to marry an old man or a widower. She might even prefer to adopt a celibate lifestyle. Even if she gets married when she is no longer an enthusiastic young woman, she is neither a patient wife nor a good mother to raise her children. Therefore keeping up with the Joneses is an obstacle to marriage, and an evil form of conduct.

In the verse 88 of Hijr and the verse 131 of Taha, the Holy Qur'an has prohibited gazing at the wealth of the rich and their life. Traditions from the holy Imams clearly state that those who are continually after the wealth of others, and hope to obtain it, are filled with envy and sorrow. One should have pure intentions for marriage, and should do it for God's sake. His/her goal should be to implement the Prophet's tradition, to have righteous children and to live under the shade of God's Mercy and Favor. Once marriage is based on these factors, it will be firmly established. God's blessings will then be manifested in such a marriage and spiritual gains will result.

Once the provisions for marriage are made, the relatives should help it take place and not improperly interfere in this divine affair. They should not ingratiate themselves, attempt to disunite, make unjust judgments or impede the marriage.

Expensive Nuptial Gift

The nuptial gift is an important, delicate and noteworthy issue in Islam. It is extremely undesirable to expect expensive nuptial gifts. Any property or action of some value can be considered as a nuptial gift. For example, a store, a garden, some land or building, cash or even teaching can be considered as nuptial gift.

Besides the verses of the Holy Qur'an, there are many credible traditions from the Prophet (Pbuh) or the Immaculate Imams which prohibit expensive nuptial gifts since they prevent young men from marrying and this will leave many young girls unmarried.

The Prophet (Pbuh) said:

The noblest woman in my nation is one with the most beauty and the least nuptial gift. [Bihar al-Anwar, v.103, p.347]

The Commander of the Faithful (Pbuh) said:

Do not set up expensive nuptial gifts since this will cause enmity. [Ibid] Verily when a young fellow goes to propose marriage and faces unbearably high nuptial gift requirements, he gets disappointed and fails to marry, then he will despise the girl and her family. Such disappointment may lead him to corruption, his life will be wasted and his youth and enthusiasm will be irreversibly harmed.

Imam Sadiq (Pbuh) said:

A woman's blessing is spending little and easy delivery, and her misfortune is heavy expenses and hard delivery. [Marriage in Islam p.95]

The Prophet (Pbuh) said:

Do not establish expensive nuptial gifts, since money and wealth do not bring affection. It is God who establishes love. [Mojazat Nabovieh, p.182]

The Prophet (Pbuh) told a woman named Haola:

O' Haola, I swear by the same God who appointed me to Prophethood, that no woman who forces an expensive nuptial gift on her husband shall be saved from fiery chains that God shall place round her neck. [Marraige in Islam, pp.96-97]

An expensive nuptial gift requirement will force the youth to escape marriage and become involved in sin and corruption. Those who require it are partly responsible for such deviations and deserve God's punishment."

The Qur'an as a Nuptial Gift

Imam Baqir (Pbuh) said: "A woman came to the Prophet (Pbuh) and asked him to find her a husband. The Prophet (Pbuh) asked who is ready to accept her as his wife? A man got up and said; "I am ready." The Prophet (Pbuh) asked what would you give her as her nuptial gift? The man said: "I don't have anything." The Prophet said it is not possible to marry her without a nuptial gift, and repeated his proposal. However no one but the same man answered. The third time around he asked if the man knew any verses from the Qur'an. He replied in the positive. The Prophet (Pbuh) said he would marry him and this woman and the man must teach her whatever amount of the Qur'an that he knew."

Imam Reza (Pbuh) said:

Whenever a believer proposes to marry a girl from the family of his believing brethren and suggests to pay five hundred Durhams as the nuptial gift, and his offer is turned down for the reason that the amount is too low, then this is an oppression. It is then appropriate for God to deprive him of seeing the companions of Heaven with lustrous eyes.

It has been said that Um Saleem who was one of the noble women in the early days of Islam required the man who had come to propose marriage to her to become Muslim as her nuptial gift. She was the same woman who consoled her husband when their child died and did not let him become impatient. In reward for her patience, God granted her another child who became one of the friends of Imam Ali, the Master of the Monotheists.

A noble girl should note that if a well-matched suitor proposes marriage to her, and the family is too strict especially in regards to the nuptial gift, then she should politely and humbly discuss the issue: By telling them the known just truth, they should not be so strict. Low expectations are among the principles of morality of the Prophets and the Imams, and it is an outstanding attribute.

The Prophet (Pbuh) established a model for all our nation when he designated a small nuptial gift for his noble daughter, who is the Lady of all Women. How awful is it for families not to follow their dear Prophet's example in regards to their own affairs, especially in marriage.

Eleven

Part 8: The Divine and Islamic Conditions for Marriage

~ ❦ ~

"Marry those among you who are single, or the virtuous ones among your slaves, male or female." [Holy Qur'an: Nur 24:32]

Religion and Piety

The revered religion of Islam is in fact a system supplied with beliefs, morals and practical matters. Religious faith in Islam consists of joining up of the heart with God and belief in the Day of Judgment; the angels; the Prophets and the Glorious Qur'an. Morality in Islam consists of humbleness; humility; etiquette; patience; submissiveness; fortitude; tolerance; perseverance; kindness; compassion; good will; having mild disposition; chastity and sincerity; justice, helpfulness; and generosity. Action in Islam consists of prayer; fasting; the Hajj(the Holy pilgrimage to Meccac); paying alms and the one fifth levy; enjoining the good and forbidding the evil; Jihad[15]; taking God as a friend and dissociation from evil; being good to one's parents; and observing the rights of those whom one encounters.

Of course, the three above-mentioned matters are not all the matters of Islam, but rather examples of the perfect, comprehensive, universal religion of Islam which is responsible in all of life's affairs for the welfare of people in this world and in the Hereafter. Actually, religion is the sun and guiding light in life; the guide towards God; and the improver of man in this world and in the Hereafter. There is no worthier jewel in the treasury of God's Creation than religion: the religion propagated by all the Prophets, the Imams, the Saints. It is the religion in which whoever becomes adorned with, puts on a semblance of God, having opened up all the doors of prosperity to himself. Whoever keeps his distance from Islam will have opened all the doors of misfortune for himself. Religion and piety hold the same worth before God. Beautifying one's self with God's religion results in the best person, the most outstanding creature and an incomparable or matchless living being in Creation.

> *"Those who have faith and do righteous deeds, they are the best of the creatures." [Holy Qur'an: Baiyina 98:7]*

If one adorns himself with the attributes of a believer mentioned in the Glorious Qur'an and religious traditions, this will result in an acceptable believer expressed in the following terms: "Being humble in prayer; protesting against false and futile talk; paying the alms tax; protecting the private parts of the body from forbidden acts; protecting whatever has been entrusted to you; keeping one's promise or oath and guarding one's prayers."

---

[15] The holy war fought by Muslim against those who reject Islam.

"Those who humble themselves in their prayers; who avoid vain talk; who are active in deeds of charity; who abstain from sex except with those joined to them in the marriage bond, or (the captives) whom their right hands possess, for (in their case) they are free from blame, but those whose desires exceed those limits are transgressors; those who faithfully observe their trusts and their covenants; and who (strictly) guard their prayers." [Holy Qur'an: Muminun 23:2-9]

We may add the following : being humble on earth; encountering the ignorant with a healthy mind; spending the night in prostration and standing; praying for being saved from the Wrath; not being extravagant when helping the needy; avoiding envy; being moderate; avoiding association of other gods to be partners with God; murder and fornication; avoiding false, oppressive witnessing; forgiving vain talk through nobility; taking a good look at God's signs; praying for the wife and the children; and praying to lead the righteous.

Those who spend the night in adoration of their Lord prostrate and standing; those who say, "Our Lord! avert from us the Wrath of Hell, for its Wrath is indeed an affliction grievous, evil indeed is it as an abode, and as a place to rest in"; those who, when they spend, are not extravagant and not niggardly, but hold a just (balance) between those (extremes); those who invoke not, with God, any other god, nor slay such life as God has made sacred, except for just cause, nor commit fornication; and any that does this (not only) meets punishment (but) the Penalty on the Day of Judgment will be doubles to him, and he will dwell therein in ignominy.unless he repents, believes, and works righteous deeds, for God will change the evil of such persons into good, and God is Oft-Forgiving, Most Merciful, and whoever repents and does good has truly turned to God with an (acceptable) conversion;those who witness no falsehood, and, if they pass by futility, they pass by it with honorable (avoidance); those who, when they are admonished with the Signs of their Lord, droop not down at them as if they were deaf or blind; and those who pray,

"Our Lord! Grant unto us wives and offspring who will be the comfort of our eyes, and give us (the grace) to lead the righteous."
[Holy Qur'an: Furqan 25:64-74]

The Commander of the Faithful (Imam Ali) stated: Among the characteristics of a believer we can state that he is not attached to financial affairs; his efforts are mainly geared to religiousness; his nobility is in contentment; and his efforts are for the Hereafter. His good deeds are increased; his ranks are elevated; and he is approaching deliverance and prosperity. [Mizan al-Hikmat, v.1, p.333]

He also said: A believer is one who is continually remembering God; thinks a lot; is thankful for all the blessings; and perseveres in the face of hardships. [Ibid]

Imam Sadiq (Pbuh) said: A believer is one whose total income is legitimately earned; is good-tempered; is not deceitful; donates some of his extra income; and avoids excessive talk. [Bihar al-Anwar, v.67, p.293]

We can see the following points in the traditions regarding the worth of the believers. Imam Sadiq (Pbuh) has been narrated as having said:

A believer's honor and respect is greater than that of the Ka'ba. [Mizan al-Hikmat, v.1, p.330]

The fifth Imam (Pbuh) said:

A believer is well-known in the Heavens in the same manner that a man knows his wife and children. And verily a believer is closer to God than the Archangel. [Ibid]

The Prophet (Pbuh) said: God, Majestic is His Praise, says: I swear by My Honor and Majesty that I have not created any creature among My Creation that is dearer than a believer. [Bihar al-Anwar, v.71, p.158]

Being Matched

Now that we have introduced the necessity of religion and piety, it should be noted that one of the most important conditions for marriage is that the couple should be well-matched. What is meant by being wellmatched is that the couple who wish to get married must have some outward and inward similarities. The most important similarity is in their piety. That is according to the holy divine culture, they must both be religious. As the Holy Qur'an states:

"And women of purity are for men of purity." [Holy Qur'an: Nur 24:26]

God's book states:

"Marry women of your choice." [Holy Qur'an: Nisaa 4:3]

The first stage of this purity of men and women is their inward purity, that is, belief in God, the Hereafter, the Prophethood, the Qur'an, the angels and having divine morality. Therefore a believing Muslim man does not have the right to marry non-Muslim, unbelieving women. If such a forbidden marriage takes place, then their children are considered to be born in sin. In the same manner a Muslim believing woman does not have the right to marry an unbelieving man, and their marriage is considered illegitimate, as are their children. Believing men or women are not matched with unbelieving men or women. Should such a forbidden marriage take place, both sides are exposed to Eternal Torture.

The Glorious Qur'an has seriously advised against the marriage of a believing person with an unbeliever:

"Do not marry unbelieving women (idolaters), until they believe: a slave woman who believes is better than an unbelieving woman, even though she allure you. Nor marry (your girls) to unbelievers until they believe: a man slave who believes is better then an unbeliever, even though he allure you. Unbelievers do (but) beckon you to the fire. But God beckons by His Grace to the Garden (of Bliss) and forgiveness, and makes His signs clear to mankind: that they may celebrate His praise."[Holy Qur'an:

Baqara 2:221]

Therefore you must be careful not to let your believing daughters marry with a young fellow who is ignorant and does not have faith. Likewise, do not choose a girl who denies divine principles to marry your believing noble son. The first and foremost condition for the marriage of a couple is their faith. Thus two believing, chaste, and shining lights will join, the fruit of which will be good children. Do not think that being handsome, wealthy or of a high status for an unbelieving man, or likewise in a woman who is not adorned with the truth can bring prosperity, health, happiness and continuity of a mutual life. It is necessary for the families not to be too strict about finding the best match. When the two sides are nearly matched in terms of faith, morality and Islamic practices, and looks and posture, then they are considered to be a good match for each other by the Holy Shariat. Consider the following traditions regarding being matched:

Imam Sadiq (Pbuh) said: A woman who is chaste and is financially easy to live with is your best match. [Bihar al-Anwar, v.100, p.372]

The Prophet (Pbuh) said: If a courter proposes to marry your daughter and you are sure about his religiousness and trustworthiness, then provide the means for such a marriage. Prohibiting marriage of a wellmatched couple may lead to sedition and great corruption on the Earth. [Ibid]

In another tradition the Prophet (Pbuh) said: Marry your daughter off to one whose morality and religiousness satisfies you. Should you prevent such a marriage, you have caused a great corruption and sedition on the Earth. [Bihar al-Anwar, v.100, p.373]

Yes, in fact the cause of self satisfaction, homosexuality, fornication, nervous problems, and psychic ailments of many young men and women is being too strict in regards to marriage; creating obstacles; insisting on wrong customs and traditions followed by imposing hard conditions; and expecting beauty, position and wealth by the families. And in fact the end results of all this will directly affect the parents, the relatives and those families who are too strict in regards to marriage, both here and in the Hereafter.

The Prophet (Pbuh) said: Provide the means for the wedding of well-matched couples. And marry with people who are a good match for you, and prepare them to marry you to bring forth good children. [Bihar alAnwar, v.100, p.375]

The essential ingredients of a well-matched couple are faith, morality, trustworthiness and righteousness. It is the moral duty of the parents and the family to prepare the grounds for the marriage of a wellmatched couple. This can be speeded up by being more lenient, not imposing ungodly conditions and avoiding unethical traditions. In this way the parents and the family can earn the blessings, pleasure and kindness of God.

Imam Baqir (Pbuh) said:

The greatest tragedy is when a young believing man proposes marriage to your daughter and you respond in the negative because he does not have the same financial status as you do. [Marriage in Islam, p.32]

Prejudices related to the family, city or tribe should be considered detrimental in marriage as such prejudices are rejected in the divine religion. So do not consider being poor or rich; coming from this city or that one; belonging to this tribe or that one as the criteria for marriage. All men and women are the offspring of one couple (Adam and Eve) and no one has any especial privileges over others except that due to being more pious and virtuous.

Imam Sajjad's Views on Being Matched

Hazrat Baqir (Pbuh), the fifth Imam said: In one of the way-stations during Hajj, my noble father Imam Zayn al-Abideen (Pbuh) encountered a lady whose good temper attracted him. He inquired if she was married, and was told that she was not. Then my father proposed to marry her without investigating about her family, and this proposal led to marriage.

One of the Ansar who became informed of this issue could not stand this simple marriage. He thought that she may not belong to a noble family, and this may cause problems for the fourth Imam. He spent some time investigating about her and finally found out that she belonged to the

Shayban tribe. He came to the fourth Imam and told him that thanks God she is from a well-known, noble family. The Imam told him that he thought the man was wiser than that. He told him "Do you not know that God the Almighty removed all inferiorities and compensated for all defects by Islam. He replaced inferiority with nobility. Now, no matter what the social status of a Muslim is, he/she is not inferior but is respectable. The inferiorities belong to the Age of Ignorance."[Bihar al-Anwar, v.100, p.374]

Therefore being of the same tribe, dwelling in the same town or having the same amount of wealth do not mean being well-matched. As decreed by Islam there exist no privileges for the Arabs over the Persians; the whites over the blacks; the Qurayshy over the non-Qurayshy. All that counts is piety. If a Muslim couple have faith, piety, morality, trustworthiness, chastity, purity and health, then they are well-matched. This is true even if one is an Arab and the other one is a Persian; one lives in a city and the other one is a villager; one is rich and the other is poor; one is white and the other is black; one belongs to a noble family and the other one does not.

Ali, the son of Isbat wrote a letter to Imam Javad (Pbuh) and stated that he had not been able to find people that match him in faith and morality to marry off his daughters to. The Imam responded by writing: "I realized what you wrote regarding your daughters. May God bless you with His Mercy and Kindness. You need not be so careful in regards to your daughters. The Prophet (Pbuh) has recommended us to accept a courter's proposal to marry our daughters should his morality and religiousness be acceptable. Else sedition and great corruption would occur on Earth." [Bihar al-Anwar, v.100, p.373]

Imam Sadiq (Pbuh) told a man called Abraham: "No believer has ever gained any profit more dangerous than wealth. The danger of wealth is worse than that of two vicious wolves which attack a flock of sheep lacking a shepherd. What do these wolves do with the sheep?" He answered: "Nothing but a great loss." The Imam said: "That is right. The least danger of wealth is that a Muslim might come to propose to marry your daughter and you reject him for not being wealthy."

Those Whom You Should not Let Your Daughters Marry

It is stated in divine books that man is entrusted with children who are God's blessing and kindness. To safeguard this "trust" we must attend to their moral and religious education and choose a pure and good spouse for them to marry. The woman who gets married and goes to her husband's home will be influenced by her husband, his family and his home. In that environment she will be asked to do things by her husband. The house she goes to must be a divine home with a believing family. Her husband must be reasonably well-mannered and goodtempered, too. It is for this reason that the divine religion has strictly forbidden marrying your daughters to those who do not fulfill Islamic conditions. The Prophet (Pbuh) has been narrated as saying: Marriage is a form of obedience, that is once you marry your daughters off to someone, you in fact make her obedient to him. Therefore you must all be very careful as to whom you entrust your daughters to. [Bihar al-Anwar, v.103, p.371]

It is not permitted to marry off your daughters to one who does not adhere to religion, divine decrees and just beliefs. Such a person is considered to be corrupt according to the divine book. It is not permitted to marry off your daughters to one who is ill-tempered, haughty, jealous, greedy, and vulgar. It is neither permitted nor humane to marry off your daughters to an ignorant, stupid, unwise man who cannot run his life and causes a lot of problems for the woman. It is strictly forbidden to marry off your daughters to an alcoholic who is so base that he does not abstain from what God has forbidden. Now consider the very important traditions in this regard.

One who marries off his dear noble daughter to an irreligious man, will be cursed a thousand times a day. [Marriage in Islam, p.55]

Husayn, the son of Bishar wrote to Musa the son of Jaffar (Pbuh) "One of my relatives who is ill-tempered has requested to marry with my daughter". The Imam responded "Do not marry her to him if he is a wrong doer." [Bihar al-Anwar, v.103, p.235]

Imam Sadiq (Pbuh) strictly forbade marrying off one's daughters to fools and the ignorant ones who cannot be trusted in social and personal affairs and those who cannot be entrusted with propertybased on verse 5 of the Chapter Nisaa of the Holy Qur'an. [Marriage in Islam, pp.54-55] The Prophet (Pbuh) said: Should anyone, who is now informed by me as the Messenger of God that drinking alcoholic beverages is forbidden, drink and go to propose marriage to the daughter of a family, he deserves no response. [Ibid]

Hazrat Reza, the eighth Imam (Pbuh) said: Be wary of marrying your girls off to those who drink, as this is like giving a virgin for fornication. [Bihar al-Anwar, v.79, p.142]

Verily those who do not adhere to God's obligatory acts, will not avoid sexual deviations. Those who do not have good morality, and are illtempered; and those who do not have a right mind and intellect; and those who are so weak that they cannot stop drinking alcoholic beverages are not suited to be entrusted with a believing pious young woman who is entrusted to us by God. If so, not only will the young woman will be spoiled, but her children too will be influenced by the man's ill effects. This fact has been stated by the sixth Imam (Pbuh) before man came to realize it through science. The effects of illegitimate acts show up in the offspring. [Vasa'il. v.17, Chapter 1, p.81, Tradition 22043]

Do Not Marry Such Women

As you read, Islam does not allow us to marry off our daughters to several groups of people including the corrupt, the stupid, the ill-tempered, and the alcoholics. Thus by prohibiting such marriages, a woman's respect and honor are safeguarded. In the same manner, Islam prohibits the marriage of young noble, believing men with those women who do not meet divine and Islamic conditions. There exist many important traditions cited in authentic books regarding this issue which have been cited from the sources of revelations. A reference is made to some of them here.

The Prophet (Pbuh) said: Avoid marrying stupid women since living with them will ruin your life and their children will be oppressors. [Bihar al-Anwar, v.103, pp.232-237]

He also said: Avoid a trashy beauty. He was asked: What do you mean by a trash beauty? He replied: I mean a beautiful woman who is raised in a bad family. [Ibid]

The Prophet (Pbuh) used to say in his prayers to God: I seek refuge in Thee from a child who orders me around instead of being obedient; from property which goes to waste without giving any profit; and from a woman who makes me old too fast due to her stupidity and bad behavior; and from a friend who is deceitful. [Marriage in Islam, pp.75-77]

The Prophet (Pbuh) said: The worst of your women are the ones who are sterile; filthy; stubborn; disobedient; disgusted by the family, and dear to themselves; disobedient to the husband and submissive to others. [Ibid] He also said: Three things have a bad omen: a woman, a quadruped and a house. A woman's bad omen is in her nuptial gift and sterility. [Ibid] He also said: A bad woman is the worst thing. [Mustadrak, Nekah book, Chapters 6 and 8]

The Commander of the Faithful (Imam Ali) stated: The worst wife is a woman who is not complaisant. [Ibid]

The Prophet (Pbuh) said: Should I not introduce the worst women? Those who are not respectable in their own family; who are haughty to their husbands; who are sterile; who are malicious; who do not stop doing evil deeds; who adorn themselves in the absence of their husbands, and do not adorn themselves in his presence; who are disobedient to their husbands, and do not please them in their own privacy; who do not accept their husband's apology and do not forgive them. [Bihar al-Anwar, v.100, p.235]

Twelve

Part 9: How to Choose a Spouse

❧

Marriage is my tradition, and whoever does not long for my tradition is not of my nation. [Bihar al-Anwar, v. 103, p. 220]

The Evil-Doer is Deprived of God's Mercy

In a very important tradition by the noble Prophet of Islam it is stated in Arabic "Al-Naqess Melown" which means "The evil-doer is denied God's Mercy." Undoubtedly, the Arabic term "Naqess" in this tradition does not carry its usual meaning. It does not refer to someone without eyes, a hand, a foot or having any other type of congenital deformity. Here it refers to one who has not taken steps to attain wisdom, to acquire good habits nor to adorn himself/herself with beneficial actions, and does not attend to himself/herself by means other than eating, sleeping and lust. In fact man has the potential to realize all the facts and attain full perfection. He should try to do so. He should constantly strive to remove his mental, spiritual and inward flaws. He should avoid listlessness. If he does not try to eliminate his imperfections, then he will be spoiled just as unpalatable water does. He will be damned and deprived of God's Mercy.

Unfortunately there are some seventy or even eighty year olds who have the mentality of a one-year old child, and their actions and morality are similar to those of a five-year old. They have not used the divine spiritual blessings such as Heavenly Books; the Prophethood; the Religious Leadership of the Immaculate Imams; the mysticism of the true mystics and the wisdom of the wise during their lifetime. They have been only engaged in eating and drinking to expand their body from a tiny sperm to some eighty or ninety kilograms. They could have turned their bodies into a good tree. They could have built themselves up to become a source of facts and perfection. However, they became proud of simply engaging in material affairs to build up their physical form. Thus they remained poor, imperfect and evil-doers as they first were. They had business deals and were occupied by their desk and chair. They had wealth, a spouse and children, but were evil-doers. Therefore, they are at a loss. They commit any form of sin or crime, they violate other people's rights. They oppress while benefiting from God's blessings without shame. Yet, they cooperate with God's enemies, being the men and jinn, in all areas.

In another tradition from Imam Musa, the son of Jafar (Pbuh) we read:

One for whom two days are the same is at a loss; one for whom the end of the two days is the worst time is damned; and one whose life passes and does not improve himself is at a loss. For such a person death is better than life. [Bihar al-Anwar, v.78, p.327; v.75, p.327, Beirut Press]

There is another tradition with nearly the same context in the authentic Shiite books from Imam Sadiq. [Bihar al-Anwar, v.71, p.173]

In another tradition from the noble Prophet of Islam (Pbuh) we read: "One who does business, is loved by God". Undoubtedly the highest form of doing business and the best trade is obtaining nobility, knowledge, good and human morality. A businessman, such as the Prophet, is a valuable being and is loved by God.

Let's try not to be evil-doers. Let's not let two consecutive days of our lives be the same. Let's avoid denying ourselves the attainment of perfection, since in the Hereafter whoever is short of spiritual affairs; intellectual development and moral and practical perfection is damned and at a loss. His balance of deeds will be light and he will deserve torture. But if the balance of his spirituality is heavy, that is, he has good faith, morality and good deeds, then he will prosper. Consider the following two verses of the Glorious Qur'an in this regard:

> *"The balance that they will be true (to a nicety): Those whose scale (of good) will be heavy, will prosper." [Holy Qur'an: A'raf 7:8]*
>
> *"Those whose scale will be light, will find their souls in perdition, for that they wrongfully treated Our Signs." [Holy Qur'an: A'raf 7:9]*

The Path to Perfection

In the Glorious Qur'an, God the Benevolent has recommended that all people realize two facts to strive towards perfection, giving due consideration to divine and humane conditions. These two are related to the material life and the spiritual life, which are expressed in four verses of the Chapter Al-i-Imran in the Holy Qur'an.

Fair in the eyes of men is the love of things they covet: women and sons; heaped-up hoards of gold and silver; horses branded (for blood and excellence); and (wealth of) cattle and well-tilled land. Such are the possessions of this world's life; but in nearness to God is the best of goals (to return to).

Say: Shall I give you glad tidings of things far better than those? For the righteous are Gardens in nearness to their Lord, with rivers flowing beneath; therein is their eternal home; with companions pure (and holy); and the good pleasure of God. For in God's sight are (all) His servants, (namely), those who say:

> *"Our Lord! we have indeed believed: forgive us, then, our sins, and save us from the agony of the Fire;"*

Those who show patience, firmness and self-control; who are true (in word and deed); who worship devoutly; who spend (in the way of God); and who pray for forgiveness in the early hours of the morning. [Holy Qur'an: Ali-Imran 3:14-17]

The passive form of the verb "Zuyanna" in the Arabic text of the first verse implies its importance, that is, God is the doer of the verb or the one who makes all those facts fair in the eyes of men. This is so that they become inclined and attracted to these issues and through this inclination, love and attraction, they get married; work; subdue the animals; irrigate or build the land; and they attain some productivity in their material life. On the other hand they are also adorned with piety, faith, supplication, and fear of the Hereafter and strive to obtain perseverance, honesty, worship, spending in charity and imploring God's forgiveness. This is so that they can attain God's pleasure, the promised Heaven and pure heavenly spouses.

Anyway according to the noble verses of the Glorious Qur'an, the cause of man's attraction to and love for women is their delicate creation, beauty, dignity, intrinsic shyness, delicate voice, amorous playfulness and coquetishness. This attraction and lust is the main drive for men to become interested and fall in love with women and get married and establish a joint life. Thus, they can have children and work hard in business, agriculture, etc. to provide for their material life and guarantee the continuation of the life of the household and the family. If this is complemented with piety and is void of sin; is accompanied with faith, supplication, perseverance, honesty, worship, spending and imploring God's forgiveness at dawn, then man's prosperity in this world and the Hereafter is guaranteed. Man can thus benefit from all worldly pleasures, and vast eternal benefits, most importantly God's pleasure.

How to Choose A Spouse in Islam

The approach to choosing a spouse is much different in the angelic spirit of Islam, when compared to those religions or schools of thought which have become void of the spirit of revelations. Islam does not allow a believing

Muslim man to choose any woman as his wife. Neither does it allow a believing Muslim woman to choose any man as her husband. This is so because there are certain things to be considered in marriage, such as their well-being and prosperity in this world and the Hereafter; immunity from corruption and Satanic plans. As viewed in Islam, marriage is not just based on lust, carnal desires, and material gains. The goal of Islam from marriage is to maintain people's beliefs; to build a divine home; to raise good children; and to seek God's pleasure. It is in this framework that all that is involved; the marriage itself; maintaining a spouse; loving a legitimate spouse; having sex as much as either side requires; respecting each others' rights; bearing children; raising them; carrying out the necessary duties such as working to provide for the housing, food and clothing of the wife and the children are all considered to be worship of God and each step taken in this regard will have a great heavenly reward. It is in this context that one can understand why Islam insists on finding a well-matched spouse. We are forced to humbly accept Islam's divine conditions for marriage, since a marriage without regard for these conditions will end up in a life full of sedition. The house will be filled with torture and suffering; pain and agony; sadness and sorrow. Such a life might end up in separation and divorce with its everlasting bad feelings. It may even end up in insanity or suicide if one party is not strong enough.

Avoid associating or marrying a woman who has not attained intellectu- al development through studying; and has not helped herself reach perfection by attaining piety, faith and morality. Such women are raised in a family void of monotheism, morality, piety, worship and belief in God's unity. They bring nothing for their husbands but sedition, corruption and destruction. An important tradition from Imam Baqir (Pbuh) has been quoted as: "The Prophet (Pbuh) passed by some women. He suddenly stopped and addressed them, and said: I have not seen any group of people lacking wisdom and religion like you, and stealing the wisdom of the wise. I have seen that your torture is greater than that of all the dwellers of Hell. I strongly recommend that you try to get closer to God, by perfecting your faith and acquiring knowledge, and good deeds." [Marriage in Islam, p.45 as cited in Vasa'il al-Shiaa Abvab Muqadamat Nikah]

Imam Sadiq (Pbuh) said: "The strongest enemy of a believing man is his bad wife." [Bihar al-Anwar, v.100, p.240]

In another tradition it has been stated: "There are six things which are essential causes of committing sins and rebelling against God: love of this world; love of power; excessive sleeping; love for women; love for eating and being lazy." [Vasa'il al-Shiaa. Abvab Muqadamat Nikah, Chapter 4; Bihar al-Anwar, v.100, p.225, Vafa Press]

Thus it is best that you confine yourself to abide by the conditions stated by Islam in choosing a spouse. I shall express all these conditions based on traditions. Try not to choose a spouse based on her beauty, love or wealth. The Prophet (Pbuh) said: "Do not choose a wife for her wealth or beauty. Her wealth will cause her rebellion, and her beauty will cause her corruption. You must consider her faith and religiousness for marriage." [Mustadrak al-Vasa'il, On Marriage, Ch.13]

The Prophet (Pbuh) has been quoted as saying: "If there is bad omen in anything, that is a woman."[Bihar al-Anwar, v.100, p.227]

In fact if a woman is deprived of knowledge, faith, morality, good-temper, dignity and nobility, then she is bad and will ruin her husband's life.

The Prophet (Pbuh) also said: "A bad woman is the worst thing."[Ibid]

An Amazing Story

It has been written in the commentary by Abul-Futuh-i-Razi: There was a young fellow who would recite the call to prayer from the top of the special place on the mosque. One night he looked at the houses surrounding the mosque when he was reciting the call to prayer. This kind of looking has been prohibited by Islam to safeguard man from sedition and for his own sake. Suddenly he saw a good-looking young girl, and fell in love with her. After saying the call to prayer he went and knocked at her door. The house owner opened the door. The young man told him that he had come and was ready to marry their daughter. The man said that they were Assyrian Christians, and they would only wed their daughter to him if he accepted

Christianity. The young fellow who had fallen madly in love with that beautiful girl did not choose a best match and let lust and beauty be the reasons for his marriage. He accepted her father's condition and abandoned Islam, but on the wedding day, he fell down the stairs and died.

Islamic and Humane Conditions in Choosing a Spouse

The respectable families should provide the means for the young man and woman to meet each other before marriage. It is not necessary to wed them to make them Mahram (lawful to see each other) for this purpose. This has been allowed by Islam, and is considered legitimate in Islamic jurisprudence. They must see each other, so that they can recognize each others' good characteristics or apparent defects, and then decide. This will also block the way for future claims. Of course, this visit should be with the intention of getting married and deciding whether or not to finalize the marriage. It should be void of sin.

Please notice the traditions in this regard:

The Prophet (Pbuh) told Mughayreh, the son of Shua'ba who had married a woman: "Had you looked at her before you got married, there was more hope for you to get along with her." [Marriage in Islam, p.47] Muhammad, the son of Muslim, the son of Muslim". said that he asked Imam Baqir (Pbuh): "Does a man who wants to get married have the right to look at the woman?" He answered: "Yes of course. He wants to purchase with the highest price, yet how can he not look?" [Vasa'il alShiia, Introductory chapters on marriage, Chapter 36]

Hassan Sary said: I asked Imam Sadiq (Pbuh): "Is it permissible for the man to take a good look at a woman before he marries her? Can he look at her face and the back of her head?" He answered: "Yes. It is not forbidden to look at the back of her head or look at her face." [Vasa'il al-Shiia, Introductory chapters on marriage, Chapter 36]

A man told the sixth Imam: "Is it permissible for a man to look at a woman's hair and her beauties when he wants to marry her?" He said: "If he wants to become aware of her characteristics it is all right." [Vasa'il alShiia, Introductory chapters on marriage, Chapter 36]

In another tradition the Imam was asked: "Is it permissible for the woman to stand up so that the man can see her?" He answered: "Yes, she can even wear clothing showing the form of her body at that time." [Marriage in Islam, p.49]

The Prophet (Pbuh) told a man from his companions who had proposed to marry a woman: "Look at her face and her hands."

These traditions and the like imply that if someone chooses a woman to marry, after he investigates about her family, her faith and morality, it is fine to look at her to learn about her physical features such as her hair, her looks and beauty, her height, and her posture. This will block any future claims about her defects which might otherwise cause disappointment or argument. This does not mean that men can go around to look inside every house and observe all the beauties of the Muslim girls to choose one if they please. [Marriage in Islam, p.49]

When you choose a wife and decide to marry her, you must intend to marry to seek God's pleasure, not her beauty, perfection, amorous playfulness or coquetishness. You must act to please God and to abide His decree and to follow the tradition of the divine Prophets, especially the noble Prophet of Islam (Pbuh) There are many important traditions regarding marriage in order to get nearer to God and attain His pleasure cited from the Prophet (Pbuh): One who marries for God's sake, and strives to provide the means for the marriage of others for God's sake, deserves to be a Friend of God. [Muhjat ul-Biyza, v.3, p.54]

Yes, people of such character and nobility deserve to be included among those mentioned in the following verse:

"God is the protector of those who have faith: from the depths of darkness He will lead them forth into light." [Holy Qur'an: Baqara 2:257]

God likes men to have a wife and children. That is why He granted John to

Zacharias and granted Ismael to Abraham when they were old. God Has stated in one of the verses of His Book to His Pure Prophet:

"We did send apostles before thee, and appointed for them wives and children" [Holy Qur'an: Ra'd 13:38]

It is not right to rush into marriage. It has been stated in Islamic teachings that to rush into something is the work of Satan. One must be careful in choosing a spouse. He/she must spend enough time, consult with others, and get to know the other party and his/her family. This is all necessary so that any great loss; spiritual, or psychological blow to either party can be avoided. In this regard Imam Sadiq (Pbuh) said: In fact a woman is similar to a necklace. Be careful about the necklace you wear forever. [Bihar al-Anwar, v.100, p.233, Vafa Press]

The characteristics of a good woman who deserves to get married to a believing young Muslim man have been carefully stated in credible traditions cited in valuable Shiite books. The Prophet (Pbuh) said: When you intend to get married to a woman, investigate about her hair as well as her face, since her hair is also a part of her beauties. [Bihar al-Anwar, v.100, p.237]

5-13Jaber, the son of Abdullah Ansari has stated: "We were sitting with the Prophet(Pbuh). Then we started to talk about women, and how some are superior to others. The Prophet (Pbuh) asked if he should talk to us in this regard, and we welcomed his proposal. He said the best of your women is one who is kind; bears children; is chaste; is respected in her family; and is humble to her husband; beutifies herself only for her husband and is respectful but indifferent to others; obeys her husband; submits to him in private but does not act like dirty old men. [Bihar al-Anwar, v.100, p.235]

14 to 18The Commander of the Faithful (Pbuh) said: The best of your women have five traits. He was asked what they were. Then he answered: leniency; good-temperedness; easy to get along with; one who does not rest until her husband is pleased and calm once he gets angry; protects her husband's honor in his absence. Such a woman is one of the agents of God

and should not be disappointed of God's Mercy. [Bihar alAnwar, v.100, p.231]

19Imam Baqir (Pbuh) said: A man consulted with the Prophet(Pbuh) regarding marriage. The Prophet (Pbuh) said: "Get married, but with a religious woman. God will give you a good reward. A good woman is similar to an especial crow which is hard to get." The man asked what especial crow? He responded: "One with one white leg." [Marriage in Islam, p.59]

20 to 21 Abraham Karkhy said that he told Imam Sadiq (Pbuh): "My wife who was my companion has died and now I am considering getting married again." The Imam told him: "Be extremely careful with whom you marry and share all your secrets, wealth, religion and trust. If you have no choice but to marry, find a well-behaved and good-tempered young woman." [Bihar al-Anwar, v.100, p.232]

The Prophet (Pbuh) said: One of the beneficial things that God has destined for a Muslim man is a woman looking at whom pleases him, one who protects his honor in his absence; and one who obeys him in his presence. [Marriage in Islam, p.60]

The Prophet (Pbuh) said: "The noblest woman in my nation is one with the most beauty and a nuptial gift of the least amount." [Bihar alAnwar, v.100, p.236]

The Commander of the Faithful (Pbuh) said: The Prophet (Pbuh) asked the people: Let me know what is best for women? Fatimah (Pbuh) responded: That she does not see men, and men do not see her, too. The Prophet (Pbuh) who was amazed at this response said: Fatimah is the chip off the old block![Bihar al-Anwar, v.100, p.238]

25-26Imam Sadiq (Pbuh) said: The best of your women is one who is grateful if you give her property, and if for some reason you denied her of some property she is pleased and satisfied." [Bihar al-Anwar, v.100, p.239]

27-30The sixth Imam (Pbuh) said: The best of your women is one who smells good; cooks well; spends properly; abstains from spending at the right time.

Such women are agents of God. For them there is no disappointment.

They shall not be sorry. [Marriage in Islam, p.61] 31The Prophet (Pbuh) said: The most blessed wife is one who imposes the least expenses upon her husband. [Marriage in Islam, p.70]

32-34The Commander of the Faithful (Pbuh) said: The best characteristics of a woman in marriage are the worst of men's characteristics: pride, fear and jealousy. If she has pride, she will not submit to anyone but her husband. If she is jealous, she protects their belongings, and if she has fear, then she gets afraid of any circumstances and tries to protect herself. Thus she will not fall prey to others. [Bihar al-Anwar, v.100, p.238] 35-38The Prophet (Pbuh) said: Marry virgin girls. They have sweeter lips, and tighter wombs. They learn faster, and their love for their husband and mutual life is more lasting. [Bihar al-Anwar, v.100, p.237]

39 to 40Imam Sadiq (Pbuh) said: The best of your women is one who is no longer shy when she is undressed in private quarters with her husband. And when she wears her clothes, she is shy. [Marriage in Islam, p.67]

These are the characteristics of a good Muslim woman. Our dear young Muslim men should look for these nearly forty traits in women. Once they find one with a reasonable amount of positive traits, then they should choose her as their wife and the mother of their children. They should try not to be too strict in choosing a spouse, since such an obsession will make it hard to marry.

Thirteen

Part 10: Islam's Original Plans for Marriage

And those who pray, "Our Lord! Grant unto us wives and offspring who will be the comfort of our eyes, and give us (the grace) to lead the righteous." [Holy Qur'an: Furqan 25:74]

Marriage Negotiations

When a marriage is being considered, it is customary among Muslims to conduct investigations about both families. Then they conduct negotiations to determine the conditions for the marriage and the wedding ceremony, and to establish the amount of the nuptial gift. Among the questions asked,

113

the families should try to answer those questions that are appropriate and within the framework of the holy religion. They should also do the same regarding the questions they ask. In these negotiations, it is best to exercise the utmost honesty. They should tell the true age of the couple, the real job of the man, his actual wealth, behavior and morality; his true spirit; relationships; degree of education; and any defects or shortcomings. The defects may be negligible. The woman's family too should be honest in responding to the questions asked by the man's family. They should not be afraid to tell the truth, since this will prevent any future problems or a probable deadlock. It will prevent any future harm, bad feelings, separation, inter-family arguments or the ruining of the relationships between the two families.

Honesty and truthfulness can protect both families against any harm, bad feelings and sorrow. It eases decision-making for both sides and causes prosperity. Concealing the defects of men and women, deception and trickery are immoral and religiously prohibited. They are considered to be great sins. The bad effects of this will not only harm the couple, but will also damage both families.

Concealing defects of men and women, deception and trickery sometimes result in the break up of a wedding, the cancellation of the nuptial gift, and the breaking up of the marriage without a divorce. This is the leeway Islam has granted to either side who may have been deceived by concealing defects. The Glorious Qur'an has prohibited any deception, trickery or concealing of defects and considers those who deceive, deserve divine punishment in this world and the Hereafter.

The Prophet (Pbuh) said: One who deceives a Muslim does not belong to our nation. [Bihar al-Anwar, v.75, p.285]

The Commander of the Faithful (Pbuh) said: Deceiving one who has trusted in you is equal to atheism. [Mizan al-Hikmat, pp.166-167]

He has also said: One who deceives people will be harmed by his/her deception. [Mizan al-Hikmat, pp.166-167]

Regarding the characteristics of the pious, Imam Ali (Pbuh) has said the following in Sermon 193 of Nahj ul-Balaghah: The pious ones do not get close to people by deception. The Prophet (Pbuh) said: Deception, trickery and treason will result in the Hell Fire. He also said: One who is a Muslim does not engage in deception or trickery. I heard from Gabriel that deception and trickery will result in the Hell Fire.

The issues related to concealing defects of men and women; deception and trickery; continued marriage; separation or divorce; the duty of man to pay the nuptial gift or not having to pay it are extensively discussed in volume 100 of Bihar al-Anwar, Vafa Press, Beirut starting from page 361 and also in the practical treatise of great Shiite scholars.

The Necessity to Pay the Nuptial Gift

The two sides should agree on a reasonable amount after honest negotiations. The less strict you are about the amount of the nuptial gift, the more God will be pleased. The leaders of Islam have instructed us to be lenient about this issue to ease the marriage of our young daughters and sons. The families should not imagine that an expensive nuptial gift arranged will prevent the disruption of the family and will help its continuation. There have been many married young women who have had expensive nuptial gifts but returned to their parent's home after marriage. They got seriously hurt and fell apart!

You should rely on God's Favor in these issues, and avoid what might cause pain, belittling or insulting of either party in the future. Once an amount has been agreed upon, and the bride and the groom have accepted it, then half of it is due to be paid immediately upon the establishment of the marriage contract, and the other half must be paid after the marriage is consummated. If it is all paid at the time of the marriage contract, it is much better. The youth must realize that the payment of the nuptial gift is obligatory, and refusal to pay it is a great sin. This necessity to pay the nuptial gift has been clarified in verses 236-237 and 241 of Chapter Baqara, verse 4 of Nisaa, verses 27-28 of Qisas, and verse 49 of Al-Ahzab.No one should impose the least harm or oppression upon women, in this respect or in any other form.

The Prophet (Pbuh) said: A man who oppressively does not pay a woman's nuptial gift is considered an adulterer by God. On the Day of Judgment God will tell him: "O my servant, I married my servant to you based on a certain contract. You did not honor that contract, and oppressed her." Then God will take away some of the man's good deeds and will credit it to his wife's record of deeds. If there is not enough good deeds to fulfill the woman's rights, he shall be thrown in the Hell Fire due to not honoring his contract. Contracts bring responsibility. [Bihar al-Anwar, v.100, p.349, Vafa Press, Beirut]

Imam Sadiq (Pbuh) said: There are three groups of thieves. Those who are envious of paying the alms tax; those who consider it rightful to devour the nuptial gift; and those who borrow money and do not intend to pay it back. [Ibid]

Imam Reza (Pbuh) has quoted his ancestors as having quoted from the Prophet (Pbuh) as saying: God, the Almighty will forgive any sin except denying a woman's nuptial gift, not paying the wages of an employee or selling a free man. [Bihar al-Anwar, v.100, pp.350-351]

Imam Sadiq (Pbuh) said: The most wicked sins are murder, not paying the nuptial gift, and not paying the wages of an employee. [Ibid]

Noble women have been instructed to forgo the nuptial gift if possible. This is a highly moral act and is a symbol of nobility and generosity. In a very important tradition from The Prophet (Pbuh) we read: A woman who forgoes her nuptial gift after the wedding and before consummation of the marriage, will be credited for the reward of freeing one slave for every Dinar of the nuptial gift. Then the Prophet (Pbuh) was asked what if she forgoes her nuptial gift after the consummation of the marriage? The Prophet (Pbuh) answered: Forgoing the nuptial gift after the consummation of the marriage is a result of love and companionship. [Bihar al-Anwar, v.100, p.351]

The Wedding Trousseau

It is customary among Muslims that the father prepares the wedding trousseau for his dear daughter who is the apple of his eye. He does this through his nobility, kindness and love for his daughter. In this regard, we should remind the groom and his respectable family not to forget contentment which is one of the attributes of the Imams, the Prophets and is a fact truly loved by God. They should be content with and grateful for whatever the bride's family sends with her. This is usually as much as they can afford. They should not let this be the cause of insults, belittlement or attacks on the personality of the parties involved. The respectable father of the bride should consider his own social status and that of the groom's family. He should also not be wasteful, since God is the enemy of those who waste. The wedding trousseau need not be extensive or extremely expensive. It need not consist of extraordinary goods. The expenditures for the wedding trousseau should not be out of traditional and religious bounds. It should not cause a great debt behind. For sure you should not try to keep up with the Joneses. Do not raise the expectations of the youth regarding the wedding trousseau, so they only go to propose to women with filthy rich fathers. This will cause a serious problem for the rest and is really inhumane; despised by God; and is a cause of torture in the Hereafter.

You should spend rightfully earned income to purchase the wedding trousseau, so that the obligatory worship rituals of the couple on the clothes and rugs that are purchased are acceptable by God. Do not put yourself through too much trouble due to your children's excessive expectations. Do not let this cause you eternal torture and punishment.

A Divine, Spiritual Model for the Wedding Trousseau

In his valuable book Bihar al-Anwar, Allameh Majlesi has narrated Imam Sadiq (Pbuh) as saying the following about Fatimah (Pbuh):

The Commander of the Faithful (Pbuh) did not have much material wealth. All he had was a couple of dresses, a camel, a sword, and an armor. He earned his daily bread by working in other people's gardens and farms. When he came to the Prophet (Pbuh) to propose to marry the Master of all women, the Prophet's daughter Fatimah, the Prophet (Pbuh) told him to get up and sell his armor. He sold his armor and gave the money to the Prophet (Pbuh). Neither did he say how much it was, nor did the Prophet (Pbuh) ask. The Prophet (Pbuh) gave a fistful of the money to Bilal and asked him to buy perfume for his daughter. He gave some of the money to Abu Bakr and asked him to buy her clothes and household appliances. He told Ummar and some of his companions to help in the shopping. The following items were purchased:

1-Shirt: seven Durhams

2-Shawl: four Durhams

3-Black Kheybar veil

4-A rope bound bed

5-A couple of mattresses with Egyptian linen cover and palm fiber and sheep wool filling

6-Four pillows with Tayef leather cover and filled with stuffing.

7- A woolen curtain

8-A straw mat

9-A hand grinder 10A copper tub

11-A water-skin

12—A bowl

13-A small bucket 14An ewer

14-A green jar

15-Several ceramic vases.

When they brought all this to the Prophet (Pbuh) he took a look at them and said: May God bless them for the Household. [Bihar al-Anwar, v.43, pp.111-112]

The author continues by writing: That simple trousseau belonged to a woman whose father had an unprecedented popularity and power. His companions were ready to sacrifice their lives instead of gold and silver. But he neither forced the sorrow of going under debt upon his groom, nor did he spend from the Muslim's treasury which must be spent for the welfare of the general public, the orphans and the poor. He did not spend a lot to show off or buy excessive luxuries. He did not raise the level of marriage expenditures to pressure others who might use this wedding as a model all throughout history. Thus he saved millions of people from hardship, stress and sorrow. The most important point is that when he recognized that he was unable to provide for the trousseau for which he was morally responsible, he asked his noble groom to sell his armor. Using the money he bought the trousseau and the living necessities, and showed how much sincerity and love existed in their relationship. He was not ashamed of this act. The noble groom, too, was so sincere and spiritual that did not think about or even say one word about it being the duty of the father of the bride to buy the trousseau. The fruit of this marriage are eleven of the Immaculate Imams. This family has so far produced thousands of jurisprudents; scientists; wise men; mystics; God lovers; religious authorities; and believers. There has never been another such marriage with all its blessings in the whole history of mankind.

Praying at the Wedding Threshold

Imploring God, praying and supplication, crying in His Presence are all desirable forms of worship at all times, especially before the wedding. This kind of prayer is closer to be accepted by God, and it can establish a background for the fulfillment of many legitimate aspirations.

The Commander of the Faithful (Pbuh) said: One who intends to get married should perform two units of prayer, recite the chapters Fatiha and Ya-Sin, and then praise God and say: O God, please grant me a deserving, kind, child bearing, grateful, content, zealous wife. She would thank me when I am kind to her; she would forgive me if I hurt her by mistake; she would help me if I remember you; she will remind me if I forget; she would protect herself and my honor in my absence; she would be pleased when I enter; she would obey when I command; she would abide if I swear; she would make me happy if I get angry. O' Owner of Grandeur and Nobility, please I ask You for I will not receive anything but what You destine for me.

The Commander of the Faithful (Pbuh) then said: Whoever does this at the wedding threshold, shall get what he wanted by God's Favor.

The Time and Etiquette for Wedding

A group of families think that the marriage or wedding ceremonies provide a permit for carrying out whatever carnal desires they please. At the time of the wedding of their children, they commit divinely forbidden acts based on the request of their children, the couple's friends, or their relatives. They think that this way they make the party more fun. However, marriage and wedding ceremonies should be accompanied by dignity; nobility; respect; and should be void of sins; forbidden acts and arousing elements. Thus they can be a cause of God's pleasure and can yield divine blessings.

Imam Musa, the son of Jafar (Pbuh) said: It is not at all required to abstain from unforbidden pleasures. Of course, we must be happy during a marriage ceremony and a wedding party. We should not forget to engage in legitimate means of entertainment like comics, jokes and singing. Even singing wise poetry, meaningful lyrics; pleasant slogans and the customs that are usual among Muslim women in such ceremonies are all fine. It is quite natural to stay up late at these times.

The Prophet (Pbuh) said: It is fine to stay up until late in the three following situations: reciting the Qur'an; studying to acquire knowledge; accompanying a bride to her husband's house.[Bihar al-Anwar, v.100, p.267]

In Islam it is considered better to perform the wedding at night. Fatimah's wedding was carried out at night. Jaber Ansari said: When the divine Prophet married Fatimah off to Ali, a few narrow minded people came to him and objected why he had married her off with a very small amount of nuptial gift. The Prophet (Pbuh) told them that this was not his decision. It was God who married off Fatimah to Ali. On the night of the wedding the Prophet (Pbuh) prepared his piebald camel. He threw a gown over it and asked Fatimah to ride it. He ordered Salman to pull the camel. He himself followed it from behind. Midway through he heard something come down. He looked and saw that Gabriel and Michael had descended from Heaven each accompanied with seventy thousand angels. He asked them the reason for the descension. They replied: We have come to see Fatimah off to Ali's house, and then they expresses their congratulations. Then they said "God is the Greatest", so did the angels. The divine Prophet too said "God is the Greatest". Thus, it became a tradition to say "God is the Greatest" when accompanying the bride. [Bihar al-Anwar, v.100, p.266]

Yes. You must prepare for and conduct the wedding ceremonies in a manner that will result in the descention of angels and God's blessings. Imam Sadiq (Pbuh) said: Take the bride to the groom's house at night. [Marriage in Islam, p.112]

Imam Reza (Pbuh) said: Wedding at night is one of the traditions of the Prophet, since the night is for resting in peace and a woman is for peace, too.[Marriage in Islam, p.112]

The Prophet (Pbuh) ordered the daughters of Abdulmutalib and the women of Medina to follow Fatimah (Pbuh) at the night of her wedding; be happy and sing; say God is great and praise be to Him; and avoid saying what God dislikes. [Marriage in Islam, p.114; Mustadrak, Chapter on Marriage, section 31]

On the night of the wedding it is recommended to feed the guests who have accepted the invitation.

The Prophet (Pbuh) said: There are only five occasions for a banquet: Marriage; childbirth; circumcision; purchasing a house; and returning from the pilgrimage. [Marriage in Islam, p114; Mustadrak, Chapter on marriage, section 31]

It has been narrated that the Prophet of Islam (Pbuh) said on the wedding night of Fatimah Zahra (Pbuh):

O' Ali. Prepare an excellent dinner in honor of your spouse. He added: We will give the meat and the bread, you provide the dates and the ghee. Then Imam Ali (Pbuh) said: I bought the dates and the ghee. The Prophet (Pbuh) rolled up his sleeves and shredded the dates into pieces and dropped them in the ghee. He mixed them until it became a mixture of dates, oil and flour. He sent a ram to be slaughtered. A lot of bread was baked. He then told Ali (Pbuh) to invite whoever he wished. Ali says: "I went to the mosque and asked the people to accept the invitation to Fatimah's banquet".

[Marriage in Islam, p.91]

Regarding being invited to a wedding party, the Prophet (Pbuh) said: Do not rush to go to a wedding party if you are invited. Wedding ceremonies remind us of the worldly issues. But rush to a funeral ceremony when invited since that reminds you of the Hereafter. The families must arrange the marriage and wedding ceremonies in such a way that it not only has a bad influence on the kids, the youth and the young participants and but not also foster or encourage them to commit any sin. It also provides a convenient place for the believing men and women invitees to participate.

Nuptial Night Customs

There are many verses of the Glorious Qur'an and traditions regarding intercourse which are very beneficial for both men and women. Consider some of the recommendations of the Prophet (Pbuh) and the Holy House-hold in this regard which have been narrated in the most authentic books on traditions.

It is polite for the groom to take of the brides' shoes once she has been brought to his house. Then he should wash her feet and spread water from the house entrance door to as far away as possible. This can block seventy thousand causes of the family becoming poor. Seventy thousand blessings will cover the house. Seven angels of mercy will start to fly over the bride's head and their blessings will fill the whole house. The bride will be protected against diseases like insanity and leprosy for as long as she lives there.

The bride should avoid eating milk, vinegar, coriander or sour apple during the first week of the marriage. These four can have a negative effect on her womb and may turn her sterile.

The Prophet (Pbuh) said: If a woman starts her period while drinking vinegar, this will slow down its termination. Coriander will extend the duration of the period, and will make delivery difficult. A sour apple will quickly stop the period and the blood which remains in the womb will cause illness.

Avoid lovemaking at the beginning, the middle and the end of the (periodic) month. Do not make love in the afternoon. It is not good to talk, it is very bad to stare when making love. It is extremely psychologically damaging to the child who may get born if the man thinks about another woman while making love.

It is better to wear a light clothing when making love.

It is inconvenient to make love standing up like animals.

Avoid intercourse on the night of Fitr Holiday (the end of the holy month of fasting); and Sacrifice Holiday; under a tree; under the sun; between the two consecutive calls for prayer (Adhan and Iqamih); the night of the fifteenth day of Sha'ban (the birth date of the Holy Twelfth Imam); on the roof; and on the night of travel. Weddings and intercourse are recommended on Sunday night; early Monday night; Wednesday night; on Thursday; Thursday night ; the eve of Friday. These times have a lot of material benefits as well as very important spiritual effects. Making love at the times that intercourse has been prohibited may result in children with insanity; leprosy; foolishness; cross-eyedness; deafness; blindness; jealousy; becoming feminine; argument and separation; being sterile; having six fingers; having four fingers; being poor; extreme desire to attack other people; blind-heartedness; ugliness and dumbness.

The times that intercourse has been recommended can result in children with such qualities as memorizing the Holy Qur'an; being pleased with divine decrees; faith; security from torture; love and kindness; compassion; nobility and generosity; being refined; having mastery over science; religiousness and prosperity; and attaining the status of God's saints.

These are issues that cannot be recognized with material tools or medical instruments. They are facts that the Noble Prophet of Islam (Pbuh) has recommended and said to the Commander of the Faithful (Pbuh), and has asked him to guard these recommendations on marriage and lovemaking as he has guarded them after receiving them from Gabriel [Bihar al-Anwar, v.100, p.280; Elal al-Sharayeh, pp.514-517; Amali Sadoogh, pp.566-570]

It has been prohibited to make love instantly. This is oppressive to women and sexual foreplay is both necessary and beneficial to both men and women.

The Prophet (Pbuh) said: Three actions are oppressive: Being accompanied by a man and not asking his name; Being invited to a party and not attending; Or not eating food if one has accepted the invitation; And lovemaking without foreplay. [Bihar al-Anwar, v.100, p.285]

The sixth Imam said: Three actions are the tradition of divine Prophets: putting on perfume; shaving the private parts and thoroughly fulfilling your wife's carnal desires. [Ibid]

The Commander of the Faithful (Pbuh) said: Not sleeping with your wife and not fulfilling her sexual instincts is a cause of torture in the grave. [Elal al-Sharayeh, p.309]

It is forbidden to make love during the period. It is forbidden not to make love for over four months without any good excuse or the spouse's consent, and it has retribution. Making love while unclean is undesirable.

Hazrat Ali (Pbuh) has said: Do not make love instantly. The woman has sensual and physical needs. Help her with foreplay, then make love. If you see another woman and feel that she is beautiful ,then immediately go to your wife. God has granted your wife the same beauties. And not looking at another woman and going home to make love to your own wife will block Satan from conquering your heart.

If you are not married, then perform two units of prayer immediately. Praise God and send benedictions upon the Prophet (Pbuh) and his Household. Then seek help from God. God may grant you what you need through His Kindness. [Bihar al-Anwar, v.100, p.287]

The reward of fulfilling a woman's carnal desires is so great that according to a tradition the noble Prophet of God told a man: Are you fasting today? The man said no. Have you gone to visit the ill today? The man said no. Have you gone to a funeral today? The man said no. Have you fed one who cannot work today? The man said no. Then he said: Go back home and make love with your wife, since this is similar to a donation from you to her. [Bihar al-Anwar, v.100, p.289]

You should not make love in the presence of a child, since this is both morally and psychologically bad for the child. The sixth Imam (Pbuh) has said that this increases the chances of the child committing adultery in the future. [Bihar al-Anwar, v.100, p.290]

One should avoid intercourse with a full stomach, since it harms your health. [Bihar al-Anwar, v.100, p.290]

Do not make love when there is a baby in the cradle who may observe you. [Bihar al-Anwar, v.100, p.295]

How wonderful is the religion of Islam in its full coverage of all issues regarding moral, educational and sensual affairs. Especially the coverage on women's rights with a precise look at all affairs of life. It really grants us a good outlook on personal, family and social issues. It must be so since Islam is the manifestation of revelations; divine knowledge and the insight of the Prophet (Pbuh) and the Holy Household, and it is not derived from a limited earthen mentality.

Fourteen

Part 11: Hygiene in the Family Structure

"For God loveth those who turn to Him constantly and He loves those who keep themselves pure and clean." [Holy Qur'an Baqara 2:222]

The Worth of Cleanliness and Hygiene in Islam

Once the marriage takes place and the young couple start their mutual life with love and affection, they must attend to basic issues in life, and seriously avoid any indifference or sluggishness in this regard. One of these basic issues is cleanliness and hygiene in all aspects of life.

We must pay close attention to the cleanliness and hygiene of our body, hair, mouth and teeth, clothing, the floor covering, living accommodations especially kitchen appliances and dishes and whatever is related to everyday life. Some young couples only suffice to eating, drinking and apparent leisure and ignore cleanliness and hygiene early in their mutual life. There is no sign of orderliness, discipline or cleanliness in their life. Not only is this ignorance not acceptable by our healthy nature, our mind or our divine religion, but it is also seriously despised. This may also become dominant in life through the passage of time, and may threaten the health of the family, both physically and mentally. It may also have grave consequences on the children, and turn them into indifferent, dumb, ill, weak, oppressive and burdensome individuals. They may get used to various sins and corruption.

God the Benevolent Has announced His love and affection for those who attend to hygiene and their cleanliness and keep their bodies and souls free of all impurities.

"For God loveth those who turn to Him constantly and He loves those who keep themselves pure and clean." [Holy Qur'an Baqara 2:222]

Islam is manifested through the Holy Qur'an, the sayings of the noble Prophet (Pbuh) and his household, that are the Immaculate Imams. The rules of hygiene of this divine school exceed five thousand. They are partly presented in volumes one and two of Vasa'il al-Shiia. They are superior to all rules of hygiene and are extremely wonderful in that they are delicate and encouraging ones to abide by. Nearly fifteen agents have been introduced as cleansing agents in Islam. This is not observed in any other existing school of thought. Islam has forbidden polluting; being polluted or causing pollution in may respects. The one who pollutes is considered a wrong-doer and deserves divine retribution on the Day of Judgment. Either of the following can be used to clean in different situations: flowing water; well-water; spring water; rain water; stale water in a volume each of its sides being nearly three and a half feet; a small amount of water being poured on a filthy object sufficient to cleanse it; dust covered earth; direct sun-light; fire; change of state or form from one to another.

In several important traditions, the Prophet (Pbuh) has stressed on the value of purity and cleanliness in such a way that it seems to be one of the surprising Islamic issues to any intellectual.

Cleanliness is half of faith. [Mizan al-Hikmat, v.5, p.558]

The first thing that is considered in the Hereafter is cleanliness. [Ibid] The Prophet (Pbuh) was extremely sensitive to the issue of oral and dental hygiene, cleaning hair and face, clothes and furniture, lanes and streets and even the dead. He was also superior to all in following hygienic rules and cleanliness. He ordered the dead to be washed with lotus and camphor water.

Also he ordered that camphor be placed on the forehead where we prostrate to worship God. Also he ordered the grave to be dug deeper and to be careful in placing a stone above the head and a little bit distant from it, and to throw dust over the dead body in an orderly fashion. Thus the body, the camphor and the dust will disintegrate and combine together in such a way as to maintain the health of citizens. These decrees are amazing ones and show the greatness of that noble Prophet's knowledge and wisdom.

The Immaculate Imam Ali's (Pbuh) knowledge and wisdom are manifestations of God's knowledge and wisdom. The Prophet (Pbuh) was so pure and clean that Imam Ali (Pbuh) introduced him as the cleanest and the purest and asked all the people of the world to use the Prophet (Pbuh) as a model for cleanliness and purity of body and soul.

Follow the example of your Prophet who is the cleanest and purest creature in existence. In fact, he is a model for anyone who wishes to follow him in all issues related to living. [Nahj ul-Balaghah, Sermon 160] The Prophet (Pbuh) said: In fact God is pure, He likes the pure. He is clean, He likes the clean. [Mizan al-Hikmat, v.10, p.92]

See how important cleaning is that there is a mention of it in God's presence.

The Commander of the Faithful (Pbuh) said: Wash yourselves free of any bad, disturbing odors with water, and be responsible for yourself.

In fact, God the Almighty is angry with those who are so filthy that others do not like their company. [Ibid]

The Prophet (Pbuh) said: Clean your body, God will clean you.

In fact there is no one who spends the night clean, and is not accompanied by an angel. And no hour of the night is passed without the angel saying: O' God, please forgive your servant since he spent the night while being clean. [Ibid]

The Prophet (Pbuh) said: The human body is filthy. [Ibid]

He also said: Filthy people perish. [Ibid]

Jaber, the son of Abdullah Ansari has been narrated as saying: The Prophet (Pbuh) saw a man with badly disheveled hair. He asked him: Did he not find anything to comb his hair with? He saw another person with filthy clothes. He shouted: Did he not find any water to wash his clothes? [Ibid]

Hazrat Baqir (Pbuh) said: Sweeping your houses will eliminate poverty. [Mizan al-Hikmat, v.10, p.93]

The sixth Imam (Pbuh) said: Washing the dishes and sweeping your courtyards will increase your daily bread. [Ibid]

The Commander of the Faithful (Pbuh) said: Do not collect the trash outside your house since it is a source of evil. [Ibid]

It is wonderful that the divine viewpoint of the Prophet (Pbuh) and the Imams informed the people about microbes centuries before their discovery.

The Prophet (Pbuh) said: Do not leave the unusable food leftovers at home overnight, and take them out of the house in broad daylight. In fact, these unusable leftovers are a source of evil. [Mizan al-Hikmat, v.10, p.95]

He also said: Attend to cleaning with all your strength, since God the Almighty has established Islam on cleanliness. No one shall enter Heaven, but the clean. [Ibid]

Imam Reza (Pbuh) said: Cleanliness is one of the attributes of divine Prophets. [Ibid]

The Prophet (Pbuh) told Ayesheh: Wash these two robes. Are you not aware that our clothes worship God as long as they are clean and will stop doing so once they become dirty? [Mizan al-Hikmat, v.10, p.94] Considering the verses of the Qur'an regarding cleanliness and cleansing agents, and God's love of cleanliness and purity, and many traditions in this regard, it is the duty of the members of the family to clean their body and clothes, the furniture and the house as much as they can. As the Qur'an has recommended mutual cooperation based on kindness and piety, the man should help his wife in cleaning. Women are morally bound to clean the house, the furniture and clothes to please their husbands and God. This will also guarantee the family's health and will defeat pain, illness, distress and suffering. Housewives should remember that working at home to provide for the family's comfort is a form of worship and it certainly has divine reward.

Oral and Dental Hygiene

Oral and dental hygiene are of the most important issues to be considered. Professionals say that the health of many parts of our body especially our sensitive digestive system depends on oral and dental hygiene. The teeth that God Has granted us are very important blessings, and are really important in maintaining our health. We chew food with them. If done properly, chewing will guarantee proper and natural functioning of our digestive system, which will in turn help maintain our health. Bad smell from the mouth is very annoying. This bad odor is usually a result of lack of attention to oral and dental hygiene and food left in between the teeth and under the gum. "Pyorrhea" is the name of a dangerous disease which destroys the teeth and the gum and is the source of many other diseases including heart disease. This disease is a result of unattentiveness to oral and dental hygiene. If after every meal you spend a few minutes to wash your mouth and brush your beautiful teeth and wash your mouth with some salt water, you will not only help the health of your mouth and throat, but will also save a lot of money preventing dental decay and future dental work. Then you can use your teeth for many years, even up until death. Although Islam first appeared in a desert-like area among illiterate people, it presented some important decrees regarding oral and dental hygiene. This shows how majestic and important this school is. It also proves that the Prophet of Islam (Pbuh) who brought this religion to guide the people was appointed by God. It also shows that the twelve Immaculate Imams were chosen by God. Consider a part of the recommendations of our religious leaders regarding oral and dental hygiene.

The Prophet (Pbuh) said: If it was not a burden on my nation, I would have decreed that they should brush their teeth before each prayer. [Mizan al-Hikmat, v.4, p.596]

The sixth Imam (Pbuh) said: Brushing the teeth and oral hygiene are of the attributes of divine Prophets. [Bihar al-Anwar, v.76, p.131]

Imam Baqir (Pbuh) said: If the people only knew how beneficial a toothbrush is, they would take it to bed with them. [Mizan al-Hikmat, v.4, p.597]

Imam Sadiq (Pbuh) was asked: Are all the people human? He answered: Yes, except for those who do not brush their teeth. [Ibid]

The Prophet (Pbuh) said: Gabriel recommended me to brush my teeth so much that I feared I would lose all my teeth if I do not brush. [Ibid]

In another statement he said: Gabriel continuously recommended me to brush my teeth, so much that I thought He wants to make brushing teeth obligatory. [Ibid]

Imam Sadiq (Pbuh) said: There are twelve benefits in brushing your teeth: It is religious; it cleans your mouth; it improves your sight; it pleases God; it brightens your teeth; it prevents tooth decay; it strengthens your gum; it improves your appetite; it removes mucus from the digestive system; it improves your memory; it adds to the goods and it pleases the angels. [Bihar al-Anwar, v.76, p.129]

Professional doctors and specialists in the field of mouth and teeth today state that we must brush our teeth slowly from its width for a few minutes. There is a very important tradition from the Prophet (Pbuh) which considering the time of his Prophethood is one of his scientific miracles. Brush your teeth vertically, and do not do it horizontally (brush the width of your teeth, not their length) [Mizan al-Hikmat, v.4, p.599] The Prophet (Pbuh) used to brush his teeth three times each night: once before going to bed, once when he got up to recite the Holy Qur'an and once before going to the mosque for the morning prayer. He used to brush with wood from Arak since Gabriel had instructed so. [Ibid]

Orderliness and Hygiene in Food

Our bodies' amazing digestive system, our mouth and teeth, and our desire to eat food and drink are of the great favors of God bestowed upon us. There are many important decrees in the Holy Qur'an and sources of Islamic traditions that are issued regarding how to obtain food legitimately and how to use it to guarantee our physical and mental health. This will also result in the family's and the society's health. It seems that some of these are religiously obligatory, some are morally obligatory, and some are strongly recommended. Disobeying those decrees which are religiously obligatory is forbidden and shall cause in retribution in the Hereafter. Disobeying those decrees which are strongly recommended will cause losses and harm to the body and its predisposition to ailment. Among the most important religiously obligatory decrees in the Holy Qur'an, we can mention obtaining clothing, food, and housing through legitimate means.

> *"O' ye who believe! Eat of the good things that We have provided for you, and be grateful to God, if it is Him ye worship." [Holy Qur'an: Baqara 2:172]*
>
> *"O' ye people! Eat of what is on the Earth, lawful and good; And do not follow the footsteps of the Evil One, for he is to you an avowed enemy." [Holy Qur'an: Baqara 2:168]*
>
> *"Eat and drink: But waste not by excess, for God loveth not the wasters." [Holy Qur'an: A'raf 7:31]*

The issues stressed here are to be clean; to have acquired goods legitimately and to avoid wastefulness. It is religiously obligatory to acquire clean food through legitimate means. It is religiously forbidden to waste. It is oppression to oneself and others and against God and certainly a cause for divine retribution to be careless about acquiring property by legitimate means; to eat of what has been forbidden or is dirty; or to be wasteful. It is necessary for the head of the household to become familiar with related Islamic teachings, and to transfer his knowledge to the house. In this way the house will be clean and the members of the family can grow up and develop to be a source of goodness for themselves and others.

The Harms of Overeating

The Commander of the Faithful (Pbuh) said: Man's soul is spoiled by overeating and oversleeping and brings losses to him/her. [Mizan alHikmat, v.1, p.117]

He also said: One who overeats is not healthy, and he/she has to pay a high price. [Ibid]

He also said: Overeating is due to abnormal appetite which is a form of disease. [Ibid]

The sixth Imam (Pbuh) said: Nothing is more harmful for a believer's heart than overeating. Overeating results in cruelty and sexual arousal. [Mizan al-Hikmat, v.1, pp.117-118]

God, the Almighty told the Israelites: Do not overeat. One who overeats will oversleep. One who oversleeps will pray less. And one who reduces his prayers is included among the ignorants. [Ibid]

The Prophet (Pbuh) said: Abstain from overeating since it will spoil your body and cause illness and sluggishness in prayers. [Ibid]

He also said: Nothing is despised by God more than a full stomach. [Ibid]

Imam Musa, the son of Jafar? (Pbuh) said: If all people eat moderately, their bodies will be moderate. [Vasa'il, v.16, p.406]

Regarding the issue of eating and drinking, the Prophet (Pbuh) said the following which is the key to health: Eat when you have an appetite, and stop eating while you still have an appetite to eat. Certainly overeating is very harmful for the digestive system, and is a great threat to our health. The best way to maintain health and vigor, and be thin and agile and live a long life is to eat only when you are hungry and to stop eating before you get full. [Mizan al-Hikmat, v.1, p.123]

An Educational Story

It is narrated that one of the great commanders dispatched an expert physician to Medina to treat the patients for free. The physician stayed in Medina for a while, but either no one or only a very few people came for a visit. He was really surprised and complained to the Prophet. The Prophet (Pbuh) told him that this is the way in this town since I have asked the people to eat only when they are hungry, and to stop eating before they get full. The physician told the Prophet: You have in one decree summarized all the rules of medicine and health. That is why the people do not get sick easily here. Imam Ali (Pbuh) has said the following regarding how to start a meal: Start your meal with some salt. If the people only knew of its benefits, they would have preferred it to established medications. [Vasa'il, v.16, p.520]

The Prophet (Pbuh) has admonished not eating hot meals. He has said that God has put the blessings in meals that have cooled down a bit, and has ordered not to blow at the food to cool it down. [Vasa'il, v.16, p.518] It has strictly been forbidden to eat food and ignore living creatures present. Najih said that he saw Imam Mujtaba (Pbuh) eating food and a dog was near him. He would eat a bit and give the dog a bite. I asked him why he did not shoo away the dog. He answered that he was ashamed before God to eat while being watched by a living creature, and not pay any attention to it. [Mizan al-Hikmat, v.1, p.125]

Yes, we must eat and feed, since this eating is necessary for our body, and feeding is a sign of morality and nobility; a means of helping the needy; a cause of God's Mercy, favor, reward and forgiveness. Strictness in this issue to your wife and children, relatives and the people is unjust and is similar to partnership with Satan.

Imam Mujtaba (Pbuh) has said that there are twelve things that each Muslim must know about food and eating: recognizing the blessings and their Provider; being content with our share of daily bread bestowed by God; starting our meals in the name of God; thanking God at the end of our meal; making ablutions before eating; sitting on the left-hand side; using three fingers; licking the fingers; eating what is nearby; eating in small bites;

chewing well; and looking less at the people who are eating around the tablecloth. [Vasa'il, v.16, p.539]

Imam Reza (Pbuh) has recommended us to eat a light meal at night since it helps your merits and also helps you to stay thin. [Bihar al-Anwar, v.62, p.324]

The Prophet (Pbuh) said: Whoever spends more time praising and worshipping God and spends less time eating, drinking and sleeping is more eagerly welcomed by the divine angels. [Mizan al-Hikmat, v.1, p.116]

He also said: Be just to your body regarding eating, drinking and clothing. Such consideration is a part of Prophethood. [Ibid]

Hazrat Ali (Pbuh) said: Eating light meals, and nobility are more lasting for our health. [Ibid]He also said: When God the Glorious wishes the well-being of His servant, He shall inspire him/her to talk less, to eat less and to sleep less. [Ibid]

Other important issues to be considered by the family and more importantly by the head of the family are to abstain from smoking cigarettes, using hubble-bubbles and narcotics. Smoking of any kind is religiously forbidden according to some Shiite jurisprudents, since it endangers our health and sometimes causes moral and social corruption.

Islam has also forbidden the joint use of personal things such as a comb, a towel or a tooth brush. It is hoped that these issues are considered by all the families, and especially by the heads of each family. This will aid in maintaining the physical and mental health of everyone. Since these are religious decrees, abiding by them is considered to be worshipping God and disobeying them is a sin and a cause of God's punishment and retribution.

Fifteen

Part 12: Islamic Ethics in the Family Structure

❦

The Prophet (Pbuh) said: I recommend you to have good morality, since verily this will take you to heaven, and you should not be foul tempered since that will undoubtedly take you to Hell. [Vasa'il, v.16, p.29, Al-i-Bayt Press]

The Value of Good Morality

It is necessary for the parents to consider a few things which are repeatedly stressed in the Holy Qur'an for the sake of themselves and their children. It is not difficult to have good morals and avoid evil acts. It is easy to put morals into action and avoid unethical acts in a short period of time. This will not only ease our progress on the highway towards God, but it will also strengthen our marriage; increase our mutual love; and serve as a lesson for others, especially our children. Mutual adherence to morals will create an atmosphere of love and affection; peace and security; and health and purity and will make all aspects of our life delightful. In several verses, the Holy Qur'an has praised the noble Prophet for being good-tempered and adhering to this attribute.

> *"It is part of the Mercy of God that thou dost deal gently with them. Wert thou severe or harsh-hearted, they would have broken away from about thee." [Holy Qur'an: Al-i-Imran 3:159]*
>
> *"And thou (standest) on an exalted standard of character. "[Holy Qur'an: Qalam 68:4]*

The Prophet (Pbuh) said: Islam means being good-tempered. [Mizan alHikmat, v.3, pp.137-138]

Imam Mujtaba (Pbuh) said: The best goodness is a good temper. [Ibid] The Prophet (Pbuh) said: Good temper is accompanied by the good of this world and the Hereafter. [Ibid]

Imam Ali (Pbuh) said: A good temper is at the head of all goodness. [Ibid]

The sixth Imam (Pbuh) said: There is not a better life than that of the one with a good temper. [Bihar al-Anwar, v.71, pp.388-389]

The Prophet (Pbuh) said: God will raise the position of the one who is good-tempered to that of the one who fasts and stays up at night standing in prayer. [Ibid]

He also said: The first thing that is counted on the Day of Judgment is one's good temper. [Bihar al-Anwar, v.71, p.385]

He also said: The one dearest and closest to me amongst you in the Hereafter is the one with the best temper, and the humblest. [Ibid]

The Prophet (Pbuh) told the Commander of the Faithful (Pbuh): Shall I inform you of your closest trait to me? He answered yes. The Prophet (Pbuh) said: The one with the best temper, the one who is the most persevering, the one who helps his relatives the most, and the one who is most fair to others regarding himself. [Bihar al-Anwar, v.77, p.58] Nobility and a good temper are so valuable that the noble Prophet of Islam (Pbuh) has declared it to be the reason for his appointment to the Prophethood. It is certain that I was appointed to perfect your good temper, and nothing else. [Mizan al-Hikmat, v.3, p.149]

I was appointed to perfect your good temper. [Ibid]

Being good-tempered and having good morals are rays of God's attributes, the way of the Prophets and the Immaculate Imams and the cause of goodness and blessings for the one with these attributes.

A bad temper and foul behavior are satanic and are the causes of disruption of life, insecurity, separation, and hatred of people; and will ruin the life here and in the Hereafter. I will refer to several points which should be adhered to by any couple in order to strengthen their relationship, and continue their love and affection. I hope that God the Almighty will adorn us all with a good temper and morals and help us avoid bad morals.

Love and its Expression

God has established love in our hearts as husbands or wives and recognizes this to be one of the signs of His Existence. This fact is a manifestation of the importance and extent of love and especially the love and affection of man towards a woman.

> *"And among His signs is this, that He created for you mates from among yourselves, that ye may dwell in tranquillity with them, and He has put love and mercy between your (hearts): verily in that are Signs for those who reflect." [Holy Qur'an: Rum 30:21]*

This love and affection blossoms early in marriage and even before the religious wedding ceremony, and it grows until it reaches its final extent. It is the responsibility of both partners in marriage to maintain this given blessing and this excellent spiritual state of love which is the main cause of happiness and pleasure in life. This can be done by mutual support, being good-tempered,forgiving, cooperation, reasonable expectations, mutual respect, avoiding arguments and fights. The couple should avoid what might harm their loving relationship. They should know that any attempt to maintain a loving relationship is considered to be worship and any act that might hurt the foundation of love is undoubtedly a sin and deserves God's punishment, and also causes grief and hurt in this life. Regarding those who have the power to attract others' affection, Imam Sadiq (Pbuh) said: May God bless those who can attract people's affection. [Mizan al-Hikmat, v.2, p.205]

If there is no intellectual or religious legitimate reasons, converting love and affection into hatred, grudges and animosity is considered to be ungrateful for God's blessings. On the other hand, maintaining a loving relationship and extending love to others is a cause of happiness in this world and the Hereafter.

Imam Sadiq (Pbuh) said: Woe to those who are ungrateful for God's blessings, and blessed and prosperous be those who love each other for God. [Vasa'il, v.16, p.171, Al-i-Bayt Press]

The Commander of the Faithful (Pbuh) said: Regarding love and affection, the best of you are those who are the ones who strive to be the first to be kind to others. [Mizan al-Hikmat, v.2, p.210]

Man is instructed to be affectionate to all the people who deserve his kindness, love and affection. Thus, our spouses and children who are even much closer to us require our love and affection. It has been written in a Qudsi Tradition: The creatures are my spouse. The dearest one to me is the one who is kindest to my creatures, and one who exerts the most effort to satisfy their needs. [Usul al-Kafi, v.2, p.199]

Based on what was said, the love of a man for a woman and the love of a woman for a man is one of the signs of God which is placed in the heart. It is one of the especial signs of God's existence, and one of His Especial Blessings. This love is the best reason for the establishment of a healthy mutual life, and its continuation. It is the cause of happiness and pleasure in life. That is why it is necessary to maintain and try to strengthen it and avoid actions which might harm it. Imam Sadiq (Pbuh) said: Love of women is one of the Prophets' characteristics. [Vasa'il, v.20, pp.22-23, Ali-Bayt Press]

The Prophet (Pbuh) said: Prayer is the apple of my eyes, women are my pleasure in life, and my scented flowers are Hassan and Husayn. [Ibid] Imam

Sadiq (Pbuh) said that there is nothing more enjoyable than women in this world and the Hereafter. God has said:

> *"And among His signs is this, that he created for you mates from among yourselves, that ye may dwell in tranquillity with them, and He has put love and mercy between your (hearts): verily in that are Signs for those who reflect. [Holy Qur'an, Rum 30:21] Fair in the eyes of men is the love of things they covet: women and sons." [Holy Qur'an: Al-i-Imran 3:14]*

The Prophet of Islam (Pbuh) said: The inhabitants of Heaven enjoy nothing more than marriage: even more than foods and drinks. [Vasa'il, v.20, pp.23-24]

The Prophet of Islam (Pbuh) said: When a man expressses his love to his wife, it will never be removed from her heart. [Ibid]

Imam Sadiq (Pbuh) said: The stronger will a woman's faith become, the more she is loved by her husband. [Ibid]

It must be noticed that love of one's wife should not become too excessive, since this will also prevent a man from walking on the right path and doing good deeds. One should especially be careful that his wife does not try to rule over him through her love, and force her excess wants upon him. A man's love and affection for his wife or anything else should be subject to his belief in God and the Day of Judgment, and it should not prevent him from his progress towards perfection and doing good deeds. If the love for women should become a bedrock for sin and wastefulness, or jealousy and greed, or abstaining from doing obligatory religious acts, then this kind of loveaccompanied by a satanic state is far away from God's pleasure and satisfaction.

Lowering Expectations

Each man and woman has his/her own physical and spiritual strength which can only be realized after some time of natural, and moral encounters. A husband and wife get to know each other's physical and spiritual status and get to understand one another after a while. They must realize that God has considered two very important facts when He ordained duties upon man. Firstly, He has not required us to do what is beyond our capabilities. Secondly, He has made our moral and religious responsibilities based on our ability not our power. Most researchers believe that our responsibility is much less than our capability. This is only due to God's kindness and mercy upon His servants. He has referred to this fact in verses 233 and 286 of Chapter Baqara, verse 152 of Chapter An'am and verse 42 of Chapter A'raf and verse 62 of Chapter Mo'minun in the Holy Qur'an.

No soul shall have a burden laid on it greater than it can bear.

On no soul doth God place a burden greater than it can bear.

For this reason, both men and women must consider this noble and kind characteristic of God in their expectations of one another. Firstly, they should not ask for anything beyond the other person's power, whether material or spiritual. This is because forcing such an unreasonable want upon the other party is considered to be oppressive, and it darkens the spirit and results in divine retribution. Secondly, they should not consider the other side's power in their expectations, rather they should reduce their wants and expectations to within their own limits. They should serve each other by performing their own duties, and invite each other to do so pleasantly. They should and can reduce their expectations of each other, since this is one of the characteristics of the Prophets and Imams.

Having excessive expectations is sometimes the same as asking the other one do what is beyond his/her power. Undoubtedly, when this want is not fulfilled, there will be bad feeling and even hatred, and this will end up in the destruction of the foundation of mutual love. Excessive expectations are a result of having a bad character, pride and haughtiness. It is a sort of mental and psychological illness. Reduced expectations however result from politeness, nobility, knowledge and humbleness. If you want your life to be sweeter than honey, and never run into any quarrels, then reduce your expectations in all aspects of life. Your spouse will then not become hurt or belittled by you. These bad feelings will also not carry over to others. God will then be pleased with you.

Anyway, both husband and wife should be good-tempered and a source of love and happiness. They should take it easy on each other. This is one of the elements of what is known as "the good way". Those who follow this way are cleansed of moral and spiritual vice, are favored by God and deserve receiving beautiful rewards. The Prophet (Pbuh) said: The good way and those who follow it will first enter Heaven and sit by me beside the Kawsar pond. [Vasa'il, v.16, p.303, Al-i-Bayt Press]

Imam Sadiq (Pbuh) said: There is a gate to Heaven called the Good, and no one but those who follow the good way shall enter through that gate, and those who follow the good way in this world, shall also be followers of that way in the Hereafter. [Vasa'il, v.16, pp.304-305]

The Prophet (Pbuh) said: Any good deed is charity. [Ibid]

The Holy Qur'an has declared a ten-fold reward for any good deed.

He that doeth good shall have ten times as much to his credit: [Holy Qur'an: An'am 8:160]

Lowering expectations is a form of doing good, is one of the good spiritual deeds, and is one of the forms of Islamic charity. It has a ten-fold reward. Why shouldn't a couple take part in this profitable business? Why shouldn't they benefit from this divine fact throughout their lifetime? Remember that forbidding oneself the Mercy and Favor of God is a great sin and a tremendous oppression which cannot be compensated for.

Forgiving

A couple may at times mistreat one another. The wife may make a mistake in her household duties, or in raising the children, or pleasing her husband. The husband too may make mistakes in running the affairs of the family, or in making a judgment about his wife. Such mistakes are forgivable from either side. It is exactly in such situations when forgiving makes sense: There is no need to forgive if all systems go. It is morally incumbent upon both husband and wife to forgive each other. In such cases haughtiness, selfishness and disrespecting the other party, and not following God and the Prophets' orders is improper, and even in some cases it is forbidden and deserves divine punishment. As the Qur'an states forgiving is loved by God:

"And pardon (all) men; for God loves those who do good." [Holy Qur'an:Al-i-Imran 3:134]

It is so important that the Qur'an has declared the reward of those who forgive to be due from God.

"But if a person forgives and makes reconciliation, his reward is due from God." [Holy Qur'an: Shura 62:40]

Imam Sadiq (Pbuh) said: There are three noble acts in this world and the Hereafter: Forgiving one who has oppressed you. Going to visit one who has cut off his relations with you, and acting with patience with one who has treated you with ignorance. [Bihar al-Anwar, v.71, p.400]

The Prophet (Pbuh) said: Truly God is Forgiving and loves those who forgive. [Mizan al-Hikmat, v.6, p.367]He also said: God will forgive one who forgives a Muslim. [Ibid]

Imam Sadiq (Pbuh) said: We are members of a household with our manhood being forgiving those who oppress us. [Ibid]

The Prophet (Pbuh) said: Forgive the people, and God shall repel the Fire of Hell from you. [Mizan al-Hikmat, v.6, pp.368-370]

The Commander of the Faithful (Pbuh) said: The worst trait for one is to be unforgiving, and one of the greatest sins is rushing to take revenge. [Ibid]

He also said: The worst of the people are those who do not forgive and do not cover up other people's mistakes. [Ibid]

Imam Sadiq (Pbuh) said: One must forgive without blaming, penalizing, and force. [Ibid]

Based upon the traditions and the verses of the Holy Qur'an, forgiving is loved by God; the reward of one who forgives is considered to be one of the nobility of this world and the Hereafter, and is a means of freedom from the Fire of Hell, and is a means of being similar to the members of the Household of the Prophet.

Not forgiving someone is a sign of illness, a spiritual defect and a sign of our soul's wickedness.

Why shouldn't a couple forgive each other's mistakes? Why shouldn't they be loved by God and benefit from divine rewards? Why shouldn't they be considered a source of nobility in this world and the Hereafter? Why shouldn't they be similar to the Immaculate Imams? All these are by-products of a spiritual and divine deal. It is not wise to lose this deal, and it is very easy to be gained. If a couple try this method for a few times, then they will soon become adorned with this divine characteristic after a short time of practicing forgiving.

Feigning

Feigning is one of the very good attributes few people have. Seeing someone's mistakes and acting as if you didn't, so that the one who made the mistake really believes you didn't notice his/her error is one of the best spiritual attributes. Feigning in regards to your wife's errors is a very noble act which must be continued into the future. The Commander of the Faithful (Pbuh) said: Half of a wise person's existence is patience and perseverance, and the other half is feigning. [Mizan al-Hikmat, v.7, p.268]

He also said: A noble man's most honorable attribute is feigning. [Ibid] He also said: There is no measure better than pretending not to notice, and no patience is better than feigning. [Ibid]

As the Commander of the Faithful (Pbuh) has said, being extremely picky and expecting total innocence and blaming others for mistakes is a cause of ruining our life. [Ibid]

It is necessary for a couple to forgive and feign and with such good attributes, life goes on with pleasure, the nerves are calm and the body is safe and immune from many diseases. Forgiving and feigning are the sweet by-products of controlling one's anger. Stubbornness, anger and quarreling are despised by God and are signs of flames of the Fire of Hell, a bad character, and a cause of the disruption of life. This may end up in divorce or separation, or delving into sin or corruption. There are many traditions regarding the harm of stubbornness and quarreling. A man addresses Imam Husayn (Pbuh), the Master of the Martyrs in a distasteful manner: Let's sit down and argue about religion. The Imam said: O' man, know that I am aware of my religion, and God's guidance is as clear as daylight for me. However if you have any problems in this regard you had better go and do something about your ignorance. What do I have to do with quarreling, as this is just a result of Satan's temptation to trap man in sin. [Bihar al-Anwar, v.2, p.135]

If verbal arguments are designed to prove the existence of God, they are considered to be good, and they will cause progress in science and discovery of the truth and God. However, if they are due to stubbornness and for defeating the other side, or for disrupting peace, then they are undoubtedly forbidden and one who argues is rebellious and deserves punishment.

Imam Reza (Pbuh) told Abdul Azim Hassany: Send my greetings to my friends, and tell them not to let Satan penetrate their hearts in any way, and advise them to be honest, truthful and quiet, and avoid quarreling over what has no profit for them. [Bihar al-Anwar, v.74, p.230]

Anger

The Qur'anic verses and Islamic traditions have advised all to avoid anger and consider it destructive; a sign of light-headedness; a cause of destruction; fire from Satan and consider it to be a form of insanity: They consider it to be the source of all evils. The Commander of the Faithful (Pbuh) has expressed these concepts in his wise words: Anger is an evil which when let free to take over will destroy you. [Mizan al-Hikmat, v.7, p.231]

He also said: Anger is the vehicle of the light-headed ones. [Mizan alHikmat, v.7, pp.230-231]

And also: Anger will raise the flames of hidden hatred. [Ibid] Imam Sadiq (Pbuh) said: Anger is the key to all losses. [Ibid]

That's right. An angry person will make many mistakes and attack the honor of the other party. It will put pressure on his heart and nerves, his face will get red and he will hit, destroy, divorce, harm, cause damages and so on. The Prophet (Pbuh) said: Anger is fire from Satan. [Ibid] Hazrat Ali (Pbuh) said: Anger is a form of insanity. One who gets angry will then become sorry. If he does not, his insanity is serious. [Mizan alHikmat, v.7, pp.232-233]

He also said: Anger will spoil the brain and terribly distract man from the truth and righteousness. [Ibid]

He also seriously condemned this Satanic state and said: One who does not control his anger is not one of us. [Ibid]

And he also said: One who is totally driven by anger and lust is an animal. [Ibid]

Regarding control of one's anger, Imam Baqir (Pbuh) has said: In the Hereafter, God will fill the heart of one who has the power to let out his anger but controls it with peace and faith in the Hereafter. Ali (Pbuh) said: God will cover up the faults of those who control their anger. [Mizan al-Hikmat, v.7, p.236]

Imam Ali (Pbuh) wrote to his loyal friend Hareth Hamedany: Control your anger, forgive when in power, be patient when angry, cover up the faults of those who make mistakes, even though you have power. Then you may prosper. [Mizan al-Hikmat, v.7, p.236]

In the books Usul al-Kafi, Vasa'il al-Shiia, and Bihar al-Anwar, we read in many traditions that controlling one's anger towards everyone will be rewarded with immunity from God's anger and receiving His Mercy in the Hereafter. Jesus (Pbuh) was asked about the cause of anger. He said: There are three roots and reasons for anger: Haughtiness, selfishness and belittling the people. The Prophet (Pbuh) has recommended the Commander of the Faithful (Pbuh): Do not get angry. Sit down when you get angry, and think about God's power and rule over His servants and God's patience. If while you are angry you are told of fear ing God, then you can control your anger and return to your normal state of patience.

Arrogance

Arrogance is one of the bad traits, and is considered to be a sin in Islam. One who has this satanic attribute deserves God's punishment unless he/she repents and returns to humbleness and politeness. A couple have religious and moral responsibilities towards each other and have seen and accepted each other before getting married, knowing about each other's family, wealth and beauty and have lived together. When they have a problem they should not use their family, wealth, beauty, knowledge and age to bother the other party. They should avoid arrogance since it will hurt and at times may cause hatred and animosity or reaction. It may even lead to quarrels or divorce, in which case the responsibility is on the shoulders of the arrogant one.

The Commander of the Faithful (Pbuh) said: There is no foolishness greater than arrogance. [Mizan al-Hikmat, v.7, p.414]

He also said in these wise words: Discard arrogance and haughtiness and remember your tomb. [Ibid]

Arrogance is so bad that in his nineteenth book, Imam Sajjad (Pbuh) has said to God: Please guard me against arrogance. Ali (Pbuh) said: How can Adam's offspring be arrogant? Their starting point is a sperm, and their end is a badly-smelling corpse. Their daily bread is in the hands of someone else, and they have no power to escape death. [Bihar al-Anwar, v.73, p.294]

God's book has mentioned the fact that God does not like the arrogant and haughty people in several verses.

For God loveth not any arrogant boaster. [Holy Qur'an: Luqman 31:18] Anyway, a couple should avoid arrogance in regards to their family, beauty, wealth, savings or knowledge and should realize that all these may vanish some day. This satanic trait is only a source of trouble, hurt, loss of love, cause of fights, and losing one's respect in God's sight.

147

Behavior

A couple's behavior towards each other must be accompanied by politeness, nobility, friendship, cooperation, love and humbleness. Their acts should be based on mutual respect and honor. A man should realize that a woman is a delicate creature with love, affection, and modesty. All these traits must be considered when dealing with a woman. A woman must realize that a man is a strong and robust creature having stronger physical and mental states and know that the stability of life is reliant upon him.

> *"Men are the protectors and maintainers of women, because God has given the one more (strength) than the other, and because they support them from their means." [Holy Qur'an: Nisaa 4:34]*

It is for this reason that noble wives respect their husbands, and gentlemen treat their wives with honor. A peaceful mutual life is only possible through mutual consideration of the above facts. We must try to be a practical model of good acts and proper deeds in the way we treat each other, so that we not only pass the days of our lives, but also gain the reward of the Hereafter and please one another with our deeds.

Talking

A couple should talk to each other in a tone which is filled with love, affection and passion, and their words must be filled with manifestations of understanding, wisdom, conscience and justness. When we speak we must follow the verses of the Qur'an regarding speaking, that is speaking justly; speaking fair; speaking mildly; speaking kindly; and calling men to God.

> *"Whenever ye speak, speak justly, even if a near relative is concerned..." [Holy Qur'an: An'am: 152]*

Speak fair to the people... [Holy Qur'an: Baqara 2:83]

"But speak to him mildly; perchance he may take warning or fear (God)..." [Holy Qur'an: Taha 20:44]

"Yet speak to them a word of easy kindness..." [Holy Qur'an: Bani-Israel 17:28]

"Who is better in speech than one who calls (men) to God..." [Holy Qur'an: Fussilat 41:33]

When what is said is Godly, when the judgment that is made is right, when what is said is simple and softly spoken, it will bless your life with love, happiness, warmth and stability. When what is said is right and it is said kindly and passionately, then it will be rewarded by being heard and realized. The Prophet (Pbuh) said: If it were not for your talking too much, and if your heart was not the place for Satan, you would see what I see and hear what I hear!

Kanzulemal

It is better to avoid talking too much or saying what is not good for either this world or the Hereafter. The Prophet (Pbuh) said: One of the good things in Islam for man is to avoid vain talk. [Mizan al-Hikmat, v.8, pp.434-440]

The Commander of the Faithful (Pbuh) once passed by a man who talked too much. He told him: "You are filling your record of deeds with extra talk. This record will be presented to your Lord, so you better say useful things and avoid vain talk". Abuzar said: You can summarize the world in two words, one in search of what is lawful in all respects, and the other in search of the Hereafter. All else is useless and harmful, and you better not engage in it. [Ibid]

The Prophet (Pbuh) said: All that the son of Adam says is to his loss, not to his benefit; except his advice to do good deeds, and remember God and his warning against doing evil deeds. [Ibid]

The Commander of the Faithful (Pbuh) said: One who talks too much shall make many mistakes. One who makes many mistakes will be less modest. One with less modesty shall be less pious. Such a person's heart shall die and he will enter Hell. [Ibid]

A couple should talk to each other about the affairs of the house, their needs and those of their children, express their love and affection for each other, advise each other to do right and to persevere, safeguard each others' secrets, and not talk about their personal affairs with their family or friends. And they should establish their home as a center of God's words, prayer, the Qur'an, no lying, gossiping, swearing or belittling, since as it can be understood from the verses of the Qur'an and the traditions, such bad deeds will deprive us of God's Mercy and may even bring His punishment. A man should avoid bringing sinful folks home, or giving sinful parties since this will bring harm to him and his household, and will cause him to lose out on the Hereafter. A wife should avoid wastefulness which is sometimes the sour result of keeping up with the Joneses, since she will be accountable for each penny wasted in the Hereafter. A man and his wife should try to practically foster nobility, politeness, and spiritual health in their children and those around them with their manners, words and deeds, since the reward of guiding even one person is equal to that of guiding all the people.

Sixteen

Part 13: The Modest Covering and Woman's Chasteness

"Thereof; that they should draw their veils over their bosoms and not display their beauty except..." [Holy Qur'an: Nur 24:31]

Veiling, or covering woman's beauty and protecting her from the evil eyes of the rude, lustfully corrupt and satanic men is a Qur'anic decree, a holy law, human duty and a moral affair. Islamic veiling, whose best form, is the long veil or chador being a reminder of that spring of chasteness Fatimah Zahra (Pbuh). The veil is not a block to acquiring knowledge and perfection for a woman. Rather, the veil protects her from many dangers and traps that animal-like people have placed before the beautiful ones, the young girls and women. The veil protects her innocence, chasteness and modesty for her husband, or if she is not married for her future husband. Whenever the precious, beautiful and costly jewel womangoes into the divine trunk called covering, she is safe from the thefts of the thieves, the looters and those corrupted by sin. When the young beautiful ones are not seen and their innocent faces are not displayed before men, the flames of lust and tendency towards disobeying; cannot burn a nation and destroy the foundations of a country's spirituality: burning instincts are not aroused.

If the young men do not see the attractive beauties of the young women and women in public places, they will not look at them lustfully, chase girls and attack women. Then there will be no mental sluggishness, nervous breakdowns, premature adulthood, masturbation, fornication, gay-like acts, sorrows and worries, lack of concentration, not being in the mood to study, love affairs, psychotic illnesses, or impotency. Based upon this, it must be said that the modest covering is a necessary matter for women and is strongly required. Without any doubt, one who denies this matter-knowing that it is necessary in Islam is an unbeliever according to the decrees of God in the Qur'an; he is not a Muslim. If a young man believes so, he cannot marry a Muslim girl since the marriage would be nullified. The marriage between these two would be worthless and their relationship would be illegal based on Islam and their children would be illegitimate; their intercourse would be considered adultery, too. A girl who denies the matter of covering cannot be the wife of a young Muslim man since the same applies to her as does to the unbelieving man.

The covering protects a woman's dignity, nobility and grandeur and protects her beauty and her benefits for her husband. Being modestly covered, she may continue her education and attain perfection and virtues. It is satanic to think that women are prevented from progressing by the veil. It is a wrong idea publicized by the looting Imperialists and the thieves of women's chastity, and the rogues of Eastern and Western countries.

All the following are related to the covering of a country's women: the warmth of the home, the strength of the relationship between a wife and a husband, the peace of mind of men, the proof of love of men for their lawful wives. All of these are based upon the home and the family and the trust of the man in his wife. They also require that men should not see the beauties of women other than their own wives. If men have easy access to women in all the scenes of society, there will be no guarantee that they will maintain their love and attachment to their own wives. The excitement of men's lustful instincts will cause them to lose interest in their mutual life and this in itself will destroy the warmth of the family center. It is impossible to assess the amount of damage done by unveiling women and the misuse of the veil and the practice of letting women on the loose as done in the West.

Up until now, the unveiling of women has caused millions of men to deviate from the straight path, many others to commit sins, the appearance of the monster called "divorce" in the families, men falling in love with married women, and illegitimate sexual relationships. The unveiling has also caused many to leave the angelic expanse of Islam and religion, just as Judaism and Christianity have wanted. The establishers of the practice of unveiling have really become frustrated themselves and recognize that the destructive influences of their action are among the evil phenomenon of this century.

The family system in Iran is a strong system based on modesty, chasteness, nobility, politeness, faith, piety and no divorces except in rare cases. However, the family and the home have experienced different times since the Reza Khan Pahlavy looted the veil from the heads of many of Iran's women. This was actually done by the western imperialists who put that rogue, base illiterate traitor, and dirty country-seller into power. At the end of his rule, the divorce rates sky rocketed so much so that the dirty dynasty had between six to seven thousand requests made to its courts for divorce every month. Thus, the young married men became womanless, and the married women became divorced.

These two groups freed of their marital obligations joined the society and spread corruption at an alarming rate throughout it.

The supreme Islamic jurisprudent -the late Ayatullah Shah Abady has been quoted as sayingwithout any fear of the government of the timethe following after the removal of the veil by the government in public and private places and on the pulpit: "By looting the Qur'an's veil and killing the protesters against unveiling in the Gohar Shad. Mosque beside Imam Reza's shrine guarded by angels, Reza Khan made the 124,000 Prophets of God cry".

O yes! That insightful mystic in love, who was an able, enlightened, peerless jurisprudent in Islamic matters, wisdom and philosophy, considered the unveiling of women and the misuses of the veil to be an affair that made the Prophets cry!!!

In the very useful book entitled "Are We Muslims"? Quttab stated : "Based on the documents I have seen, one of the Popes invited all the cardinals and the priests in the Vatican and asked them to comment on how to destroy Islam and eliminate the illuminating light of religion in a way that does not cost Christianity and the Vatican too much. Committees were formed and several views were expressed. Among these, the view that was accepted by all the priests, the cardinals and Pope himself was that the cheapest plan and the strongest weapon to destroy Islam was to unveil Muslim girls and women and make them freely available to young boys and men in the allies, the markets, the parks, the public places, the offices, the theaters, commercial and social centers." This plan was carried out by the traitors and was reinforced by the lustfulness of unfaithful girls and women who added to the flames burning the religion and the family.

The situation became so bad in Islamic countries and Iran that the product of the efforts of the Prophets, the Imams, the scholars and the wise being God's religion, was about to be abolished. And the light of guidance was about to be extinguished. However, God's hand extended out through a man from the descendants of the Prophets and the Imams in Iran. Khomeini, the idol-breaker, appeared on the scene and saved the religion from the evil ones. He re-established the practice of the Qur'an's veil.

It is incumbent upon the Islamic nation to protect the Revolution of that divine individual as well as the values of that great divine movement. The people must not let the injured enemy decrease or extinguish the light of the movement and return the Iranian nation to its previous state. The nation must assertedly export the culture of the Revolution and bring the rest of the nations from outside the circle of Islam back into the orbit. Considering what has just been said, we can understand the value of that enlightened martyr's words who stated several times in his speeches: "The veil is a protection, not a limitation."

O' yes! The veil is a protection from thousands of dangers for a woman, her husband, her family, the society, and especially the youth and those who have not married. It protects everyone from corruption and prevents the warmth of the family center from getting cold. Researchers have stated that the issue of covering has been presented in fourteen Qur'anic verses and some believe that close to twenty-five verses make use of the meaning of the concept called "veiling".

The Commander of the Faithful (Pbuh) said to Imam Mujtaba and in reality all people: Truly adhere to the restrictions regarding veiling near those who are forbidden to see each other, as this will safeguard youand all women you are not allowed to see from thinking about or falling into sin. And if you can, try not to let your women know any man other than you yourself. [Bihar al-Anwar, v.77, p.214]

A narrator has stated that one rainy day he was sitting in Baq'ih Cemetery with the Prophet (Pbuh). A woman riding a donkey passed by us, when its foot got caught in hole and the woman fell off the animal. The Prophet (Pbuh) turned his face and I told him she was wearing pants. The Prophet (Pbuh) asked God for forgiveness of such women three times and said: "O 'people! Put on such clothes as they are the best covering for the body and women should wear such clothes when they leave the house." [Mizan al-Hikmat,v.2, p.259]

The short veil, the scarf, the long cloak are the various titles which are used in the Qur'anic verses and Prophetic traditions for a woman's modest covering. A woman must consider herself a slave of God, and must be grateful to God. Being grateful means to consider His grandeur, the Hereafter and the Trial. She must pay strict attention to the fact entitled the Resurrection Day and the Last Judgment. She must wholeheartedly obey the decrees of her God in the Qur'an, on the tongues of the Prophets and Imams, so that she may protect herself, her family and society from the harmful effects of not veiling properly or at all.

"And for such as had entertained the fear of standing before their Lord's (tribunal) and had restrained (their) soul from

lower desires, their abode will be the Garden." [Holy Qur'an: Nazi'at:40-41]

Sorrowfully, it must be said that some girls and women living today in various parts of the world follow the school of lust and sinning. They have freed their lusts and sexual desires and spread corruption in every corner of the world which is unprecedented in history. And it must also be sorrowfully stated that some females in Islamic countries who belong to the nation of the Prophet (Pbuh) are imitating those deviant Westerners. The Commander of the Faithful (Pbuh) said the following regarding such women: "Near the end of time when we are approaching the Hereafter, there will be women with such characteristics: Lacking any modest covering and nearly naked; showing off their private beauties outside the house in the streets and the markets; irreligious; malicious; inclined to lust; accelerating towards pleasures; considering divinely forbidden acts as legitimate: such women with these characteristics will abide in Hell forever. [Vasa'il, v.14, p.19]

A Surprising Fact

In one of the issues of the newspaper KAYHAN having a high circulation, I read (I cannot remember which issue): "There was a young woman who was an example of those women noted in the afore-mentioned tradition of the Commander of the Faithful (Pbuh). She fell in love with a youth even though she had a three year-old daughter, because she was free as the Western women's style to come and go as she liked and because her husband's friends visited the house freely. She did not cover herself Islamically and exposed her body to them. She would attend frequent parties where men and women were mixed.

The young, lustful, irreligious man was excited sexually even more by the young married woman and told her the child was an obstacle in their way and must be eliminated. They argued over this matter for nearly four months, and finally lust and the inclination to make love with others overcame the mother who was created to be a center of love and affection. She took her innocent, beautiful blonde girl to the bath and choked her to eliminate the obstacle to her lust and to let the married woman and the strange man reach a few moments of carnal desire.

She became corrupted forever and left her poor husband with a devastating state of life." If the husband of this woman had shown some manliness and prevented his young beautiful wife from freely being seen by others and being attractive to men around, then a sinless child would have been left for the unfortunate father and a married woman would not have spoiled her chasteness forever. A youth was thus made to experience a terrible misfortune and the warm, family center of another youth who had just married was completely wrecked. O 'yes! The modest covering is a protection not a limitation.

The View of Some Eminent Westerners in Regards to the Situation of Western Society

Disraeli, one of the Prime Ministers of Britain, a country leading in corruption and its spread, wrote in an article:

"I am at the verge of committing insane acts, but always try to avoid one being a love affair with a woman in the street and say this is my ideal woman!" Under the guise of freedom, the unwise took the Creation's valuable and chaste jewel out of the guard for chastity being the veil and let her totally free in any program deemed necessary by lust. Then they discarded her with the excuse of escaping from a love affair, since this valuable jewel has now lost its worth and is with someone else at each moment. And she is in bed with others at different times constantly delving into immoral, inhumane acts.

Miss Alzeemary, a Swedish writer and poet, has stated the following regarding the European society in an important article in the Daily Express: "The men know nothing about loyalty and trick girls and women". She must be told that men lost their loyalty, to their wife, home and the family when you guided the women towards unchastity, bad covering or no covering of the body at all. And men turned her into an unconditional slave of man's lust and inclination so that men could easily see her halfnaked while being tempting, whenever they desired. It was then that the men turned into tricky people.

The side-effects of poor veiling, or no veiling at all and the woman's freedom to have a relationship with whomever she desires are not few in number. And the sour results of this issue are unnumerable. When the men saw these scenes, they left their spouses; in other words, they quit the responsibility to support their family. They went to the free market to satisfy themselves. When the young men realized how cheap it was to satisfy their lusts, they rejected establishing a mutual married life and pursued their lusts. It was in this way that the family structure in the West and those Eastern countries which followed it, fell apart and a situation similar to a jungle was the result.

Miss Alzeemary added in her paper that there are many young beautiful girls who hope to find a husband, but are forced into sexual relations with men. Verily they are awaiting a husband but none is to be found, since young men have access to women in whatever form they desire and see no need to marry. Even many married men separate from their wives to be able to satisfy their lusts freely. She adds that she recommends that young girls have no relations with any men before they get married. Her request is very important but this is not practical given the current state of women in the world and the loose behavior of men in the Western society.

If the world decides to approach an appropriate state it must put the legitimate, natural and humane Islamic regulations into practice. First and foremost, they must return the veil and proper covering to women: They must return chastity and shyness to her. Otherwise, there exists no cure for all the corruption which destroys the family order.

The oppression against women in the West is unprecedented in man's history. They have guided women's intent, will and effort towards appearance in public places for corruption and seduction of men. They have turned her into sexual goods to be used for gaining wealth and pleasing their lust.

Hazrat Ali (Pbuh) has said in Nahj ul-Balaghah: The animals strive for food; the beasts strive for animosity with others; and the women strive for adoration of life and corruption in the world. It is believing men and women who submit to God, fear God, are kind and benevolent. [Nahj ulBalaghah, Ibn Abi al-Hadid, v.9, Chapter 153, p.160]

A Case From Imam Husayn's Life (Pbuh)

It has been narrated that before going to fight the enemies, Imam Husayn (Pbuh) told Hazrat Zaynab (Pbuh) to gather all the women's jewelry and throw it in front of the tents after Imam Husayn got martyred and the enemies attacked the tents. Then their poor materialist enemies, who were unaware and attached to this world would get busy gathering them, and the women would get a chance to find a secure corner safe from the eyes of the strange men. It has been said that when Yazeed was hitting Imam Husayn's chopped off head's lips and teeth, one of his maids dreamt of Hazrat Zahra (Pbuh) being sad and upset, and complaining of what Yazeed was doing. Then she woke up and got so afraid that she rushed out yelling into Yazeed's court without a scarf and veil. Yazeed who saw her in this state covered her up with his own cloak and shouted: "Why did you appear in front of strange men without the proper head and face covering?" How strange it is that this atheist, alcoholic, dog and monkey-keeper Yazeed could not bear to see his maid without any modest covering and covered her with his own cloak and sent her out of the meeting where there were strange men; but there are men who are so careless about their women and let them appear everywhere in public with their hair and face made up and without any cover. The Prophet (Pbuh) said regarding the sense of honor A sense of honor is due to man's belief in God and the Hereafter. [Mizan alHikmat, v.7, pp.357-358]

Verily God is religiously zealous, and loves any one with a sense of honor. It is due to His sense of honor that He has forbidden the exposure of private parts. [Ibid]

Seventeen

Part 14: Security in Life

⎯⎯ ❧❦❧ ⎯⎯

"Whatever good, (O man!) happens to thee, is from God; But whatever evil happens to thee, is from thy (own) soul." [Holy Qur'an: Nisaa 4:79]

The Good and the Bad

Man is a creature consisting of the intellect, the heart, the soul and the body. Good and bad aspects exist for each part of man's being; all the good ones originate in God and all the bad ones originate in man himself. Nothing but benefits, goodness, mercy and blessings come from the Sacred Existence, God, Who is mentioned in the Glorious Qur'an as having the following attributes: the All-Benevolent; the All-Merciful; the Lord; the All-Loving; the All-Forgiving; the Generous; the All-Subtle; the Compassionate; the Creator; the Shaper; the Holy and the All-Mighty.

Nothing but evil and damage are the products of ignorance, rancor, envy, spite, short-temperedness, greed and laziness. An individual must strive to attain enough wisdom, knowledge and insight so as to make a living; to thoroughly illuminate one's worldy life and spiritual life; to manage the affairs of his wife and children; and to acquire the correct outlook on Existence and the world, as much as his personal and social duties requires.

Learning about the basic matters such as belief in God and the Day of Judgment, knowledge about the Prophethood and the leadership of the Imams, is a necessary affair and one's personal duty. One is duty-bound to learn the matters related to jurisprudence and the worldly sciences as much as he needs to. God has bestowed upon man the beneficial elements of science and knowledge, wisdom and insight as powerful goods and benefits along with the necessary success in growth, perfection of the intellect and the power to understand. Whenever the intellect, itself being one of God's blessings, accompanies other blessings like success and insight, then a sea of light appears in the individual's spiritual domain. This illumination and good will guarantee a part of the security of man's spiritual domain. Naturally, this security will be passed on from a man to his wife and children, and they too will benefit from peace with him. As a result, life will to some extent be illuminated by the light of peace and quiet.

In the first stage, it is essential for the head of the household, who is responsible for managing life's affairs to have enough knowledge of religion as required by his personal duty and, as much as is necessary of religious jurisprudence knowledge: this means to be informed of the religiously lawful and forbidden actions and things. He must have as much as necessary of worldly knowledge in order to run life. In the next stage and under the support of the man of the house who provides the necessities of the family, the wife and the children can live as a small nation in the small country of the home. They can live together with knowledge, wisdom, insight and awareness, and be secure from the evils of ignorance, illiteracy, jealousy and foolishness. Verily knowledge provides security and ignorance and illiteracy will result in loss.

Ignorance and Illiteracy

In a very important statement made by members of the Prophet's family, ignorance is considered to be a kind of spiritual death and to be more detrimental to one's life than a harmful meal. Ignorance is an illness, some sort of suffering, a source of deviation bringing on ever-lasting misfortune. It ruins one's future life, is a mine of evil and a dangerous enemy. Ignorance is the cause of unbelief and deviation, and prevents sermons and advice from being accepted. It also is the cause of excesses in life. The Commander of the Faithful, Imam Ali (Pbuh) said: Ignorance is death; ignorance is destruction; ignorance is an incurable disease; ignorance is a cause of man's slippage; ignorance ruins the Hereafter; ignorance is the source of all evils; and ignorance is the main stock of evil. [Mizan al-Hikmat, v.2, p.154]

The Prophet (Pbuh) was asked about the signs of the ignorant. He answered as follows: An ignorant will trouble you if you socialize with him. He will blame you if you stay away from him; he will mention it if he grants you something; he will be ungrateful if you grants him something; and if you trust him with your secrets, he will misuse your trust. [Tuhaf ul-Uqool, p.28]

Consider the following matter for yourself. If the head of the household is ignorant, does not consider spiritual and doctrinal matters to be important and has no worldly plans in mind, then he will be a great source of stress, insecurity, trouble, suffering and torment in and outside of the home. Wealth and property, the home and life, the wife and children, are faced with danger and damage, and loss and insecurity in the presence of an ignorant individual. Islam stresses that one must acquire wisdom and insight in worldly and spiritual affairs as much as necessary, so that security is created in the individual's spiritual and worldly life. Islam wants an individual's innocent wife and children to live in peace with him, and not suffer any physical blows, loss and damages at his hands. It does not want his family's worldly and future lives to suffer any loss and the distressful monsters of war to be at their throats.

In Islamic literary traditions, it is written that Jesus (Pbuh) was wholeheartedly on the run. A friend of his asked him why this was so. Jesusf (Pbuh) replied he was fleeing from the ignorant. O' yes, one must be wholeheartedly on the run from ignorance and the ignorant, and follow the Prophets' way so as to secure one's prosperity in this world and the Hereafter. Even if the ignorant has the elixir of life, he is poor, but the informed and the wise is rich beside poverty.

Knowledge and Wisdom

According to the decree of the Glorious Qur'an, the wise and the foolish are in no way equal: Say:

"Are those equal, those who know and those who do not know?"
[Holy Qur'an: Zumar 39:9]

And as the Prophet of Islam (Pbuh) has said: A day in which I acquire no knowledge or science which would help me approach God is not a blessed day for me. [Mizan al-Hikmat, v.6, p.449]

He also said: A heart without any wisdom is like a ruin. So learn, teach and understand and do not pass away as an ignorant. Verily God will not accept the excuse of the ignorant in the Hereafter. [Ibid]

The Commander of the Faithful, Imam Ali (Pbuh) described knowledge and wisdom, and their attributes in the magnificent book entitled "Ghurar al-Hikam" as follows: Knowledge brings forth success and is a dam against catastrophes and calamities. Wisdom is the highest degree of self-sufficiency. Knowledge is the light of the intellect; a good reason; the best guidance; obvious beauty; the best companion; the most worthy measure; the believer's lost one; the guide to patience; the most beneficial treasure and the most excellent truth. In one sentence, the Prophet (Pbuh), expressed all the realities in this world and the Hereafter resulting from knowledge and wisdom: Knowledge, insight and wisdom are the source of all goodness. [Bihar al-Anwar, v.77, p.175]

Hazrat Ali (Pbuh) recognizes that there are seven basic differences between material wealth and knowledge. Knowledge and insight are the legacy of the Prophets. Wealth and property are the legacy of the Pharaohs. Knowledge will not decrease once taught, but wealth once spent will. Wealth requires a guard, while knowledge guards an individual. Knowledge accompanies an individual all the way to his future life, while wealth remains in this world. Acquiring wealth is feasible for everyone, but knowledge, wisdom and insight belong to the believers. Concerning the affairs of religion, all people are in need of a wise man but do not need a wealthy one. Knowledge will help one pass over the bridge to the Hereafter, but wealth will prevent one from rendering one's accounts. [Bihar al-Anwar, v.77, p.185]

An empty ship will face many dangers such as terribly bad weather, strong winds, wreckage or getting lost while sailing at sea, while a full ship will move on safe and secure to approach its destination. This is similar to an ignorant man versus a wise, knowledgeable one. How does the person behave whose spiritual life is enlightened by the light of monotheism; whose heart is sure of the truth and whose soul is pledged to the Resurrection Day; and who knows that the day is the Day when:

> *"Then shall anyone who has done an atom's weight of good, see it! And anyone who has done an atom's weight of evil, shall see it." [Holy Qur'an: Zilzal 99: 7-8]*

How does the person behave who knows himself to be only a traveler in this world and who knows the future life to be the everlasting home for life in the Hereafter? The one who considers all blessings to be entrusted to him by God; the one who considers himself responsible for every blessing; the one who knows that God gave him a wife, children, a house, a factory, wealth and property, etc. In short, how does a person behave whose relationship with everything is determined by wisdom? This sort of person's behavior is actually wisdom itself; his actions are just like enlightenment; his movements are pure truth; and his interactions with everyone and everythingespecially his wife and childrenare based upon peace, straight forwardness, compassion, mercy, genuineness and generosity. A Lot of security and tranquillity are expected from such a person at home, with the family and outside the home. Everyone who comes into contact with him lives in security, at ease and in peace and quiet along with having trust in him. Islam wants the man of the house, the spouse of a lady and the father of children to be exactly like the man described above.

The Heart is the Source of Truth

In Islamic works there are various, surprising explanations about the heart:

The territory of God[Bihar al-Anwar, v.70, p.25] A spring [Mizan al-Hikmat, v.8, p.212]

An Imam (leader) [Bihar al-Anwar, v.70, p.53] A monarch [Mizan al-Hikmat, v.8, pp.216-218] A container.[Ibid]

Other attributes have been ascribed to the heart (soul) such as: health, illness, innocence, mischief-making, soft-heartedness, harshness, enlightenment, blindness, destruction, prosperity, misfortune, life, death, courage, termination, calmness, deviation and hard-heartedness. These interpretations of the heart are mentioned in the Glorious Qur'an and other books like Usul al-Kafi, Shafi, Bihar al-Anwar, Vasa'il al-Shiia, Mustadrak al-Vasa'il, Tuhaf ul-Uqool, Ruzat al-Vaizin and Muhjat ulBiyza, with various words given a meaning. Really, the heart is a container and what an amazing one it is!

If room in it is made for faith in God and the Resurrection Day, innocence, enlightenment, life, fear of punishment, fear of God, sincerity, and in short-sympathy, compassion, loving-kindness and lovethen the owners of this heart will enjoy peace, security, health and tranquillity. Everyone who comes into contact with such a person will be secure, healthy and at ease. If this container, however, is a place for greediness, stinginess, avarice, envy, spite, hypocrisy, unbelief, polytheism, hard-heartedness, suspicion and the like, the heart is a dangerous, harmful, corrupt, base and oppressive creature: no one will be safe at his hands.

The following must be mentioned to the youth who have still not gotten married. If you recognize that your heart has been polluted by these hideous qualities, then try and reform it and then get married. This is so because the woman who marries you, who comes to your house with thousands of desires and has abandoned her home, neighborhood or city, and loving bosoms of her parents, and after a time gets pregnant by you, will then feel secure and have some peace and quiet. She can then properly perform her marital and domestic duties and raise your children. An insecure home and a person who destroys security is Hell and the punishment of Hell. Woe unto the man whose wife and children are not safe with him, and continually live in bitterness and trouble.

And woe unto the woman whose husband and children are bothered by her and live in suffering. Woe unto her who without fear of God, changes the peaceful home environment into one of terror and stress. And woe unto those children whose mother and father are not at ease due to their offspring's trouble-making. Amir al-Mumeneen (The Commander of the Faithful) (Pbuh) believes that if a person's heart is not linked up to God and his heart is not full of faith, the love and kindness of God, then amazing catastrophes will befall him. If he becomes attached to the baseness of greediness and is polluted by the excitement of it, then avarice will attack and destroy him. And if he becomes coldhearted, sorrow will kill him. In the case he is subject to someone's anger, he gets angry and the fire of anger will blaze. If he gets too involved in happiness, he will lose control of himself. If he becomes fearful, his life will be wasted in abstention. If he finds security, his existence will be devastated by pride. If he is struck with a misfortune, he will go crazy and disgraced. If he attains some wealth, wealth and riches will make him rebel. If poverty attacks him, calamities and troubles will entertain him. If hunger presses down upon him, weakness will make him bedridden. If extravagance in anything attacks him, gluttony will prevent him from breathing.

Whatever is given to such a man in small amounts is harmful to him, and whatever is given in excess causes corruption in him. These astonishing words of the Prophet, Muhammad (Pbuh) concern the health and the illness of the heart: There is a piece of meat in our body which when healthy guarantees that the rest of our body is healthy and when sick, the rest of our body gets sick. This is nothing else but the heart! [Mizan al-Hikmat, v.8, pp.216-218]

The Prophet (Pbuh) also said: There are containers on the Earth for God the Almighty. Know that those containers are hearts. The most beloved of those hearts is the kindest, most pure and the strongest: The kindest towards the believing brethren, the most pure from sins, and the strongest in attachment to the Lord. The Commander of the Faithful, Imam Ali (Pbuh), stated a very important tradition concerning the health of the heart: Your heart will not be healthy for you unless you prefer for the believers whatever you prefer for yourself. What an amazing way has been suggested for the heart to be healthy!

What an enlightened and wise saying has been quoted from one of the Saints and Lovers of God!

O 'yes, if a person wants for others what he wants for himself, the heart will gradually be freed of all vices and corruption, and changed into a healthy heart. At this moment, the expanse of the heart will be overfilled with faith, love, compassion, mercy, nobility and sincerity. All those coming into contact with such a person, especially the wife and the children, will benefit from goodness in this life and the Hereafter. If a youth has still not married and if he finds some imperfections in his heart, he should try to reform it. If he does not do so, his future wife and children will be oppressed. If married men find some dark defects in their hearts, they must strive to correct these problems. If they do not do so, their wives and offspring will not be safe at their hands.

Everyone must know the following fact: A great punishment awaits those men whose wife and children are endangered with being corrupted by their husband's ill-temperedness and bad actions. If the intellect is fed with knowledge and one's behavior is endowed with divinity, then the soul is enlightened and all of one's actions become heavenly. An individual is changed into a source of goodness and a spring of virtues who insures the security of others. Concerning this matter, pay close attention to the following Qur'anic verse from the Book of God:

"It is those who believe and confuse not their beliefs with wrongthat are (truly) in security, for they are on (right) guidance." [Holy Qur'an: An'am 6:82]

O 'yes, just as has been mentioned at the beginning of this discussion, all goodness comes from God and all evil from man himself. One can acquire all the virtues and wipe out all the evil from his being by turning to God, following the Prophets, the Qur'an, the Imams and by utilizing one's worldly and spiritual power. Once an individual has acquired virtues, it is his duty to relay them, as much as is within his power to others, especially his wife and children. If one is indifferent in this area it is considered a great sin causing God's punishment. Our Imams (leaders) have stated that we must be a model for others in our words and actions, so that whenever anyone sees goodness and the soul's beauty in someone else, he desires to acquire such virtues. The man of the house must be a proof of God for his family and the symbol of goodness at home. He must be a model of spiritual, moral and practical goodness at home. The man of the house will not be such unless his intellect, heart, soul and body -as much as is within his powerare fed with knowledge, morality, pleasantness, innocence, piety, honesty, and good acts. This is so because his house and his household must be a branch of the Household of the Prophet (Pbuh) and a manifestation of the Saints of God. At this point, it is felt necessary to participate in useful, religious meetings and to go to the mosques and to have discussions with clergymen and jurisprudents about religion and the spiritual world. If one avoids these actions, it is the source of increasing one's ignorance, the appearance of mental illness and deviation in the soul and practical affairs. There shall be no excuse for anyone in front of God, in this world, the Purgatory or the Hereafter given the manifestation of revelations in the Qur'an, the effects of the Prophethood of the Prophets and the leadership of the Imams in valuable authentic books; all these mosques and religious ceremonies; the availability of clergymen to help one walk on God's path, reach perfection and acquire the good of this world and the Hereafter.

Torture in the Expanse of the Hereafter

The fire of Hell is burning because of ignorance, corruption of the heart and deviation. It is not God the Compassionate who has willed punishment to be necessary for anyone he decides to punish. It is sin, evilness and moral vice that appear in the form of punishment and fire, and imprison the beings of the sinners. If there were no sinning, denial of God and unbelief, and disobeyance of God, there would also be no punishment in Purgatory and on the Day of Judgment. It is stated in the Supplication of Kumayl: I know for sure that if it was not for Your decree to punish the rejecters and opponents everlasting in Hell, You would have cooled down all the Fire, and made it healthy, and there was no room for punishment for anyone. But You have sworn that You shall fill Hell with the pagans, and those who are ungrateful.

Therefore, there are some people who pollute themselves with sin and thereby create their own punishment. It is God the Merciful and Forgiving who has created everything needed to adorn His servants with goodness resulting in security in this world and the next. Men and women try to bring about an acceptable amount of security in their lives for themselves, their children, relatives and others, with the help of faith, morality, good deeds, sincerity, fidelity, honesty and patience. Thus, these people will enjoy peace and security on the Day of Judgment due to the security they created in this world. According to the Prophet (Pbuh): This world is the field of cultivation for the Hereafter. And according to Imam Baqir (Pbuh): Truly this world is a good home for the pious ones. The pious ones make supplies for the Hereafter out of all the activities of this world. Out of their own world, they establish their own Hereafter. They are happier in their own world and the Hereafter. Abdullah ibn Ya'fur who ranks among the eminent Islamic personalities stated: "I said to Imam Sadiq (Pbuh) that I was in love with this world. He asked what I did in the world. I said I used it to marry, go on pilgrimage to Mecca, earn the living expenses for my wife and children, attend to the needs of my needy brothers in their affairs and pay charity. Imam Sadiq (Pbuh) said: These affairs are not of this world but of the Hereafter. You can see that the faithful and pious run business, farms and have income. They marry, manage the home and life in the best manner, help others, go on pilgrimages and pay alms.

In short, they spend their time in this world in a healthy way with security, faith and a good temper, and then benefit in a better way from the Hereafter. I wish that all the homes would be filled with security and healthiness. I wish that faith, morality and good deeds would govern over all homes and that all men and women were adorned with goodness and lacked any vices, so that no one would have any problems. I wish that all would live together in a healthy way and in peace, and enjoy God's blessings. The sixth Imam (Pbuh) introduces the real believers in an important tradition, a part of which goes: All the people are in comfort because of the believers, and the believer is put to some trouble due to creating this security and comfort. [Bihar Al-Anwar, V.78, P.37]

Good Mothers and Fathers

A wife and husband who are adorned with goodness and cleansed of vices are a source of peace and security for each other. They are a source of development, perfection and peace and quiet for their children. They are never indifferent to their offsprings' needs: the parents kindly and politely answer the request of their children for kindness, material expenses, education, visiting, recreation and marriage. If they cannot answer positively to some of their children requests, the parents persuade the children with good manners and patience. And the dignified children accept their parent's answers and explanations. Enlightened and good children refuse to do evil if their parents sometimes invite them to do so due to not paying attention to the children. They refuse their parents request respectfully and politely and do not deviate from the right way. At the time of the Prophet (Pbuh) there was a mother who did not like her children becoming Muslim and even she refused to eat any food. But when she heard that God approved of her child becoming a Muslim and did not value her disapproval, she broke her fast and remained silent before her children.

O' parents, the Prophet (Pbuh) pays strict attention to your aborted fetus; so much so that he stated when the fetus is told to enter heaven; it will answer in the negative saying: I will not enter until my parents enter heaven before me. [Vasa'il Al-Shiia, V.20, P.14, Al-i-Bayt Press]

Why don't you take especial care of your honorable offspring who are God's blessing and goodness. Taking care of offspring and paying good attention to them and their human needs is an affair that is very beneficial here and in the Hereafter.'

Eighteen

Part 15: The Aspects of Virtue in the Family

The Prophet (Pbuh) said: Whoever marries and visits his relatives for the sake of God, God shall attend to him by placing a crown like that of the angels on his head. [Vasa'il, v.20, p.51, Al-i-Bayt Press]

The Sincerity of One's Intentions

These wise and important words have been reported on the authority of the Prophet (Pbuh): Whoever marries to please Allah and establish a family, God will adorn his head with the crown of angels. Marriage produces numerous benefits: the loving-kindness of a wife and a husband; relief from loneliness; increase in one's daily sustenance; the happiness of two families; maintaining half of one's religion; attaining God's satisfaction; sexual pleasure; having children in one's life and finding support in life, etc. In addition to all these benefits, if one marries for the sake of God and with the best of intentions, then due to his good intentions he has engaged in a great act of worship. Marriage will make him equal in worth to angels and a crown like that of the angels will adorn his head. Why not act in such a way that God's acceptance illuminates it and places a highmost value on it?

From the very beginning, let's base the foundation of marriage and the establishment of a new life upon sincerity. Our men and women must give their total attention to this matter so that both the worldly and spiritual aspects of their lives will enjoy the attention, mercy and acceptance of Allah. Imam Ali (Pbuh) has been narrated as having said that none of our acts is of a higher value than the ones accepted by God. This has been narrated in the book Mava'ez al-'Addadiyi.

The Peak of Sincere Intention

Considering this matter, pay especial attention to this very amazing story told by the Prophet Moses (Pbuh) (Musa ibn Umran).

One day Moses (Pbuh) watered the Prophet Jethro's flocks of sheep and then in return Jethro (Pbuh) invited him to come home with him. Moses entered that great Prophet's house where the table was already spread for dinner. Jethro requested the young man to sit down for dinner. Moses replied that he could not partake of the food, so Jethro asked Moses if he was hungry. Moses replied he was hungry, but was afraid that the dinner before him was in recompense for his previous good deed. He said we are of a family who will not even exchange a bit of our good deeds for the Hereafter, even an earth full of pure gold. Jethro said: "O, young man! I swear to God that this was not what I had in mind when inviting you to dinner. I didn't intend to recompense your divine deed with food from my table. It is my father's and my custom to entertain guests and serve them food. After this discussion, Moses sat down at the table to eat. [Bihar al-Anwar, v.13, p.21]

Really, it is very astonishing that Moses had left Egypt some time ago and been wandering around in the wilderness, but during that time was not able to find any suitable food. He had eaten the sweet plants of the desert and upon entering Jethro's house he saw a prepared and pleasant table of food. Even though he was terribly hungry, he would not partake of the food because he thought that this deed only for God's sake (watering the sheep) might possibly be lessened in the sight of Allah. However, when Jethro insured Moses that he also intended to please God and had sincere intentions in entertaining his guest, then Moses sat down to eat. Jethro's sincerity was the reason why Moses[16] became Jethro's shepherd for the next eight years. And Moses sincerity was the reason why the Prophet Jethro (Pbuh) became Moses's father-in-law.

A Surprising Example of Sincerity

For many years I had been a friend of one of the sincere men of the cloth in love with the Prophet Muhammad (Pbuh) and his Household. His morality and behavior had taught me some good lessons. He told me that when he had left Tehran for Qum so as to become educated in theology, Ayatullah Al'Uzma Hajj Sheik Abdulkarim Haeri" . Abdulkarim was the head of the Qum Seminary. After some time, I was introduced to the Ayatullah as having an especial zeal for and way of reciting the tragedies of the Household of the Prophet Mohammed (Pbuh). I was requested to recite those tragedies for him at specified times. Gradually, I became renown for this type of recital and I was honored to be in the line of the professional reciters of the elegies for Imam Husayn (Pbuh).

One Thursday night I was taken to the home of one of the great clergy-men who lived in the poorer parts of town and was asked to make a speech where I spoke for a few minutes about death referring to some lines from the book Nahj ul-Balaghah (The Peak of Eloquence).

The house owner sobbed too much and even continued doing so until the end of the meeting. I was invited to go again next Thursday night and was instructed to speak about a lighter and more down to earth subject. Whenever the distinguished house owner remembered the sermon subject from the week before, he sobbed his heart out.

Then I was told a surprising story about that man's sincerity. He was

---

[16] Ola 'Azam or the decision-maker

single, but our insistence upon his marrying was to no avail. After a while he accepted to get married, so a young, unmarried woman was suggested to him to be his suitable match. According to the principles of Islamic law he saw her one time, but he rejected the marriage. Later on I heard that the man had married a dark-complexioned, ugly widow having three offspring. I was really surprised to hear the news, so I asked him why he had done so. He replied that he had seen the first lady who was a virgin and accepted to marry her, but as much as he tried to do so out of sincere intentions and for the sake of Allah he found it to be impossible. So he decided to forsake the marriage. Then he said he saw the second woman whose husband had died and therefore had no one to bring in the daily bread. She was left with three orphans so no one was ready to marry her. He noted that he had found the field of sincerity of intentions and married for the sake of Allah. He also mentioned that the real benefits of this good deal would be bestowed upon him on the Day of Judgment. The Commander of the Faithful Ali (Pbuh) stated: Blessed is the one whose actions, knowledge, kindness, revenge, taking and not taking things, speaking and not speaking all stem from his sincerity for Allah. [Mizan al-Hikmat, v.3, pp.56-58]

He also said: Sincerity is the most honorable ending. [Ibid] Hazrat Ali (Pbuh) said: Freedom is found in sincerity. [Ibid]

And he said: Sincerity is the support for the worship of Allah. [Ibid]

The Prophet (Pbuh) said: Blessed are the sincere ones. They are the lights on the path of guidance and are free from any wickedness. [Mizan alHikmat, v.3, pp.59-62]

Imam Hassan Askari (Pbuh) said the following about the very impressive value of the sincere ones: If I reduced the whole world into a bite of food and fed it to the one who worships God out of sincerity, then I would still think I had not done right by him. [Ibid]

The Prophet (Pbuh) stated: Do all your actions out of sincerity for God. God will not accept those actions except the ones done out of sincerity for Him. [Ibid]

Imam Ali (Pbuh) said: The one whose goal is other than God has been ruined. [Ibid]

The Prophet (Pbuh) stated: Sincerity means to avoid all divinely forbidden things and actions. [Mizan al-Hikmat, v.3, p.63]

The flower of sincerity in each action would blossom from the garden of the spirit and its scent would fill all spheres of life, if passion, lust, the instincts, keeping up with the Joneses, attachment to material affairs over and above the lawful limits and forgetfulness in one's affairs did not rule over us. O' how pleasant is the life of a man and his wife who have based their marriage on sincerity and during the course of life continue to be sincere even in the face of limitations. Say:

Truly, my prayer and my service of sacrifice, my life and my death, are (all) for God, the Cherisher of the Worlds: [Holy Qur'an: An'am 6:162] Hypocrisy and showing off in the performance of the obligatory acts would void them and hypocrisy and showing off in the lawful acts would reduce their value.

Piety and Justice

A woman and her husband must observe the divine matters and Islamic decrees when interacting with each other. Enacting these truths in life is impossible unless one puts piety and justice to work in his life. Piety means avoiding evil deeds, bad-temperedness and unacceptable behavior. Justice means to avoid going to extremes in one's daily affairs. Oppression of a woman by a man and vice versa to whatever degree it may be is shameful, even though some may not think it is important. A woman does not have great physical strength and at times is not in good spirits. In his encounters with his wife a man must consider the various aspects of her creation, just as God has taken into consideration a woman's abilities and powers and exempted her from carrying out some duties. Woman's weaknesses must be compensated for by the graceful encounters of the man with her. The Prophet (Pbuh) said: Whoever gets married for the sake of God and observe the relations of the womb, then God will crown him with the angels' crown.

The Manifestations of Virtue in the Family

She is not in a position for man to fight with her and turn the house into a field for combat and struggle. Consider the following two excellent traditions in this regard: The Commander of the Faithful Ali (Pbuh) has mentioned various detailed and important issues including the nature of woman's creation in his letter to Imam Hassan Mujtaba (Pbuh): Truly, a woman is like a bunch of scented flowers, not a source of physical power. [Vasa'il al-Shiia, v.20, p.168]

Imam Sadiq (Pbuh) said: Most residents of Heaven are from amongst the oppressed. God was aware of their weakness, so that is why He was merciful to them. Then it is incumbent upon men to obey Allah and treat women with kindness, patience, love and affection. In encounters with them, men must consider their physical and spiritual states to be a similar to bunch of scented flowers. Men should avoid going to extremes in oppressing women in any way since God who is the Creator of women has ordered men to fear Him in their dealings with women. And man must entertain God's maid in his house with all possible material and spiritual benefits. This delicate interpretation about women which shows God's especial mercy and consideration for woman has come in a very important tradition regarding the marriage of Adam and Eve in Vasa'il al-Shiia. [v.20, p.13, Al-Bayt Publications].

However, a woman must remember that a man has to suffer many hardships to run the affairs of the house. He has to worry about providing for proper housing, clothing and food for the comfort of his wife and children; things which cannot be provided for except by suffering many hardships, working, traveling and encountering various people. Thus, when the man comes home the woman should kindly receive him, take care of him with pleasant conduct and give in to his natural desires. She should welcome her life partner and fill the atmosphere of the house with the good scent of her proper behavior and smile at him thanking him for his hard work. She should attract his love. Then justice, piety, good conduct, a proper attitude, smiling, showing satisfaction, maintaining the peace, and proper entertaining are all considered to be good acts. These must be mutually embarked upon by both sexes so that their joint life is filled with these blessings. The proper treatment of a husband by his wife and that of a husband for his household constitutes a very important section of Shiite traditions being amazingly large in number.

The contents of these divine traditions are also amazing. The oppression of anyone of any other, even in the slightest amount, is not justified and the oppressor must know a terrible punishment awaits him. A man does not own his wife so that he can implement any plan he desires. And a woman in respect to her husband is not free to do as she wishes. Allah, the Prophet of Islam (Pbuh) and the Infallible Imams have designated duties for every woman and her husband. The couple may only interact with each other within that framework of duties. It is oppressive to act outside the divine limits and human, moral responsibilities and such actions have reactions in this world and the Hereafter.

A very important tradition on the authority of the Prophet (Pbuh) concerns a wife oppressing her husband and vice-versa which are satanic acts not associated with nobility. It is really important to pay close attention to it. "Neither the prayers nor any of the good deeds of a woman who bothers her husband will be accepted by God, unless she changes her ways, becomes an assistant to him and pleases him. That annoying woman should know that in case she continues to bother him, she shall be the first person to enter Hell even though she spends her entire life fasting, saying night prayers and frees slaves in the way of God. The Prophet (Pbuh) said: Such punishment exists for a man if he bothers his wife or oppresses her [Vasa'il, v.20, p.160, Al-i-Bayt Press]. Such men or women should know that God has announced his hatred of oppressors in the Holy Qur'an and has expelled them from his circle of love. But God loveth not those who do wrong.[Al-i-Imran 3:57]

Men and women should note that oppression is not just physical, but mean looks, paying no attention and not giving in to one's spouse, bad behavior, being vulgar, swearing and belittling are all cases of oppression, too. The woman who oppresses her husband and the man who oppresses his wife are not true Muslims. They have left the circle of guidance and are wading in the marsh of deviation.

"Nay, but the transgressors are in manifest error."[Holy Qur'an: Luqman 31:11]

The Prophet (Pbuh) stated: There are seven mountain passes between Heaven and a servant of Allah: The easiest one is death. Annas asked the Prophet (Pbuh) which was the most difficult for the servant. He replied: Standing in front of Allah (on the Day of Judgment) while the oppressed ones are clinging to the oppressor's collar. [Mizan al-Hikmat, v.5, p.596]

The Commander of the Faithful Ali (Pbuh) said: The evil provisions for the Hereafter consist of oppressing God's servants. Oppression unsteadies one's steps, deprives one of blessings and wipes out whole nations. [Mizan al-Hikmat, v.5, pp.595-6]

I swear to Allah that if seven countries were given to me so that I would commit a sin by taking the husk of a barley seed from an ant's mouth, I would not do so. The Prophet (Pbuh) has prohibited men from eating whatever is being transported by the mouth and feet of an ant. [Ibid]

The Prophet (Pbuh) said: Avoid oppression: Verily it is the darkness on the Day of Judgment. [Mizan al-Hikmat, v.5, p.599-600]

A man said to the Prophet (Pbuh) that he would like to among the guided ones on the Day of Judgment. Imam Sadiq (Pbuh) said: Any type of oppression is infidelity and he who beats his innocent servant is an unbeliever. [Ibid]

A Virtuous Countenance

Believing men and women have especial characteristics which are manifested in their lives, cause enjoyment in life and the appearance of a new, pure generation. These characteristics cause them to be prosperous in the Hereafter.

The believers, men and women, are the protectors, one of another: they enjoin what is just, and forbid what is evil: they observe regular prayers, practise regular charity, and obey God and His Apostle.

"On them will God pour His mercy: for God is Exalted in power, Wise."[Holy Qur'an: Tauba 9:71]

From many verses about believers, I think this one alone is enough to learn about their physical and spiritual attributes. Once such men and women establish a joint life, their mutual life will be filled with light, sincerity, goodness, blessings, truth and honesty. In this type of life, the man is an ideal man and the woman is an ideal woman, too. Also their life is a good life, and they are prosperous in this world and the Hereafter. The late Majlesi said: There were people whose wife and children would tell them to avoid earning illegal property when they left the house to go to work. We can tolerate hunger and difficulty but cannot tolerate the punishment of the Resurrection Day.

Truly, what virtue is greater than patience and tolerating hardships so as to protect one's self against the punishment on the Last Day. I, myself, saw a great man who sometimes would prohibit his family from buying the things they wanted in a convincing tone. He would promise to fulfill their needs at a later date when business was good. His wife and children would submit to his request and did not bother him. Family life abounded with peace and quiet, divinity and enlightenment. Khadijah the Great (the Prophet's wife) was a woman who patiently bore the hardships during her noble husband's times of difficulty. She shared in his sufferings and sorrows, and lived with the Prophet (Pbuh) in such a way that after her death he would ask God to be merciful to her whenever he remembered her and tears would flow from his eyes. At the beginning of their marriage, she devoted her great and rare wealth of those days to the Prophet's movement. The Prophet (Pbuh) gradually spent that wealth to relieve the problem of the needy and to aid God's movement: finally nothing remained of the wealth. Near the end of her life she lived with her husband in a humble house without too many furnishings. She lived in hardship and the only thing she said to her husband in those difficult days was during the last moments of her life. With tears in her eyes she asked him if God was satisfied with her. The angel entrusted with revelations descended from Heaven and asked the Prophet (Pbuh) to give his best regards to Khadijah and announce God's satisfaction with her. Khadijah became really happy and said to the Prophet (Pbuh) that life and death were now very sweet for her. Fatimah Zahra was only four years old at the time. When she felt the absence of her mother at home, she asked her kind father where her mother was, and the Prophet (Pbuh) answered that she was with the angels. Verily, a believing woman whose faith is manifested in her actions and behavior is an angel-like creature and a source of satisfaction for God and a spring of virtues and perfection.

An Instructive Story

My maternal grandmother and grandfather lived with each other for almost seventy years in peace and quiet, honesty and with faith and morality. Till the end of their lives, they never forgot the following: to lovingly perform the obligatory and recommended Islamic duties; to perform the night prayers; to recite the Qur'an; to make pilgrimages to the Saints; to hold religious meetings; to entertain guests; to solve others' problems; to visit relatives and to attend the congregational prayers.

My paternal grandfather and grandmother lived with each other in the same way (maybe even more devotedly) for more than fifty years. As is inevitable for everyone, my grandmother passed away near the midday call to prayers early in Muharram, the month of mourning for the Master of the Oppressed Imam Husayn while my grandfather was in perfect health. The children and the relatives were about to write announcements for her mourning ceremonies after burying her. But my grandfather told them not to do so since he was going to pass away the next night after the Isha (night) prayer. He asked them to wait until then and hold just one mourning ceremony. Everybody got worried but he pacified them.

No one could believe him, but the next night after finishing his prayer he spoke to God saying: O' God, you have promised to attend to the call of the needy and now that I am traveling to the Hereafter, please help me since I am in need. Then he recited some holy words and passed away next to his prayer mat. They buried both of my grandparents in the same grave. I saw him in a dream one night and asked him where they were. He said that he and his wife stayed where they were buried for three days, and then they were taken to the Master of the Martyrs Husayn (Pbuh). Then he said they now have a pleasant life in the divine atmosphere of Purgatory.

An Amazing Event

I became really fond of religious life, the mosques and religious ceremonies during my childhood and adolescence after witnessing my father's religious states of mind and his encounters with men of letters, mosques and religious ceremonies. During the era of the ungodly rule (the Shah's regime), a percentage of the people, especially the youth, were corrupt. Going to religious centers and my interaction with clergymen was very beneficial for me and the development of my spirit. Based on the background that I received from the family, the mosque and the religious clergy, I was attracted towards the religious centers in Qum at the age of sixteen in the year 1963 AD. There, I naturally had more encounters with religious knowledge and the men of the cloth. I had the opportunity to visit with many outstanding successful men during my studies of Islamic sciences.

I do not remember whom I heard this amazing story from, but the story is very interesting and educational showing the mental and spiritual states of a woman when her existence is combined with faith, good deeds and morality. That noble man told me: The Gohar Shad. Mosque next to the Holy Shrine of Imam Reza (Pbuh) is one of the most widely frequented mosques on the earth where thousands of prayers and pilgrimages are performed each day. And tens of classes for teaching Islamic sciences and training religious clergy are held there. The founder of this mosque was an educated, wise, chaste and noble woman. Before building the mosque, she ordered the architect and those in charge to place water and hay along the path of the animals who were to carry the building materials to the mosque. This was so that none of the animals would have to carry any load while hungry or thirsty, since it is not accepted by God and one's conscience. And their owners did not have the right to beat the animals.

The work schedule had to be clearly defined, the workers had to be treated with compassion and kindness and their wages had to be paid according to their efforts. When they needed to be admonished, it had to be done so in a gentle tone and no one's feelings were to be hurt. The surrounding houses had to be purchased according to their current market prices, since a place of worship was to be built and a center for pilgrimage as well as a school for the discussion of divine sciences. The lady admonished everyone not to oppress any man or animal in the least amount, since that would lessen the value of the work done.

The Commander of the Faithful Ali (Pbuh) said in Nahj ul-Balaghah: Truly, you are all responsible for pieces of land and the animals.

Lady Gohar Shad used to visit the mosque to check the progress of the work and issue the necessary orders. Gohar Shad was the wife of Shahrukh Mirza and the daughter-in-law of Taymor Gurkany. By chance, during one of these visits one of the workers saw her face and fell in love with her, but he did not dare express his feelings since the condition seemed dangerous. This affection was a ridiculous affair, but that naive worker did not understand these things and fell ill. From the daily mosque work report Lady Gohar Shad became informed of his illness: he lived with his mother in a half-ruined house. She went to visit him. In a weak state, the poor man was pale and waning out of his love for her. After she asked about his health and insisted on finding out the reason for his illness, his mother, who was even more naive then the son, divulged the secret.

Lady Gohar Shad complained to the mother about the young worker without getting angry or using her high social status. Then she told his mother that she was ready to marry him after having separated from her husband, but he must first give her nuptial gift being forty days and nights of worshipping God and prayer in the prayer niche of the semibuilt mosque. She was aware of the result of such an effort, but the young fellow accepted her proposal and out of his love and excitement he prayed there for a few days. However, his state of mind changed with God's favor and Imam Reza's attention. After the forty days had passed, Gohar Shad sent a messenger to him to inquire about his health. He told the messenger that if he only knew the pleasure of abstaining from pleasure, he would never call carnal desires pleasure. I heard a passer-by say that wine will get pure when it stays in glasses for forty days. (A poem) By profitting from belief in God, paying attention to the Hereafter, having good attitudes and proper behavior, we can make our home a place for the manifestation of humane, divine and spiritual virtues. This is not too difficult, and if God helps one he can easily walk on this path, although it may be most difficult for others.

Nineteen

Part 16: The Material Issues of the House and the Family

"O ye people! Eat of what is on earth, lawful and good; and do not follow the footsteps of the Evil One, for he is to you an avowed enemy." [Holy Qur'an: Baqara 2:168]

The Virtues and Vices of Wealth

A man's need for property and wealth to manage his life's affairs, and especially with the burdensome responsibility of managing a family, is a completely natural need. Wealth and property, business and commerce are not in any way connected with virtue or vice when they are not related to man. For example, iron is a type of property and may be molded into many shapes. Many tools are made from it, but until man gains control over it, it is simply a material having no benefits and no evilness. Iron is beneficial when managed by a polite, dignified and noble believer. When iron falls into the hands of a rude, forgetful, lustful rogue, it becomes an evil material.

When Ibn Muljam had a sword, he could kill the Imam of the Lovers - Imam Ali (Pbuh) in the mosque. Thus, he became the worst of all people and this can be traced back to his bad spirit: And this damage is irreplaceable. When Imam Ali (Pbuh) had a sword he established and spread guidance: the reward of one time of stabbing as the Prophet Muhammad (Pbuh) says is superior to the all of the worship of the genie and Adam. One stroke of the sword on the day of the Battle of Khandag is superior to all the worship of the Qur'an and the Prophet's Household. For those adorned with divine etiquette and the Lovers of God, money and commercial goods act as a take-off platform towards Heaven and a means for acquiring His Mercy and Blessings and attaining an eternal and great reward. Truly, wealth is the commerce for heavenly trade for believers who are noble, kind, generous, compassionate and have divine ethics. For such people, wealth serves as a vehicle driving them towards God's eternal blessings. And it is a means to obtain the good of this world and the Hereafter.That is why God has called the property of one who has died "his good leftovers" in the blessed chapter of the Qur'an entitled Baqara. God considers the wealth and property of a believer to be a manifestation of the belief of that believer, his nobility, generosity, mercy and passion. One-third must be spent in a good way according to his will and the remaining two-thirds are to be distributed amongst his inheritors according to the Qur'anic verses. Imam Sadiq (Pbuh) has said the following in interpretation of a verse in the Qur'anic chapter Baqara.

*"Our Lord! Give us good in this world and good in the Hereafter...
"(verse 201)*

The good in the Hereafter is God's Pleasure and Heaven, and the good in this life is a good temper and bountiful daily bread. [Bihar al Anwar, v.71, p.383]

Thus, we can conclude that the believers wealth and property are similar to a factory in which God's Pleasure and a musk-scented Heaven are produced. Believers earn their income through legitimate business transactions, abiding by the law and avoiding unlawful transactions. In short, they earn money through continuous lawful transactions and by obeying God. They spend their income for the expenses of their household, paying the alms-tax and the one-fifth levy. They spend the rest to help the deprived, the oppressed, the weak and to aid relatives and friends. Spending legitimately earned income in these ways is natural and lawful and is in fact considered to be worship and obedience: Or as the Holy Qur'an has said It is the good of this world and the Hereafter.

It is for this reason that wealth and property has been interpreted to be good and blessed in God's Book. Earning and spending it is considered to be worship for the believers and a cause of great reward and infinite divine gifts. It is interesting to hear the viewpoint of the Commander of the Faithful (Imam Ali) about wealth in the hands of irreligious, lustful people: Property is the material of lust, is subject to catastrophes, strengthens aspirations and entertains the inheritors. Wealth will raise the status of the owner in this world and lower it in the Hereafter. [Mizan al-Hikmat, v.9, pp.277-78]

The Prophet (Pbuh) said: Gold and silver destroyed those before you and will destroy you, too. [Ibid]

He also said: For each nation there is a calf and for this nation the calf is silver and gold. [Ibid] (the calf refers to the golden calf idol made by the Israelites). Truly, wealth enslaves those of weak faith with illegitimate lusts and excitement of their aspirations. They become base in this world and in the Hereafter, and as the Prophet of Islam (Pbuh) has commented: people began to worship the calf in the form of the worship of wealth.

The Forbidden and the Unforbidden

Undoubtedly, whatever a person earns from working and from his business affairs is lawful. Concerning lawful earnings, God has issued many orders and the Prophet's Household has completely described the religiously legal ways to earn money. Any money gained in illegal ways such as bribery, usurpation, theft, deceit, looting and usury is illegal. Whoever tries to make lawful money is worshipping God and God will reward him. Whoever tries to illegally make money is sinning and God will punish and curse him. If one makes money illegally and does not listen to anybody's advice saying God has desired so, then he has insulted God, speaks satanically and has lied.

There are many Qur'anic verses stating God has provided lawful daily bread for everyone. The Qur'an invites everyone to make a lawful daily living and has given no illegal earnings to anyone, since thinking in the wrong way causes one to make illegal money. Saying that God allows forbidden actions is an insult and a great sin which will cause one to be punished on the Day of Judgment.

Man's intellect dictates that it is illogical to say God gives illegal provisions to man, but rather He has placed emphasis on benefiting from lawful and completely legally earned money. It is paradoxical for God to give illegal earnings to man and there are no paradoxes concerning God. Stupid people foolishly and ignorantly insult God. Imam Baqir (Pbuh) has stated: God has ordered all men to make a lawful living. This money will cause man to be healthy. It is not God's fault that some make an illegal living: The forbidden way to earn a living is not the Right Way. Satan is the designer of the forbidden ways to make money. If one illegally makes money, his lawful daily bread will be lessened to the same extent. If we consider lawful and legal means of earning money, God respects us a lot. [Bihar al-Anwar, v.5, p.147]

Don't Deprive Yourself of the Lawful Things

Imam Ali (Pbuh) entered the mosque and told a man to keep an eye on his camel. The man stole the camel's bit in Imam Ali's (Pbuh) absence. When Imam Ali (Pbuh) came out of the mosque to pay the man two Durham's (coins), he saw his camel without the bit. He gave the money to his servant and asked him to go and buy a bit. The servant went and bought the same bit from the thief without knowing who he was and took it to the Imam (Pbuh). When he saw the bit the Imam said that a servant deprives himself of lawful daily bread due to his impatience, but he does not get more than is determined for him by God. [Mizan alHikmat, v.4, p.123]

Provide Your Family's Needs Through Lawful Means

There is a sequence of outward and inward effects for using lawful or unlawfully obtained property, and no one can avoid them. Lawful goods result in the pleasure of God, spirituality, energy to worship, pacification of the heart and the curing of illnesses. However, the opposite holds true for the unlawful goods. The necessity of providing for the family by the man of the house is one of the most important issues in Islamic jurisprudence and is extensively discussed in the Holy Qur'an and traditions of the Prophet's Household. As much as possible, a man is religiously bound to provide housing, food, clothing and transportation for his wife and children.

In addition to this, the man is required to obtain his family's expenses through lawful means. The man of the house should whole-heartedly thank God for these two requirements. By attending to the needs of the family, moral realities will blossom. By working to obtain lawful income which is similar to a Holy War (Jihad) in God's way, man can get a lot of divine rewards. The heavenly and positive effects of using lawfully obtained goods will appear in the family, and this will substantially aid mental and spiritual peace and security for the family.

The Prophet of Islam and Lawfully Obtained Food

Consider the following tradition. A man came to the Prophet (Pbuh) with a bowl of milk and asked him to break his fast with the milk. The Prophet (Pbuh) asked him who had sent the milk. The man said it was a gift from a woman and the Prophet (Pbuh) told him to return with the milk and ask her where she had got it from. So the man went to the woman's house to ask her. The woman said she had obtained it from her own sheep. The man returned to the Prophet (Pbuh) to tell him. He was told to return and ask her where she had got the sheep from. He returned to ask her and she replied she had bought the sheep by working hard. The man returned to the Prophet (Pbuh) and explained. Then the Prophet (Pbuh) said he would break his fast with the milk. The following day the owner of the milk came to him and asked the reason for returning the milk several times. He said God the Almighty had ordered the Prophets to partake of only lawfully obtained food. This must be a lesson for all Muslim people to pay enough attention to the issue of what is lawful and unlawful, so that they do not pick up a burden which is either too difficult or impossible to bear. The Prophet (Pbuh) said: Seeking the lawful is obligatory for each Muslim man and woman [Bihar alAnwar, v.103, p.719; Mizan-al-Hikmat, v.4, p.119]

Seeking the lawful is obligatory for each Muslim. [Ibid]

Seeking the lawful is a form of Jihad (Holy War). [Ibid]

The gates of Heaven are open to anyone who obtains lawful food through hard work, and he can enter Heaven from any gate he wishes.[Ibid]

There are ten parts to worship. One is seeking the lawful.[Ibid]

Imam Reza (Pbuh) said: The reward of one who seeks his daily bread from God's Grace to provide for his family's needs is greater than that of the one who fights in God's way. [Bihar al-Anwar, v.78, p.339]

Imam Baqir (Pbuh) said: Whoever seeks worldly goods to protect his family, and to be kind to his neighbors will meet God in Heaven with his face shining like a full moon. [Vasa'il al-Shiaa,v.12, p.11]

The sixth Imam (Pbuh) said: There is no good in one who is not interested in saving money to protect his honor and pay back his debts. [Bihar al-

Anwar, v.103, p.7]

The Prophet (Pbuh) said: The one who falls asleep at night being tired from hard work because of seeking the lawful, is forgiven his sins by God. [Bihar al-Anwar, v.103, p.2]

God likes to see His servant working hard to seek the lawful. [Mizan al-Hikmat, v.4, p.119]

In the traditions it is stated the increase or decrease in one's daily bread is simply a test for God's servants to obtain a holy rank from God. The woman who is patient in the face of shortage of her daily bread, does not commit any sins to obtain more, and is grateful for the increase of her daily bread has successfully passed the test. [Nahj-ul-Balaghah, Sermon 91].

A believer does not become base in the face of shortage of his daily bread, and does not get drunk when his daily bread increases. He is content with the low amount of his daily bread; and when his daily bread increases, he eats, feeds others and rushes to pay the necessary dues.

How to Increase One's Daily Bread

There are some ways in the Holy Qur'an and the Prophetic traditions to increase one's daily bread, which will also improve people's morality and affection in the family and the society. The Commander of the Faithful (Pbuh) said: Good temper is the treasure of daily bread. [Bihar al-Anwar, v.77, p.389]

To be too strict spoils your temper, and to go easy on others increases your daily bread. [Mizan Al-Hikmah, v.4, p.117]

Co-operation and helping your Muslim brothers increases your daily bread. [Bihar al-Anwar, v.74, p.395]

Being trustworthy increases one's daily bread. [Bihar al-Anwar, v.75, p.172]

Imam Sadiq (Pbuh) said: One who treats his wife and children kindly will get an increase in his daily bread. [Bihar al-Anwar, v.69, p.407]

Good deeds increase one's daily bread. [Bihar al-Anwar, v.74, p.81] Good temper increase one's daily bread. [Bihar al-Anwar, v.71, p.396]

Imam Ali (Pbuh) said: Attract your daily bread to yourself through charity to others. [Bihar al-Anwar, v.78, p.60]

Imam Baqir (Pbuh) said: Pray for your brothers and this act will bring in your daily bread. [Bihar al-Anwar, v.76, p.60]

The Fifth Imam (Pbuh) said: Giving alms will increase your daily bread. [Bihar al-Anwar, v.66, p.15]

The Commander of the Faithful (Pbuh) said: The daily bread of one with good intentions will be increased. [Bihar al-Anwar, v.103, p.21]

Unlawful Property

The Prophet (Pbuh) said: God said, If one does not care how and where he gets his money from, I do not care by which gate I will let him enter into Hell in the Hereafter. [Bihar al-Anwar, v.103, p.11]

God will make the one who earns unlawful money poor. Whatever one earns unlawfully becomes provisions for the Hell Fire. Wealth from which religious dues are not paid is considered to be property containing unlawful property. Its use is not allowable and giving it to the family or others is another wrong act. The Commander of the Faithful (Pbuh) said: The worst property is that from which God's dues have not been paid. [Mizan al-Hikmat, v.9, p.308]

Imam Baqir (Pbuh) said: There are people who shall leave their graves with their hands tied to their necks, lacking any power to get anything even as much as an ant can. They are seriously blamed by the angels saying: These are people upon whom God bestowed wealth but they did not pay God's dues. [Bihar al-Anwar, v.7, p.197]

Imam Hassan Mujtaba (Pbuh) said: One of the signs of generosity is to legally earn your property. [Bihar al-Anwar, v.103, p.6]

O' dear brothers who are responsible for the financial expenses of your family and their spiritual training, and also you who shall marry later: your wife and children only deserve their rightful dues. However, they are not responsible for your job or business, and will not accept the responsibility for unlawful property which you brought home and they knew nothing about. The punishment in Hell for unlawful property is for the one who earns it. There are two punishments: one for earning unlawful property and the other is for giving it to others. Then be content with lawful property given by God, and be careful about how you earn your income. Avoid obtaining unlawful property and pay the lawful dues, so that you can prosper in this world and in the Hereafter.

One Who Repents is Loved by God

During a visit to Mashhad, I met a man one night at the time of the call to prayers. It seemed he had known me for many years. He asked me to accompany him to his residence, so after a few minutes of talking I accepted his invitation even though that was the first time I had met him. Then I found out that he was one of the people who had attended my lectures during the mourning ceremonies in the months of Muharram and Saffar. He knew me but I did not know him. I asked who he was from one who had accompanied him when he left us for a few minutes. I recognized him when the man told me his name. When he was younger, he was a man who was strong and brutish, so much so that the strongest men of Tehran were afraid of him. His activities included taking bribes from the casinos and banks, smuggling and distributing wine. No one in Tehran could confront him. He had earned a lot of wealth unlawfully.

God guided him and his conscience bothered him. His pure nature and his intellect brought him down from his previous position. He then converted all his property into cash and put it all in a suitcase. Immediately he went to Qum to meet the Grand Ayatullah Boroojerdy. The noble Shiite authority kindly accepted him when he was informed about that man's past. The man told the Ayatullah that what was in the suitcase was all absolutely unlawfully earned. He said he could not bear the reckoning on the Day of Judgment and asked the Ayatullah to relieve him of this heavy burden. The Ayatullah told him that if he really wanted to repent he should take off his outer garments and return to Tehran wearing just his pajamas. The man took off his clothes, and the Shiite authority was really impressed.

193

Boroojerdy found his repentance to be a serious one, returned his clothes, paid him five thousand Tumans from his personal property, and gave him the good news of a brilliant future. The repenter returned to Tehran with that lawfully earned money. He quit all his past deeds and started to work with his new capital. He settled down, really changed, and guided his wife and children towards the Right Path. He then founded one of the most fruitful religious meetings in Tehran.

At the end of his life in 1992A.D., he talked to Imam Husayn (Pbuh) while he was crying one Friday night a few minutes before he died. He said: I spent most of my life in your service, and now I hope I can gain your favor. His wife and children said that suddenly he stared at the corner of the room, respectfully greeted Imam Husayn (Pbuh) and passed away with a smile on his face.

Thus everyone can repent. Repentance will purify one's soul, illuminate one's heart, improve one's temper, cleanse one's wealth and all aspects of life of impurity. Why not benefit by repenting and spend the rest of your life moving from darkness into light? Let's repent since God loves those who repent and it is not worth the whole world to stay sinful.

> *"For God loves those who turn to him constantly..." [Holy Qur'an: Baqara 2:222]*

The Prophet (Pbuh) said: There is nothing dearer to God than a believing man or woman who repents. [Mizan al-Hikmat, v.1, pp.540-541]

I swear to God, God is more pleased with one who repents than a man who is pleased when he gets his food. [Ibid]

God is more pleased with the repentance of his servants, than an infertile man who becomes a father, or one who has lost something and finds it, and one whose thirst is quenched by water. [Ibid]

One who repents is just like one who has never committed any sin. [Ibid]

Repenting will purify the soul and wash away the sins. [Ibid] Repentance actually has consequences which the Prophet of Islam (Pbuh) has pointed out. One can be sure of the acceptance of his repentance if these consequences are manifested. If not one must repent again. If the consequences of repentance do not show up, then the repentance is not accepted. The consequences of repentance include gaining the satisfaction of those involved; performing undone prayers; humbleness with people; protecting the soul against lust; and losing weight through fasting. [Bihar al-Anwar, v.6, pp.35-36]

1.The Commander of the Faithful (Pbuh) said: Repentance holds the uppermost place in Heaven, and consists of six parts:

2.Regretting the past

3.Determination to stop sinning in the future 3Returning people's rights to them

4.Performing undone duties

5.Losing all the weight gained during the period of sinning

6.Exposing the body to the trouble of worship, and asking for God's forgiveness [Ibid]

Twenty

Part 17: The Principles of Spirituality in the Family

~⚬⚬⚬~

"Help ye one another in righteousness and piety, but help ye not one another in sin and rancour: Fear God." [Holy Qur'an: Maida 5:3]

Spiritual Blessings

Many blessings have been bestowed upon man by God to live a pure life, and only God knows the value of these blessings. Some of these blessings left for us are the intellect, the Qur'an, Prophethood, Imamat, religious scholars and the literature on practical, moral and religious issues. We will briefly discuss the meaning of each of these blessings for the readers' information.

Intellect

Intellect means the power to understand, to theoretically distinguish between right and wrong and practically understand the difference between good and evil, and profit and loss. This unique blessing is equipped with the outer senses by which it can recognize the appearance of things. It is also equipped with spiritual senses by which it recognizes spiritual affairs such as will, love, hatred, hope and fear. And it uses each accordingly. In theoretical issues the intellect makes practical decisions. The illuminating activities of the intellect continue as long as it is the outstanding force in man; other forces being subject to it. However, should another force within man overpower the intellect, it becomes weak and man will deviate from the right path going to either extreme. This deviation towards either extreme in our life is the result of lust, anger, or greed overpowering the intellect. Letting loose the instincts and following lust, meeting with the sinful ones and disregarding realities are all factors which weaken and disable the heavenly force and angelic light of the intellect. Once the intellect is disabled, it is either too difficult or impossible to distinguish between right and wrong, and recognize spiritual realities. Then man deserves to be at a loss in this world and suffer retribution in the Hereafter, even if he mischievously gains a lot of financial property, or remains secure from apparent losses. [Adopted from an article in Al-Mizan, v.2, pp.447-450]

The directors of Hell say to those there: Didn't a Prophet come to you to inform you about your present situation? The inhabitants of Hell will say: Yes, but we denied him and God's laws. Then they will tell the directors of Hell: If we had listened to the call of God in the world and the invitation of the Prophet (Pbuh) and had thought about what we were doing in all daily affairs, then today we would not be the inhabitants of Hell: It is impossible to reason if there is no other power holding first place in one's being. If lust and satisfaction of one's lust does all the talking in you, the intellect will not be empowered to guide man. It was asked of Hazrat Sadiq: What is the intellect? He answered: It is something with which God is worshipped and heaven attained! [Bihar al-Anwar, v.1, p.131]

It was asked what did Muaviyah have? He said he had cunningness, wickedness and something which resembled the intellect but was not the intellect. What great blessings are bestowed upon the true servant of God and make him a buyer of Heaven? Amir al-Mumineen Ali (Pbuh) said: The will and high ambition of the intellect manifests itself in man through the abandoning of sins and reforming the apparent and hidden mistakes. [Mizan al-Hikmat, v.6, p.419]

The enlightenment of these blessings is so great that Ali (Pbuh) said: Had God, the Almighty not forbade us from doing the unlawful acts, the intellect would forbid us from doing them. [Ibid]

Imam Ali's (Pbuh) opinion is that this spiritual faculty, the intellect, possesses great powers of understanding. In the noble book entitled Ghorar al-Hikam the Commander of the Faithful has been quoted as saying the following about the intellect: The intelligent person is one who can overcome his lust; not trade in the Hereafter for this world; rebel sagainst his carnal desires; obeys the Lord; and is in full command of himself at times of anger. The ethics of the intelligent ones is to have little lust and little ignorance. [Ghorar al-Hikam, Chapter on the intellect]

The Prophet (Pbuh) said: All good is attained via the intellect and one who lacks intelligence lacks religion. [Bihar al-Anwar, v.77, p.158]

In many important traditions we can read that man's prosperity or punishment in the Hereafter depends upon his/her intelligence as it is the intellect which is the measure for responsibility and duties. It is incumbent upon man to use his intellect in order to face reality and recognize the difference between good and evil, and truth and falsehood. It is an unforgivable sin to not use the intellect. As the intellect is the lantern of truth, a divine prophet within and the essential element to distinguish truth from falsehood, and good from evil, it is incumbent upon the head of the household to protect the intellect from the inrush of lust, desires, instincts and corruption. He should use his intelligence and not let his intellect or that of his family become enslaved by carnal desires and excessive lust, since the loss of the intellect's control will pull man down from his rank as a human to the rank of an animal.

Therefore you should not associate with corrupt people, but rather associate with the lofty Islamic principles.

The Prophet (Pbuh) said: The disciples asked Jesus whom they should associate with. Jesus replied: The ones whose encounter shall remind you of God, whose speech shall add to your knowledge and whose actions shall attract you to the Hereafter. [Bihar al-Anwar, v.77, p.147]

The fourth Imam said: Association with good-doers attracts man towards good deeds. [Bihar al-Anwar, v.78, p.141]

The Prophet (Pbuh) said: Association with credible, wise men shall direct you from five states to five other states:

1) from doubt to certainty; 2) from hypocrisy to sincerity ;3) from undue excitement to fear ;4) from haughtiness to humbleness ;5) from wickedness to benevolence [Bihar al-Anwar, v.74, p.189]

The Commander of the Faithful said: The gatherings of the evil-doers are not safe from catastrophes. [Mizan al-Hikmat, v.2, p.63]

The Prophet (Pbuh) said: Avoid associating with the dead. They asked him who are the dead? He replied any rich person whose wealth has caused him to rebel. [Ibid]

Imam Ali (Pbuh) said: Avoid the evil-doers and associate with good people .[Ibid]

Guard yourselves and the family against lust and association with the evil-doers if you want your intellect to rule over you. Two of the widespread evils of today are the corrupt films and videos of the satellite channels. Watching such programs will corrupt the intellect, destroy morality, and wipe out humanity.

Qur'an

The Qur'an is a divine book, being the light of guidance and the cure for the soul of moral evils; a guide towards better life; a remembrance of God; and an interpreter of realities and an organizers of the affairs. It is a source of guidance and a producer of knowledge and wisdom; a cure for hard-heartedness; the straight path; the criteria to distinguish truth from falsehood; the statement of high moral issues and the manifestation of the life of the good and the pure; and God's final say in this world and the Hereafter. Both men and women are equally responsible and dutybound to this unique divine blessing. This duty is to learn the Qur'an and acting accordingly in all facets of life.

Indifference to God's book is a great sin. The Qur'an is God's letter to his servants : The servants are obliged to respond to this letter by being adorned by the right belief through their hearts, enacting out their morals via their souls and turning to good deeds via their bodies. The Prophet (Pbuh) said: Seek refuge in the Qur'an when you are attacked by vices as the darkness of the night attacks you. And repel the attack by enacting out the orders of the Qur'an in your life and do not let your lives be darkened by the rule of wickedness. The Qur'an is a mediation whose mediation is accepted at God's threshold and whose complaint is also accepted. Whoever lets the Qur'an lead him or her shall attain Heaven through its blessing. And whoever is indifferent to God's book is heading towards Hell. The Qur'an is the reason for and a guide towards the best path. [Bihar al-Anwar, v.92, p.17]

The Commander of the Faithful said: The Qur'an is the best remembrance, and courage and spiritual enlightenment are attained with it. [Mizan al-Hikmat, v.8, pp.67-69]

Imam Sadiq said: Whose does not recognize the truth from the Holy Qur'an, does not avoid sedition. [Ibid]

Ali (Pbuh) said: In fact, the book of God the Glorious, and the Almighty contains the best stories in the most fluent speech and the most beneficial admonishment. [Ibid]

In fact, the remedy for the worst ailments being unbelief, hypocrisy, and deviation is in the Qur'an. [Nahj ul-Balaghah, Sermon 176]

The Prophet (Pbuh) said: The Qur'an is wealth and there is no wealth other than it and there is no poverty after it. [Bihar al-Anwar, v.92, p.19] Imam Sadiq said: A believer deserves not to die until he learns the Qur'an and teaches it. [Bihar al-Anwar, v.92, p.189]

The Prophet (Pbuh) said: The best of you is one who learns the Qur'an and teaches it. Thus, considering these very important traditions, one can more clearly see the heavy responsibility of the head of the household. He must learn the Qur'an, and provide the means for his family members to learn it. Then they can all act according to it. Their living atmosphere will be cleansed from impurities and be adorned with good deeds and characters. And the house and the family will be a sample of Heaven. It will be a house in which there is no oppression or animosity; one filled with piety and purity; an atmosphere of security and comfort, truth and honesty, righteousness and trust. A house whose members are followers of the Qur'an will attain mental and intellectual development from the blessings of the Qur'an. An intellect which follows the Holy Qur'an is an angelic intellect; it is the essential ingredient for Heaven and the Hereafter, and its profit is the worship of God and the achievement of the eternal Heaven.

Prophethood

The Prophets are guides for men towards the straight path, invitors to the unity of God, and the expressors of physical and spiritual reality. They invite us to worship God, and they admonish us not to worship the ungodly. They show men the way to live a good life, to be adorned with virtue and to be cleansed from iniquity. The invitation of the Prophets is inviting us to God. Accepting their invitation will result in the revival of spiritual life. Regarding the Prophethood of the honorable Prophet, Ali (Pbuh) has said: He came to guide the servants of God away from the worship of idols to God's worship, and away from obeying Satan to obeying God. [Nahj ul-Balaghah, Sermon 147]

The Prophet (Pbuh) was appointed to recite the verses of God for the development of the people, the cleansing of their souls from impurities, and for teaching the Qur'an and wisdom. He uprose to take the people out of darkness, and to help them enter a region of light. He came into the arena of life to command us to do good deeds. Admonish us against evil acts; to allow us to use lawful and clean goods; to forbid evilness; and to lift off the burden of forced cultures; and to open the satanic neckbands. Those who believe in him, respect and honor him, help him and obey His Qur'an shall prosper.[A Summary of Verses on Prophethood in the Holy Qur'an]

The Prophets came to bring God's final say so that tomorrow on the Day of Judgment the deviated ones could not say that if they had a Prophet, they would not have been deviated. God the Kind has made the acts, the statements and the morality of the Prophets necessary for all the people. And has made the Prophets a model to follow. Among the behaviors of the Prophets, we can mention the use of perfume, having a happy face, cleanliness, liking women, establishing prayer, uprising for the rights of the believers, kindness and generosity. The Prophets have invited the people to piety, purity, trustworthiness, honesty, bravery, loyalty, righteousness, truth, kindness, mercy and good deeds; and have admonished them against committing any evil acts and having a bad temper. In the Hereafter they are the criteria for action. The condition of the people will be measured based upon their condition. If there is sufficient coordination between them and the Prophets, they will be saved, else they deserve punishment.

Leadership

In order to complete His blessing, and perfect His religion, God appointed the Commander of the Faithful and the twelve Imams who followed him to their posts. This was done so that the people would stay on the Straight Path of their Prophet by following the Qur'an and the members of the Prophet's Household, and never face deviation. Even though the noble Imams themselves suffered from the ungodly government and the deviated people, they never stopped expressing what was right, ordering the people to do good deeds, admonishing them against iniquities, and praying for what was divinely guided to help man's spiritual development. They fully delivered God's religion to the people with their actions, conduct, sayings and martyrdom. On the Day of Judgment the Imams are also the criteria like the Prophets are. If the people's lives are in accordance with theirs, then they shall be saved or else they will be condemned to divine punishment.

Religious Scholars

The Prophets and the Imams are Allah's authority for the people: Likewise are the jurisprudents, the experts of divine knowledge and those familiar with the traditions and the Holy Qur'an. It is incumbent upon the people to follow such religious scholars after the Prophets and the Imams. Such obeyance is like following the Imams and the Prophets and a cause for prosperity. The head of the household should allocate some time to make his family familiar with the Qur'an, the Prophethood, the leadership and the following of the jurisprudents. As this theoretical and practical supplication should cause good in this world and the Hereafter. Disregarding the intellect and separation from the Qur'an, ignoring the Prophethood, the leadership and the scholars is harmful. The family must help the father in this regard, should thank him for this beneficial program and become reasonably acquainted with divine facts.

If the head of the household is not strong in these areas, then the family members should encourage him to do so. They should ask him to provide the necessary means for this. If he disagrees, they should politely disobey him and, they themselves should try to learn about the Qur'an. the Prophet, the Immaculate Imams, and the religious scholars so that they may prosper. The head of the household should fill the atmosphere of the house with the recital of the Qur'an, prayers, supplications, and God's remembrance. Thus, he can combine this world and the Hereafter, and will create a blessed ending for all members of the family.

Prayers

It is not obligatory for the head of the household to only say his prayers. He is also responsible to gently direct the members of his family by advising and encouraging them.

Enjoin prayer on the people, and be constant therein. We ask thee not to provide sustenance:

"We provide it for thee. But the (fruit of) the Hereafter is for Righteousness." [Holy Qur'an: Ta-Ha: 20:132]

We read in the Qur'an that one of the attributes of Abraham was that he invited his wife and children to prayer.

"It is We Who will inherit the earth, and all beings thereon: to Us will they all be returned." [Holy Qur'an: Maryam 19:40]

And we also read in the Qur'an that Abraham requested God that he himself and his progeny establish prayer till the Day of Judgment.

"O my Lord! make me one who establishes regular prayer, and also (raise such) among my offspring." [Holy Qur'an: Abraham 14:40]

In many traditions the Prophet (Pbuh) has called prayer the apple of his eye. [Bihar al-Anwar, v.77, p.77]

The Sixth Imam stated: There is nothing other than prayer which can be compared to knowledge. [Bihar al-Anwar, v.69, p.206]

Imam Ali said: I instruct you to say your prayers which is the best act and the pillar of religion. [Bihar al-Anwar, v.72, p.209]

The Glorious Qur'an recognizes the prayer to be what keeps man from evil inwardly and outwardly.

For prayer restrains from shameful and unjust deeds; [Holy Qur'an: Ankabut: 29:45]

Hazrat Baqir said: The first affair of a human which will be judged on the Day of Judgment is prayer. If his prayers are accepted, the rest of his actions will be accepted.

Negligence of prayers, or quitting to perform this great worship will cause us to lose the possibility of the mediation of the Prophet (Pbuh) on our behalf; It will also be a cause of bankruptcy in the Hereafter; losing the possibility of benefiting from God's Mercy. and never being allowed to enter Heaven.[Bihar al-Anwar, v.83, pp.9-19]

They will say:

"We were not of those who prayed." [Holy Qur'an, Muddaththir 74:43]

Do not forget about your prayers and that of your family members, so that on the Day of Judgment you do not have to answer to the complaints against you made by your family members. They may tell God that if we were called to say our prayers, we would have accepted. The fact that our file is void of prayers is at first the fault of our husband and father, then it is our own fault. Since he was indifferent to us, we neglected our prayers. O' God, please take our revenge, damn him and let him suffer double our torture. Children are wonderful imitators. They mimic the states, actions and behavior of adults. If we pray, they pray. If we fast, they fast. If we recite the Qur'an, and are pleasant, kind and polite, then they follow us in all these respects, and after a while get used to doing so.

It has been stated in a very important tradition that Jesus passed by a grave in which the person who buried there was being tortured. The next year he passed by the same grave. He noticed that the person was no longer being tortured, so he asked God the reason for this. Then a revelation came down to Jesus that the man had a good child who had reconstructed a road and had provided shelter for an orphan. For the good deeds of his offspring, We forgave him. [Vasa'il, Al-i-Bayt Press, v.16. p.338]

Raising good children who are religious and do good deeds is good for this world and beneficial for the Hereafter. Try to benefit from this fact.

Twenty-One

Part 18: Responsibilities of the Head of theHousehold

"O ye who believe! Save yourselves and your families from a Fire whose fuel is Men and Stones, over which are (appointed) angels stern (and) severe, who flinch not (from executing) the Commands they receive from God, but do (precisely) what they are commanded." [Holy Qur'an: Tahrim 66: 6]

Protect Yourself and Your Family From the Fire of Hell

A verse in chapter Tahrim places an extremely heavy responsibility on the head of household. If all the people, especially those responsible for their wife and children, paid close attention to this verse, then a large portion of family problems would be solved. There would be no more tension or insecurity in the house and all things would get settled easily.

> *" O ye who believe! Save yourselves and your families from a Fire whose fuel is Men and Stones, over which are (appointed) angels stern (and) severe, who flinch not (from executing) the Commands they receive from God, but do (precisely) what they are commanded." [Holy Qur'an: Tahrim 66: 6]*

It is the responsibility of the head of the household to guide his family members towards unity, faith in the Hereafter, fear of God's punishment, piety, Islamic behavior; and to provide the means for their development, education and training. Hence he shall protect them from the torture of the Hereafter. Take note that the Qur'an says that men are the fuel for the Fire of Hell in the above verse. It is clearly understood from the Holy Qur'an that the roots of the torture in the Hereafter are sins; and the nature of crimes and their punishment is the same. As opposed to crimes in this world which have a different form of punishment, like demanding fines for driving rule violations; in the Herafter crimes are human acts, but their fine is not financial. The nature of property and action is different; however, in the order of the Creator, the nature of crimes and punishment is the same. This means that the penalty for a criminal in the Hereafter is the crime itself which shall blaze out of the criminal like fire.When man commits any crime, be it a criminal action, a financial crime, a moral or spiritual crime, he has accepted the fire, which will appear and burn him in the Hereafter. Many people commit lots of sins for much of their lives and leave no part of their body pure from committing sins. In fact they have stored up much fire within themselves. This fire shall physically appear in the Hereafter when the curtains are drawn aside and the unseen becomes visible, and it shall enslave its owner forever. Please note the following two verses from the Glorious Qur'an.

> *"Those who conceal God's revelations in the Book, and purchase for them a miserable profit, they swallow into themselves naught but Fire; God will not address them on the Day of Resurrection, nor purify them: grievous will be their penalty." [Holy Qur'an: Baqara: 2:174]*
>
> *"Those who unjustly eat up the property of orphans, eat up a Fire into their own bodies: they will soon be enduring a blazing Fire!" [Holy Qur'an: Nisaa: 4:10]*

In both verses, eating what is unlawfully earned is known as eating the fire. Although it looks like a delicious bite today; it will show its inherent nature as fire in the Hereafter. There are the words of the Glorious Existence which has willed and created the beings, the Jinns, the angels, the heavens, and men and women. He is the one who sees sins as being fire while we see a bad act as being a pleasant one. He sees the Fire of Hell blazing brightly while we do not even feel the heat. In the Hereafter, fire shall blaze from the eyes for looking at forbidden scenes; the ears for listening to forbidden sounds; the tongues for swearing, gossiping or vain talk; the stomach for eating what is unlawfully earned; from the lust for fornication, masturbating or gay acts; the hands for oppressing, cheating, deceit, forging signatures, corrupt writing; and feet for going to forbidden parties. The owner of these body parts shall suffer tortures from which he cannot escape.

O' heads of the households, protect your family and yourself from such a fire which is a result of committing sins. Adhere to divine piety in all aspects of life. Do not let this life's few days of temporary pleasure, or wealth which may be lost, cause you to suffer from eternal torture in Hell, whose fuel is man himself. Stone is one of the materials which can burn. You all know coal is a hard substance with high heat production capability, and a long burning time. For millions of years, rocks and lava have been burning at a high pressure such that at times they appear as a volcano. The flowing lava will burn and destroy everything in its path. This fire does not end, and as noted by the Holy Qur'an, it will cover all the earth, and put aflame all the seas.

"When the oceans boil over with a swell." [Holy Qur'an: Takwir: 81:6]

This is a fact which scientists have now discovered. One day in the future, the earth will turn into a ball of fire.

"One day the Earth will be changed to a different Earth." [Holy Qur'an: Abraham 14:48]

Thus considering the internal conditions of the Earth being a sea of molten rocks and lava, and the future of the Earth as a ball of fire, we can better understand the traditions which state that Hell and all its stages exist here on Earth. On that day, men and rocks will be the fuel for the fire. The combustible materials in the Earth are the rocks and the lava which may become eternal if God wills, as man which can become eternal if He wills. Then the family and its head should pay close attention to the following divine words.

"O ye who believe! Save yourselves and your families from a Fire ..." [Holy Qur'an: Tahrim 66: 6]

It is not easy to deal with the fire managers being angry angels. The residents of Hell are weak and there is no escape for them. Base people have a base place in Hell. The Hell that is on this Earth, whose fuel is rocks and men, whose managers are angry and harsh, whose torture is all-encompassing, burdensome, burning and ever-lasting. The residents of Hell neither die nor do they have a desirable life.

"In which they will then neither die nor live." [Holy Qur'an: A'la 87:13]

A Scented Heaven

When the head of the household encourages his family members to do their obligatory religious duties, and abstain from doing physical, financial or moral wrong acts, then he has saved himself and his family from the Fire of Hell. Their road towards heaven will be paved. The Heaven which is near the lote-tree, its width being similar to that of the Earth and all the heavens.

"Near the lote-tree beyond which none may pass:Near it is the Garden of Abode." [Holy Qur'an: Najm: 53:14-15]

It is clear that the above verse points out to a vast universe, so vast that the divine Heaven which is the same width as the Earth and all the heavens is a part of it. The Holy Qur'an instructs all people to become adorned with faith, good deeds and a good temper; and rush towards Heaven:

"Be quick in the race for forgiveness from your Lord, and for a Garden whose width is that (of the whole) of the heavens and of the Earth, prepared for the righteous." [Holy Qur'an: Al-i-Imran: 3:133]

Dear readers, beware that sins are savings which you take with you to Hell, while faith, worship and serving the people are savings which you take with you to Heaven. Protect yourselves and the family members from saving for Hell, and encourage them to put things aside for Heaven. Your responsibility as the head of the household is a heavy one. Take the Prophet (Pbuh) as a model for your behavior with your wife, children and servants. Then you may be secure from the torture of the Hereafter, and may reach the eternal blessing of God, being the lote-tree leaves. The Prophet (Pbuh) was the best husband and father. He did not go to any extremes in kindness, love and affection, actions and behavior and was moderate in all respects. He was friendly and kind with them, and also admonished them regarding their religious duties, God's worship and the fear of the punishment of the Hereafter. He treated women as women, and acted like a child when he was dealing with children. He was a light of guidance and an example of politeness, nobility, morality, belief in the unity of God, and God's worship.

Four Important Duties

Several important duties of the head of the household have been mentioned in what follows. These help protect the family members from the fire.

Invite them to obey God. The head of the household should invite all members of his family to obey God's orders which are issued to improve our life in this world and the Hereafter. He should invite them in such a manner that it is not difficult for them to follow. It should be said kindly, so that the wife and the children become interested in obeying God, and consider this to be of the highest priority. I have tested this at home and it was useful. You should try it too. I am sure you will benefit from it. When your children start to obey God, you should encourage them, give them a prize, and hug them. Thus they will get used to obeying God. Woman too should readily accept their husband's call to obey God, so that the children learn to obey God.

Teach them about their religious duties. The head of the household should teach his family their religious duties, part of which is described in books on Islamic jurisprudence, Islamic ethics and in the practical treatise of Muslim scholars. If he cannot do this himself, he should take them to the mosque and religious ceremonies, or invite religious scholars to his house, so that his family members receive some training about their religious duties. It may be difficult for some people to read, yet understand the practical treaties of Muslim scholars. In this case, the children should be sent to classes so they learn about their religious duties near the time of maturity.

Instruct them to avoid doing what is considered to be bad. It is incumbent upon the head of the household to admonish the members of his family against wrongful acts and sins, and to eliminate any grounds for commiting sins at home.

Encourage them to do good deeds. It is incumbent upon the head of the household to encourage the members of his family to do good deeds such as charity; humbleness,;respecting the elderly; helping to strengthen people's friendship; saying what is right; seeking what is right; and whatever is considered to be a good deed.

The late Islamic scholar Allameh Majlesi has said that following these four guidelines is a sure way to protect one and his family from the Fire of Hell. Working for God's pleasure as such is extremely rewarding. When the Prophet (Pbuh) decided to dispatch the Commander of the Faithful to invite the people of Yemen to God's way, he told him: I swear by God that should God guide even just one person through your efforts, it is better for you than whatever the sun sets and rises on. [Bihar al-Anwar, v.21, p.361]

What a good deal, and how profitable a business it is to gain such a reward for guiding the wife and the children by being a good teacher! This reward is in addition to that gained by going to work to earn your living by lawful means. Such heads of household will receive a double reward; one for providing the material necessities of their family members and one for providing the spiritual necessities.

Twenty-Two

Part 19: The Rights of Wives and Husbands in Islam

⟨~⟩

"Those are limits set by God: those who obey God and His Apostle will be admitted to Gardens with rivers flowing beneath, to abide therein (forever) and that will be the Supreme achievement."
[Holy Qur'an: Nisaa 4:13]

An Outlook on Family Rights

The rights of wives and husbands are completely described in the Glorious Qur'an. When studying them one can recognize these mutual rights as being one of the miracles of the pure culture of Islam. No other school of thought has so thoroughly attended to the rights of wives and their husbands until now, and none can do so from now until the end of time. These rights include obligatory and recommended rights. Disrespecting the obligatory

213

rights without the other person's consent is the cause of divine punishment, and not honoring the recommended rights will lessen the sweetness of life. A major portion of these mutual rights are described in Vasa'il al-Shiaa, volumes 20-22, printed by Al-i-Bayt Press. As much as is required, I shall quote traditions from this volume, and instruct my dear readers to carefully read over those volumes.

Firstly, to bless the discussion I shall mention a few Qur'anic verses related to the matter and then I shall quote the traditions.

> *"I will mislead them, and I will create in them false desires; I will order them to slit the ears of cattle, and to deface the (fair) nature created by God. Whoever, forsaking God, takes Satan for a friend, has of a surety suffered a loss that is manifest." [Holy Qur'an Nisaa 4:119]*
>
> *"And women shall have rights similar to the rights against them, according to what is equitable."[Holy Qur'an: Baqara: 2:228]*
>
> *"And yet they had already covenanted with God not to turn their backs, and a covenant with God must (surely) be answered for." [Holy Qur'an: Ahzab 33:15]*

Isaq, the son of Ammac, said that he had asked Imam Sadiq what right does a woman have whose fulfillment by her husband implies that he is a good doer. The Imam replied that he should feed her properly and provide her with clothing. And when she does something out of ignorance, he should forgive her. Then the Imam said my father had a bothersome wife but he would always forgive her. The sixth Imam quoted the Prophet (Pbuh) as saying: Gabriel recommended on behalf of wives so much so that I thought divorcing her is not permissible unless she commits adultery. He also said good mercy be upon the man who performs all the affairs for himself and his wife well, since God the Almighty has granted to men the control of women, and established the husband as her guardian. The Prophet (Pbuh) said: One who ignores his wife's rights is deprived of God's Mercy. He also said: The best of you is one who is the best for his family and I am a model for you in this regard. He also said: A man's wife is his slave and the person most loved by God the Almighty is the one who treats his slaves kindly.

The rights of the wife:

1-Providing the means for living. The Prophet (Pbuh) said one must provide the foodstuffs and clothing of his wife in the best manner. Imam Sajjad said: Going to the market and buying one Durham of meat which my wife desires is better than freeing a slave. The sixth Imam said: The most fortunate man is the one who manages the affairs of his wife and children.

2-Sexual intercourse. The eight Imam was asked about a man who had a young wife whom he had not slept with for nearly a year due to a disaster that had come upon him. He had no intentions to bother his wife but the disaster caused him to do so. Was he sinning? The Imam answered: Of course. After four months passed, he was sinning. Abuzar asked the Prophet: Is a man's love-making to his wife divinely rewarded even though it brings pleasure? The Prophet (Pbuh) answered: Yes, of course. Is it not forbidden to satisfy your sexual desires unlawfully? Abuzar answered yes. Then the Prophet (Pbuh) said: Certainly its lawful form is divinely rewarded. It is considered desirable in divine teachings for a man to sleep with his wife for love-making once every four nights.

3-Improving the Living Conditions The Prophet (Pbuh) said: When a man goes to shop for his wife, he is similar to one who takes charity to the house of the needy. When he gets home, he should first give what he has bought to his daughters. This is so because one who makes his daughter happy is similar to one who frees a slave from Ismael's generation. And one who makes his son happy by giving him something is similar to one who cries for fear of God given that God shall take such a person into Heaven filled with blessings.

Imam Musa said: Men's wives are their slaves. When God gives blessings to anyone he should use it to improve the living conditions of his slave or

215

else that blessing might be taken away from him. The Prophet (Pbuh) has admonished against a man being full while his wife is hungry. The sixth Imam said: A man should try to do the following things even if it is against his own desires.

(1)Treating the family well

(2)Trying to improve his living conditions without being wasteful

(3) Being concerned about protecting the family's honor.

The fourth Imam said: God is more pleased with the one who brings about more improvement in his family's living conditions. The Prophet (Pbuh) said: Whatever a Muslim man buys for his wife has a reward similar to that of charity.

(4)*Respecting the wife* The Prophet (Pbuh) said: Anyone who gets married should respect his wife. He also said: Anyone who hits his wife more than three times (at once), will be disgraced by God in the Hereafter. The Prophet (Pbuh) said: Can you expect to hug your wife at night, having beaten her in the day time? He also said: In fact a woman is a doll; Anyone who marries one should not commit sin with it. He also said: I wonder about a man who beats his wife, while he himself deserves to be beaten more. Do not beat your wives with a stick since there is retaliation for this act. The Commander of the Faithful said: The women you are responsible for are a trust for you. Don't be strict with them and leave them up in the air. Haola asked the Prophet: What rights does a women have over a man? The Prophet (Pbuh) replied: Gabriel made so many recommendations on behalf of women that I thought a man cannot say the slightest thing to her. Gabriel said: O' Muhammad, be afraid of God in regards to women. They bear the sufferings and hardships of life. Women have rights over you since they have placed their bodies in your control for pleasure, they carry your children within their bodies until the time for delivery and they experience dangerous pains. Be kind to them. Keep them satisfied so they'll get along well with you. Don't say your wives are ugly or you don't like them. Don't be greedy about what you have given as the nuptial gift or take any of it back by force.

(5)*Grooming oneself and keeping clean*

Just as men like to see their wives looking pretty, clean, wearing nice clothes and using good scent, women have the same desires for their husbands: cleanliness, grooming, taking baths, brushing teeth, washing one's hair, combing one's hair, cutting one's nails, using scent, wearing proper clothing and the rest of the allowed grooming. These acts will please the woman and increase her chastity. She will not go after other men and think about getting another husband. Hassan ibn Jahm said: The 8th Imam dyed his hair and I asked him why. He said that a man's grooming himself increases the chastity of his wife. Women abandon chastity because they never saw their husbands grooming themselves. Then the 8th Imam asked if I would like to see my wife in a disheveled state. Hazrat Reza quoted on the authority of his grandfather that the women of the Israelites turned away from chastity for no reason at all, except that their husbands didn't groom themselves. Then the Hazrat said: Women expect the same things of men that men expect of them.

Some men are really unfair and don't groom themselves. They don't go to the barbers often and they smoke cigarettes. Therefore their teeth and mouth are dirty and bad-smelling. They don't wear the appropriate clothing and don't care about their looks. Yet they expect their wives to submit themselves to them. These men are oppressors who deserve to be blamed and punished.

(6)*Speaking Decently and Courteously* Swearing, or using a vulgar language will force the person we are facing to react no matter who they are. When you complain too much your wife will be upset, and this will ruin your mutual life. The Commander of the Faithful has ordered men: Be patient with your wife under all circumstances and treat her with kindness.

(7) *Be content with your share of control over life* Some men give up all their God-given free will and totally submit themselves to the will of their wives. Some women take full control of their husband's will and try to run their lives in any way they wish. This sort of life usually turns into a Satanic life with a lot of sin, waste and unlawful desires. The house and the family deviate from the main and divine principles when life is void of spirituality. Today, a large percentage of families suffer from this devastating catastrophe.

Instead of life being dependent on the man's decision, it depends on the woman's. Instead of the man being the husband of the wife, the wife is her husband's master. God forbid that the man disobeys the woman's wants even if it is unlawful and ungodly. A fight will be started by the woman which will not end until the man surrenders or divorces her. Regarding such men who have lost control over their wives, Imam Ali said: Any man who gives his control over to his wife is damned. He also said: The man who totally submits to his wife shall be thrown into the Fire of Hell by God with his face down. They asked him why and he replied: Because the wife requests see-through clothing and he accepts it.

Regarding this issue, Imam Ali conducted a public sermon when a man complained against his wife: O' people! Never obey your wife. Do not give her any property. Do not grant the control of your life to her. If such people are left free to do as they wish, they will ruin everybody's life and disobey their husband's orders. We have discovered that these people are not pious when in need; quickly submit to lust; think about collecting gold and silver until very old and are selfish and haughty when they are weak. If some of what they want is not provided to them, they ignore all your kindness and favors and will always remember your bad actions.

They will accuse without any hesitation and will never stop their rebellion and are constantly trotting on Satan's path. [Vasa'il, v.20, p.180, Al-i-Bayt Press]

The Rights of the Husband

A major factor in strengthening the ties of mutual life is dependent upon the woman respecting her husband's rights. The wife should only consider God and the Hereafter and not let anyone else interfere in regards to her husband's rights. Others may be mistaken or have bad intentions and it may even be that the cause of such interference in the life of the newly-wed couple is pure jealously. Women should remember that they are easily influenced by others. They should consider this element of their nature, and pay close attention to the possibility of others being wrong. They should remember God and their situation in the Hereafter and respect the man's humane, divine and religious rights.

The man likes the woman to be his woman. She should maintain her sex role as a woman, as this is her nature by creation. She should limit her beauty, appeal, seduction, and coquettishness to her husband. She should neither follow others nor should she accept the interference of distant or close relatives, neighbors or guests. Anyway, she should be the wife of her husband, and live based on his lawful desires. She should run the affairs of the home according to her husband's will, and be a good mother to her children. Some women forget that they are feminine. They become rough, harsh, bitter and man-like. This shall make man's life really bitter, and make him sorry about getting married. They may even get fed up with life. Some of the rights of the husband include: The woman should submit herself to her husband's sexual desires whenever he needs her. The woman should obey her husband in all moral and religious affairs. The woman should seek her husband's permission to leave the house, except for the required pilgrimage to Mecca.

1-Obedience: Imam Baqir said: A woman came to the Prophet (Pbuh) and asked him what rights does the husband have over the wife? He said: She must obey the husband, and not be rebellious. The Prophet (Pbuh) said: A woman who performs her five required daily prayers, fasts for the month of Ramadan, performs the pilgrimage to Mecca obeys her husband, recognizes the rights of Imam Ali, being that he must be obeyed, shall enter Heaven from anyone of the eight gates which she desires to. Pay close attention to this very important tradition from the noble Prophet of Islam: Any good woman who worships God, performs the obligatory religious acts, and obeys her husband will enter Heaven. Any woman who says her prayers, does not leave the house unnecessarily, and obeys her husband shall be forgiven all her past and future sins by God. The Prophet (Pbuh) told a woman named Haola: By the God who entrusted me with Prophethood, a husband has rights over his wife. She should submit to his sexual desires. She should not disobey his orders, and not oppose or quarrel with him. In a very important and strong statement the Prophet (Pbuh) said: A woman has not fulfilled God's rights as long as she has not fulfilled her husband's rights. You should not conclude from the above traditions that the key to a woman's prosperity is solely obeying her husband. But she should also have faith, worship God, do her religious duties, and avoid doing what is forbidden. This means that she may prosper in this world and the Hereafter only if she gathers all these realties within herself.

2-Sexual submission: It is obligatory for the wife to sexually submit herself to her husband at times when there is no religious excuse. It is even recommended that she declares her readiness to him. The Prophet (Pbuh) said: A woman should use the best perfume, wear her prettiest clothes, and groom herself in the best possible form. She should appear in front of her husband every morning and night displaying her beauties. The husband has even more rights than this. If a woman carries out the instructions of the Prophet (Pbuh) exactly, she can keep her husband for herself, and keep him away from looking at or chasing other women, even in a lawful manner. This is exactly the situation which causes conflicts. The wife wants to wear her best clothes, perfume, and make-up for going out to wedding parties or visit her friends and relatives, but appears in front of her husband as she is. Even after she returns from the party, she does not give her husband the slightest chance to see her. This hurts the husband's feelings and weakens their relationship and may prepare the grounds for other problems. Many young and middle-aged men have come to me to complain about their wives' indifference and lack of interest in sexual submission and not making themselves up for them. They have expressed their interest in temporary marriage or divorce and re-marriage and have asked me to solve their problem. My only recommendation to women at this stage is to wholeheartedly follow the instructions of the Immaculate Imams and the Noble Prophet. This way their husband will not become lustful outside the house and they will not have any marital problems. Or else your life will be ruined and you will be responsible for it in the Hereafter. In regards to man's attraction to his wife and her submission to him the Prophet (Pbuh) said: Do not elongate your prayers to avoid submitting to your husband.

3-Going out of the House:

Unfortunately, many women who have quit being a woman, and consider themselves to be men do not obey their husbands in regards to seeking permission to go out of the house. If it was deemed proper for women to freely go out of the house, then God would not have made it conditional upon the husband's permission. Some women left the house without their husband's permission. They caused sedition and corruption. They let out their hair and showed their face. They disturbed the pure atmosphere of the society. They acted sexy and coquettish in the streets. They even sometimes forced the men not to object in an attempt to protect their honor, so that these women could act as they pleased.

They imitated the Western culture, that of the Jews and the Christians.

They made such catastrophes for Islam and the Muslims that can never be compensated for. The Prophet (Pbuh) has ordered a woman not to leave the house without her husband's consent. And if she does so without his permission, all the heavenly angels and each jinn or man who passes by her will damn her until she returns home. Imam Sadiq said: One of the men from the Helpers (Ansar) went on a trip and ordered his wife not to leave the house until he returned home. Her father got ill while her husband was away. She sent a messenger to the Prophet (Pbuh) asking him if she could visit her father. The Prophet (Pbuh) replied that she should obey her husband and stay at home.

Her father got worse and she sent another message but received the same reply. Her father passed away and she sent another messenger to go and pray for her father, but she received the same reply. They buried her father but the woman stayed at home. The Prophet (Pbuh) sent a messenger to her and he said that God forgave you and your father for obeying your husband. The Commander of the Faithful has instructed men as follows: Protect your women from the eyes of strange men, since this will better guard their chastity. The bad influences of bringing untrustworthy men to your house is the same as letting them go out to be seen in public. Make an effort so that they know no one but you.

4-Don't bother your husband, and don't be vulgar and ill-tempered:

The Prophet (Pbuh) has made an amazing speech regarding this issue.

He delivered this lecture for women. O' women, pay charity in God's way, even though it be your ornaments, even a date, since many of you swear and are ungrateful to your husband and will be the fuel for the Fire of Hell. A woman said are we not mothers. Don't we carry the babies in our wombs for many months. Don't we breastfeed them. Aren't these girls the heads of some households, and these sisters sympathetic to their brothers? The Prophet (Pbuh) said yes. You get pregnant. You deliver children. You breastfeed them. You are kind. If women did not bother their husbands and got along with them, then no praying woman would burn in the Fire of Hell.

The sixth Imam said: These people's prayers are not accepted: A maid's prayers who runs away are not accepted until she returns to her owners huose; a woman whose husband is dissatisfied with her from night until the morning; and a leader who leads the people, but the people do not want him. Ali, the son of Jafar asked his brother Imam Musa Kazim: What is the status of a woman's prayers and conditions who angers her husband with her bad temper and vulgarity? He answered she is sinful until her husband is pleased with her. The Prophet (Pbuh) told Haola: I swear by God who appointed me to Prophethood through my honesty and trustworthiness that when a men gets angry with his wife, God too will be angry with her. The Prophet (Pbuh) has asked women not to expect of their husbands more than they can provide for them and not to degrade their status before anyone whether it be a relative or a stranger. The sixth Imam said: A woman who bothers her husband, and makes him sorrowful is damned. A woman who obeys her husband under any circumstances and respects him and does not bother him is prosperous.

5-Working at home:

The Prophet (Pbuh) told Haola: God shall prepare various delicious meals in Heaven for women who prepare delicious meals for their husbands. He will tell them to eat and drink as a reward for their efforts in this world. The Prophet (Pbuh) said: God shall look favorably at any woman who changes the decorations in the house to make the house look better. Whoever is favorably looked at by God will be saved from punishment. Imam Baqir said: Zahra (Pbuh) took care of the work inside the house such as preparing the dough and cooking the bread, and the Commander of the Faithful took care of the work outside the house such as shopping and collecting wood.

6-Respect your husband and treat him well: The seventh Imam said: A woman's Jihad is to take good care of her husband. A woman Jihad is being grateful to her husband; being kind with him; bearing with him when he is poor; seeing him off when he leaves, and welcoming him when he comes home; totally submitting to her husband at allowed times; putting on good clothes and make up for him; properly running the affairs of the house; avoiding wastefulness and not asking him for more than he can buy. Such acts which are defined by the Prophet (Pbuh) and the Imams as a wife's duty towards her husband are her Jihad (Holy War) Imam Baqir said: Nothing can intercede on behalf of a woman in God's presence than her husband's consent. The sixth Imam said: Some people went to see the Prophet (Pbuh) and said we saw some folks who prostrated in front of their leaders. Will you let us do so in front of you? The Prophet (Pbuh) said: No, but if I were to issue such an order, I would order women to prostrate in front of their husbands.

The Prophet (Pbuh) told Haola: God will make any woman who obeys her husband, and is patient with him under all circumstances a companion of the wife of the Prophet Jacob (Pbuh) in the Hereafter. God will grant any woman a reward for bearing the bitter words of her husband. For each word, He will count one day of fasting of a fighter in the way of God as her reward. The Prophet (Pbuh) said: A husband's right over his wife is that she should turn up the light of his house, cook the food; welcome him at the door when he comes home; prepare water and a towel for him to wash his hands and face; and submit herself to him sexually whenever she does not have a religious excuse. The Commander of the Faithful stood by the dead body of his wife Fatimah upon her death and said:

O' God. I am pleased with your Prophet's daughter. O' God, please be her companion, and alleviate her fears.

7-Do not make yourselves up except for your husband : The Prophet (Pbuh) told Haola: Do not let anyone other than your husband see your ornaments and jewelry. Do not put on any perfume in the absence of your husband. Do not show off your attractive scarf and wrists. If you do so, you will ruin our religion and make God angry. The Prophet (Pbuh) admonished women against wearing attractive clothes outside the house. He also forbade wearing jewelry that might make noticeable noise. A very important tradition exists from the Prophet, and must be seriously considered by the Muslims. Any man, whose wife puts on make-up and leaves the house to go out and be seen in public with his consent, is a cuckold, and it is not a sin to call him so. For each step that she takes, a house full of fire will be prepared for him. Limit them in this respect, since these limitations are a cause of happiness and pleasure for you and family.

8-Do not use your husbands property without his consent: The sixth Imam said: A wife is not free to let a slave free, give charity or bet without her husband's consent, however, the payment of the obligatory alms tax,visiting her relatives and doing good deeds do not need his permission. The Prophet (Pbuh) said: A woman should not donate any of her husband's property without his consent. Should she do so, she will be sinful and the reward of her act will belong to the man. I shall once again say that the material presented here regarding the rights of husbands and wives mostly comes from volumes twenty-one through volume twenty-two of the noble book "Vasa'il" printed by Al-i-Bayt Press, and several traditions have been cited from volume 103 of Bihar al-Anwar. Those who wish to study this subject further should refer to these valuable books.

Twenty-Three

Part 20: Pregnancy

"In travail upon travail did his mother bear him, and in years twain was his weaning: (hear the command)" [Holy Qur'an: Luqman: 31:14]

The Period of Pregnancy

The time of pregnancy is a very difficult period with anxiety and various physical and spiritual stresses, although a mother is the center of love and affection, an example of God's Mercy and eager to have a baby and see her child's pretty, innocent face. The husband, the relatives of both and their friends should all take care of her at all times, since any yelling or screaming, vulgarity or bad-temper, or any form of bothering the pregnant women will not only hurt her, but it will also have a bad influence on the baby. If the couple lives in the house of either one of their parents, then their parents are morally bound and religiously obliged to not only avoid provoking the husband against his pregnant wife, but also to be considerate of the pregnant woman. The man's parents should seriously avoid interfering in the couple's peaceful life and the woman's parents should try not to be picky about the husband. Both sides are seriously responsible for the couple and the unborn baby.

If the fetus is harmed even slightly by the quarrels, bad tempers or excessive expectations of either relatives, they must undoubtedly answer to God in His just court. Then they shall be seriously punished for their oppression. The Holy Qur'an holds every one responsible for the slightest to the greatest sins they commit.

> *"Therefore, by the Lord, we will, of a surety, call them to account, for all their deeds." [Holy Qur'an: Hijr: 15:92-93]*
> *"But stop them, for they must be asked: [Holy Qur'an: Saffat: 37:24] For every act of hearing, or of seeing or of (feeling in) the heart will be inquired into (on the day of Reckoning)." [Holy Qur'an: Bani Israil: 17:36]*

I have received many letters from young couples during my religious lectures all over Iran. I have helped resolve many family conflicts, and have noticed that a major portion of these problems are related to the relatives of the couple, usually some unreasonable expectations of the husband's father or mother, or the pickiness of the woman's parents or of the groom's. Imam Sadiq has said the source of many of these immoral encounters is the result of jealousy. In some cases, of course, the newlywed wife is at fault since she is young and inexperienced. In these cases, the elders should forgive her, but they do not, and the fights get worse. Sometimes religious or moral shortcomings worsened the situation to the point of divorce. As you know, any man or woman is seeking freedom and independence by nature. Restriction of this God-given freedom by anyone is a great vice and a sin. Stressing on the needs of a pregnant woman for security and attention does not mean that we should ignore her needs or treat her badly at other times. This is only because of the subject of the discussion in this chapter, and a pregnant woman's special conditions.

In fact, it is necessary for all to respect human rights of freedom and independence at all times and under all conditions. If the two families can provide for a separate housing arrangement for the newly-wed couple without experiencing real difficulty, it would be great. They should treat them kindly and with love and affection. Both parents should associate with the young couple, and avoid gossiping or interfering in their life while doing so. If they cannot provide a separate house for them, then they should let them live in a part of their own house. However, they should try not to bother them, since in the beginning of the couple's life they are filled with love. The bride is God's trust in the family of the groom. She has left her own family with lots of hope and aspirations and has entered a new life. The groom , also, is God's blessing in the family of the bride. They should take care of these blessings just like their own children. Such caring is in line with the Holy Qur'an and traditions and is considered to be God's worship with the reward being God's pleasure and the eternal Heaven.

The parents of both the bride and the groom have either experienced the kindness and nobility of their near relatives, and started a good life or have been seriously hurt by them when they first got married themselves. In either case, they should now help safeguard the ties of marriage of the newly-wed couple by providing for their peace and security and avoiding undue interference. This way the young couple can enjoy their life and benefit from God-given blessings, instead of being hurt or separated due to improper interventions or unreasonable expectations. I remember seeing the following tradition in Usul-i-Kafi: The sixth Imam said the first piece of advice given to Adam by God when he first started his life on Earth was:

"Want for others what you want for yourself, and do not approve of for others what you do not approve for yourself."

Thus, the relatives and friends of both the bride and the groom should follow these words, since then there will be fewer problems, and these problems can easily be resolved, too. Now consider the following verses of the Glorious Qur'an regarding pregnancy:

"In travail upon travail did his mother bear him, and in years twain was his weaning: (hear the command)" [Holy Qur'an: Luqman: 31:14]

"We have enjoined on man kindness to his parents: In pain did his mother bear him, and in pain did she give him birth." [Holy Qur'an: Ahqaf: 46:15]

Do you not think that we should respect the pregnant woman during this strenuous period of weakness, anxiety and suffering? Being considerate of her is at first her husband's moral and religious duty, and next it is the responsibility of all her relatives, so that the physical and mental health of both the mother and the baby are guaranteed.

Duties During Pregnancy

The time of pregnancy is a boring and difficult period during which the various systems in the body undergo strange changes. If it was not for the love of the child, mothers who have once become pregnant would refuse a second pregnancy. In this period some of the internal glands start to increase secretions, and the body uses more and more nutrients. However, the pregnant woman cannot eat food property due to nausea, and a lack of appetite. Some women go on a rigid diet to be slim and not let the fetus grow too big and hurt their good looks. They avoid eating good foods so that the baby does not grow so much that their skin wrinkles, or they have to undergo a hard delivery. They do not realize that now they are two people, and their diet must be such that it provides the necessary nutrients for the growth of the baby, too. To keep at a reasonable weight and provide for the health of the mother and the proper growth of the child, a well-balanced diet must be established. During this period of over secretion of the glands, food is absorbed and burnt rapidly. Much of the food intake is absorbed by the fetus, else the women would get really fat.

Should the pregnant woman not consume sufficient food, reserves in the kidney, bone marrow, and other parts of the body would be depleted. The fetus needs lime and iron to build up its various body parts: The iron is needed for the blood. Without it hemoglobin which is the fundamental elementt of blood cells would not be formed. Then the fetus will extract it from the mother's iron. Thus the mother will slowly develop blood deficiency as will the baby. To be able to provide the iron necessary for her body and the baby, she must daily eat some grains, some liver, meat and some fruits like apples, grapes, dates, etc. Lime is the basic material for the baby's body. It is needed in the amount of 40-50 grams to build up the bones. The mother should eat this much calcium every day, otherwise the baby will extract calcium from the mother's body. Then the mother will slowly get weaker, her bones will deteriorate, her teeth rot and her hair will fall out. We can compensate for this need by feeding the mother dairy products, wheat or barley, pears or apples. Thus we can help the fetus grow. [Mother's Guide, p.6.]

There are many books which explain ways to help safeguard the health of the child and the mother. There are many details like the kind of clothes, their color, the shoes, the mother's associations, and so on which affect the baby. If the mother neglects God and does not pay enough attention to her religious duties and reading the Qur'an, then the baby's mental and spiritual growth will be affected. Pregnancy itself is considered a form of worship with a great reward. The Prophet (Pbuh) said: When a woman becomes pregnant, she is similar to one who fasts, stays up at night to worship God, and fights for God with her wealth and life. [Bihar al-Anwar, v.101, p.106]

Of course, a couple could use birth control with mutual consent. However, this way they will lose out on a profitable deal. They should also not lose control and have too many children, since raising kids requires financial, physical and spiritual strength. Should parents not be able to properly raise their children because they have too many, the kids may turn out to be bad kids and then damn their parents.

Delivery

Although childbirth is a very pleasant experience for the mother, the father and the relatives, it is very painful for the mother. The Imams have said that labor has a great reward and is considered to be worship. The Prophet (Pbuh) said:

When she delivers her baby she will have a reward which is so great that it is incomprehensible. [Bihar al-Anwar, v.101, p.106-107]

Imam Sadiq said:

A woman who dies during delivery will not be accountable for her deeds in this world since she has died with the sorrow of childbirth.

The Prophet (Pbuh) said: Give your wife a few dates as soon as she delivers her child, since God ordered Mary to eat dates at the time of delivery. Give her seven dates from Medina or your own town. God has said: I swear by my Majesty, Grandeur, Nobility and Highness that if a woman eats dates on the day of childbirth, then the child shall be patient whether it is a boy or a girl. [Bihar al-Anwar, v.101, p.116]

In Islam, all aspects of childbirth including the delivery room, the midwife, and the people present are closely considered so as to guarantee the physical and mental health of the mother and the baby.

New-Born Clothing

The Prophet (Pbuh) ordered the people in charge of the affairs of the house to put white clothes on Imam Hassan Mujtaba when he was born. By mistake, they put yellow clothes on him and handed him over to the Noble Prophet. The Prophet (Pbuh) took him, kissed him, put his tongue in the mouth and sucked his lip. Then he said:

Did I not order you to put white clothes on him?

Then he asked for the white clothes and put them on the baby, and put the yellow clothes aside. Then he said the general call to prayer (Adhan) in his right ear and the specific call to prayer (Iqamah) in his left ear. He named him Hassan. He did the same things when Imam Husayn was born

(Vasa'il, v.21, p.409).

The First Food for the Baby

The Noble Kulayny, author of the book Usul al-Kafi has narrated the following tradition:

Feed your baby first with the water from the Euphrates River and then the dirt from Imam Husayn's grave: if not possible use rain water. [Vasa'il, v.21, p.407]

Adhan and Iqamah (The general call to prayer and the specif-ic one)

It is said the first part of the body of the baby which works is the ear. The Qur'an has placed especial emphasis on the ear. From the very first moments of birth the ear hears and the brain receives and records what the ears hear. Sounds affect the child's mind. The house should be void of forbidden and polluted sounds or else the child will become mentally and psychologically polluted. Saying the Adhan and Iqamah in the child's right and left ears at the first moments after birth was a tradition of the Prophet (Pbuh) and the Immaculate Imams. The child should hear the call to God's unity, Prophethood, leadership, and prayer so that he/ she starts life with these concepts and ends it with the same concepts. He/she will be born a Muslim and will die as a Muslim. Do not say that he/she is only one-day old, does not understand, does not see, cannot receive any information. The baby has all these fresh and powerful powers. I heard from Professor Tabatabaee (may God bless him):

A twenty-three year old American girl got a brain disease. They operated on her brain, and then after waking up she sang a religious song in French. The parents were really surprised. The doctor asked why they were surprised. They said our daughter does not know any French, does not have any French books, and nor does she have any French friends. Then the girl's mother solved the problem by saying that when the girl was only there months old, some French refugees of World War 2 came to the US. There was a Christian nurse who had rented a house next to their house: She used to come to our house, hug the baby and sing her a lullaby to pacify her. It was obvious that her lullaby was religious. Those words were recorded in her brain then, and were retrieved 23 years later when she became conscious after surgery. Therefore, saying the call to prayer in the early moments of life, and saying things to the ears of the dead person just after death are not useless. The ear is the first part that works and is the last one that stops to function.

Childbirth Etiquette

The author of the book, Makarim-al-Akhlagh has narrated the Immaculate Imams saying there are these traditional acts for the time of childbirth. The first of these is naming the child, then shaving the head, giving charity equal in weight to the cut hair, sacrificing an animal, rubbing saffron on the head of the baby, circumcising the boys, and feeding sacrificial meat to the neighbors. [Vasa'il, v.21, pp.411-413]

Imam Sadiq has highly recommended to sacrifice an animal, so much so that he has nearly considered it obligatory [Ibid].

Imam Musa, the son of Jafar was asked about circumcision, he replied: Circumcising boys on the seventh day after birth is a tradition [Vasa'il, v.21, p.439]

Mother's Milk

Breast feeding for two years is prescribed in the Holy Qur'an:

> *"The mothers shall give suck to their offspring for two whole years." [Holy Qur'an: Baqara: 2:233]*
> *"In travail upon travail did his mother bear him, and in years twain was his weaning: (hear the command)" [Holy Qur'an:*

Luqman: 31:14]

In fact, God has provided for the sustenance of the baby's milk in the mother's breast. A mother does not have the right to deprive the baby of his/her God-given milk and give powdered or animal milk for some personal, imaginary or physical reasons. The best way to start the breasts to produce milk is through sucking them. No drug can do a better job. Once the baby starts to suck the mother's breast, her milk secretions become regular, and she starts to feel healthier too. Breast milk contains 1.6 percent of albuminoidals, 0.4 percent fat, 3.8 percent sugar and some salt and vitamins. This combination is only found in the mother's milk, and nowhere else. By God's will, only the mother's breast has the potential to produce such food for a newborn guest. The formula for animal milk is slightly different. Animals like cows which grow faster have more albuminoidals. While the breast feeding progresses, the combination above changes slowly. The sugar and fat reduce, while the albuminoidals increase. The sucking action of the baby not only helps him/her feed and get full, it also causes an increase in the secretions of the glands in the breasts. In the first fifteen days after birth, the child must be breastfed seven times per day. This starts from nearly 6 AM and continues to 12 PM once every three hours. Then we must reduce this frequency of breastfeeding six times per day, and let the child go to sleep at 9 PM. This way the mother can get a chance to rest, as does the baby's digestive system, which should be prepared for the next day. The mother should try to let the baby get full at each breast-feeding session. This requires some patience. The baby must be then put to sleep on his/her right side. Then the mother can go and get busy doing her own household chores. A child that sleeps well after each breast feeding session is perfectly healthy, and one must be glad to have such a baby. [Mother's Guide, p.30]

Even though the Prophet (Pbuh) was very busy, he paid special attention to the feeding of the children. He would come to Fatimah Zahra's house, put his finger on Husayn's mouth and by observing his sucking tested his appetite. If he was really hungry, he would be breastfed. If not, he would not be fed just for crying, since feeding the baby too often would cause illness and slow down the children digestive system. This would make him/her grow up to be weak. The Prophet (Pbuh) said:

There is no milk for babies better than mother's milk. [Bihar al-Anwar, v.103, p.323]

This was said centuries ago by the Noble Prophet of Islam. It is a fact that has been recently discovered by great scientists. In the West where families leave their children to be raised in day care centers and be fed powdered milk, the researches have stated that there is no better food or milk for the baby than the mother's milk. In rare instances where the mother lacks sufficient milk, it has been stressed in traditions to be very careful when choosing someone to breastfeed the baby instead. This is so because the milk is very effective on both the spirit and the body of the child. Based on traditions, one should avoid choosing a dumb, psychotic, evil-doing, weak-eyed person, Jew, Christian, Magi, or an alcoholic person to breastfeed your baby. This is because their condition will be transferred to the baby through the milk. [Bihar al-Anwar, v.103, Chapter on Breast-feeding; Vasa'il, v.15, Chapter on Breast -feeding].

The main point about breast feeding is the reward which is surprising.

Um Salmeh asked the Prophet:

Men get all the good rewards but what about poor women? He replied:

The reward of pregnancy is the same as fasting and night worship, and fighting in the way of God with one's wealth and life. Delivery has such an extensive divine reward which no one can realize. And for breastfeeding, each suck of the baby has the reward of freeing one of the slaves from the generation of Ismael. When the mother stops, a noble angle shall hit her on the side and tell her, start over since you are forgiven [Vasa'il, Al-i-Bayt, v.21, p.451]

It is important for mothers to note the following point that Imam Sadiq told a woman named Um Ishaq:

Breastfeed your baby with both breasts, since one is like a source of food while the other is like a source of drinking.

Naming

Some people consider naming an unimportant issue, and put any name on their child. However, naming is very important, and it affects the child's mentality and future. For this reason, there is one detailed chapter dedicated to naming in the books on traditions. The seventh Imam said: The first kind act of a man towards his child is choosing a good name. Each of you must choose a good name for your child.

The Prophet (Pbuh) said:

Choose good names for yourselves, since you will be called by the same names in the Hereafter. [Ibid]

A narrator said that he went to see Imam Sadiq when he was sitting by Imam Musa's cradle. I sat and waited for him to stop caring for the child. He called me and I greeted him. He answered and then yelled at me, saying that I should immediately go and change the name I had chosen for my baby the previous day. I had named my newborn daughter Homeyra, but God dislikes this name, so I went and changed it. [Vasa'il, v.21, p.389]

Imam Sadiq has narrated his ancestors as saying:

In fact, the Prophet (Pbuh) used to change the bad names of towns and people. [Vasa'il, v.21, pp.390-391]

Imam Baqir said:

The most loudable name is the one which conveys the meaning of being a servant of God. And the best names for your children are the names of the Prophets. [Ibid]

Imam Musa, the son of Jafar, said:

Poverty shall not enter a home in which a girl is named Fatimah, or a boy is named Muhammad, Ahmad, Ali, Hassan, Husayn, Jafar, Talib or Abdullah. [Vasa'il, v.21, p.396]

To please the Prophet (Pbuh) and the Imams, you should change the names of your children if they are different from the names of the Prophet, the Imams or their mothers; lest your children file a complaint against you in the Hereafter for the bad names, symbolizing the wicked heroes of sin and corruption, which you named them with.

Twenty-Four

Part 21: Raising Children in Islam

~~~~~~~~~~~~~~~~~~~~~~~~~~~~~~~~~~~~~~

Imam Sajjad said:

One thing guaranteeing men's prosperity is to have children whom they can help. [Kafi, v.6, p.2]

The Position and Worth of Children

Children, whether male or female, are the greatest and most beneficial blessing that God has favored his servants with. The Prophet Abraham (Pbuh) did not have any children and was sad about this. When he was very old, God gave his worthy servant two sons: Ismael and Issac. Issac is the source of the divine Prophets until the time of Jesus and Ismael is the source of all the Prophets to the time of Muhammad, the last Prophet (Khatim-al-Anbiyaa), the Immaculate Imams and thousands of wise men, mystics and religious jurisprudents A child is a great blessing, a source of goodness, nobleness and benefit in this world and the Hereafter for an individual. Of course, the reference is to an individual believing in God and due to his belief trains his child to be a believer and a good and worthy person. Abraham wholeheartedly praised God for being granted offspring: Really, being granted offspring requires one to praise God.

> *"Praise be to God, Who hath granted unto me in old age Ismael and Isaac: for truly my Lord is He, the Hearer of Prayer!" [Holy Qur'an: Abraham: 14:39, p.631.]*

We understand from this noble verse that the position of offspring is so important in life that Abraham requested children from God in his old age and his prayer was answered. When Zacharias was old he prayed to God in the prayer niche to give him a child.

> *"So give me an heir as from Thyself, (One that) will (truly) represent me, and represent the posterity of Jacob." [Holy Qur'an: Maryam: 19:5-6]*

Ishaq ibn Umar quotes on the authority of the sixth Imam:

Mothers and fathers depart from this world and benefit completely from the worship, supplications and good deeds of their offspring in the case that their children were believers.

The Prophet (Pbuh) stated:

Five people have left this world but their files have not been closed: Reward continually is bestowed upon them. 1) The one who plants a tree 2) The one who digs a water well for others to use 3) The one who builds a mosque 4) The one who has taken down the Qur'an and 5) The one who leaves behind a worthy child. [Bihar al-Anwar, v.104, p.97]

The sixth Imam said:

When Joseph saw his brother he asked him:

How are you going to make the preparations for marriage. His brother said that his father Jacob instructed them in the following way: If you can raise heavenly children, do so. [Vasa'il, v.21, p.356]

Imam Sajjad said:

A Muslim man is fortunate in these regards: 1) His place of business is in the small city he lives in, so he can see his family after a day's work. 2) His friends are worthy and pious 3) He has a child whose help he can benefit from. [Bihar al-Anwar, v.103, p.7]

How blessed is a worthy child that the Glorious Qur'an says:

And God has made for you mates (and Companions) of your own nature, and made for you, out of them, sons and daughters and grandchildren, and provided for you sustenance of the best. [Holy Qur'an: Nahl: 16:72]

Imam Sadiq stated:

In the Hereafter, Muslim offspring will intervene on their parents behalf and the intervention will be accepted.

The seventh Imam said:

The man who does not die until he sees his offspring is fortunate. [Vasa'il, v.21, p.351-8]

The benefit of having children is so much that the Commander of the Faithful (Amir al-Mumineen) said:

A child's illness is the penalty for the parent's sins. The Prophet (Pbuh) said:

Worthy offspring are a bunch of sweet-smelling flowers which God has distributed amongst his servants.[Ibid]

And the Prophet (Pbuh) said:

Worthy children are a bunch of sweet-smelling flowers from the Heavenly flowers. [Ibid]

In a tradition it was stated:

The Prophet (Pbuh) was on the Medina mosque pulpit preaching to the people when Hassan and Husayn (peace be upon them) entered the mosque. They were both wearing red shirts and while walking fell down. The Prophet (Pbuh) quickly came down from the pulpit and picked up both children. [Bihar al-Anwar, v.42, p.284].

Then he recited the Qur'anic verse:

"Your riches and your children may be but a trial: but in the Presence of God, is the highest Reward." [Holy Qur'an: Tagabun: 64:15]

In Tehran, a subterranean water canal had been dug whose excavator was a man named Hajj Alireza Zaba. For more than one-hundred years people from some parts of Tehran used that water. One of the great theologians said that someone saw him (the excavator) in his dreams. He was in a great orchard standing by a big river. The excavator told the man that his orchard was one of Heaven's orchards and that river was one of Heaven's, too. Those two blessings were the reward for excavating that canal in Tehran. But, alas! I wish I had a child who had said "There is no God but God" just once and then died. By stating his belief in monotheism, a great benefit would have been mine.

Love for children

The Sixth Imam quoted upon the authority of the Prophet:

Love your children and have mercy on them. [Vasa'il, v.21, p.483]

Some people do not show much affection for their children or do not show their affection. They are harsh and strict when interacting with their children. These people must know that using this method, which is inhumane and unIslamic, will deprive them of God's Mercy. Imam Sadiq said:

In fact, God shows mercy upon his servants, just for the strong love they have for their offspring.[Ibid]

The Seventh Imam said:

God the Great does use things like His Anger against women and children. [Vasa'il, v.21, p.484]

God's Anger is shown for the faithlessness and bad-temperedness to the family. The Sixth Imam said:

Moses said the following to God when he was on the Tur Mountain: God, which action according to you is the best one? God said that loving children is the best one.

Kissing the Children

In the valuable book Ruzat al-Vaizin Fatal Nayshaboori being one of the great Shiite scholars has narrated an Immaculate Imam as saying:

Kiss your children a lot. For each kiss you will get a divine heavenly rank which would otherwise take 500 years to achieve.

A man came to the Prophet (Pbuh) and said: I have never kissed my child. The Prophet (Pbuh) said that in fact this man was a resident of the fire of Hell. There is no difference between boys and girls in this regard. Those who look sad when God grants them a daughter, are similar to the Arabs of the Age of Ignorance: They are terribly stupid. God willing, I shall discuss later about raising daughters, so that it becomes clear how valuable it is in Islam to raise a daughter. Another important consideration regarding child rearing is stated by the Immaculate Imams , and is very important to follow: Separate the sleeping place of boys from girls at the age of ten. [Vasa'il, v.21, p.361]

The Prophet (Pbuh) has issued a very important recommendation in this regard:

Separate the sleeping place of boys from boys, boys from girls, and girls from girls from the age of ten. [Vasa'il, v.21, p.460]

It is not appropriate for two kids to sleep in the same bed, whether they be both boys, a boy and a girl, or both girls. Islam does not approve of this. Imam Sadiq said:

Let your children be free to play until they reach the age of seven. For the next seven years, keep a really watchful eye on him/her. If he/she accepts to be religious, it is fine. Else there is no good in him/her. [Vasa'il, v.21, p.473]

The Prophet (Pbuh) said:

Teach your children to swim and shoot. [Kafi, v.6, p.473] He also said:

Respect your children, and improve their behavior. Then you shall be forgiven. [Vasa'il, v.21, p.476]

Malik Denyar said:

I was ignorant, a loafer and I married three times. I divorced all of them for being infertile. I had a son from my next wife. I took him to school at the age of six. When I returned home in the evening, I saw that he was ill. Then I found out that the following verse is the first thing that he was taught:

"A Day that will make children hoary-headed?" [Holy Qur'an: *Muzzammil : 73:17]*

We could not treat his ailment, so he died. I went to stay beside his grave. One night I dreamt that I was alone in a scary desert. A strange creature attacked me. I started to run away, and then reached a wall. I tried to climb over the wall to get over to the other side and escape. But suddenly I saw a few kids playing. I called out to my son and asked where he was. He said that after he died he was taken to a Qur'an class, so that by learning the Qur'an, he could become qualified to enter Heaven, and gain God's Mercy. I asked him about the nature of the creature that followed me. He said that was the manifestation of my own ugly and immoral acts. I fearfully woke up and stopped all my wicked acts and repented. Then I trotted down God's path.

Twenty-Five

Part 22: The Worth of Raising a Daughter in Islam

⁓❀⫯❀⫯❀⁓

The Prophet (Pbuh) said: A female child is a blessing.[Furu al-Kafi, v.6, p.5]

God's Will in Granting a Child

The Holy God is the Creator of all He wills, the owner of the heavens and the Earth, the Wise, the Powerful, the Just, the Merciful and the Benevolent. His will and decision regarding his servants is pure kindness and favor. He is the manifestation of love, mercy and nobleness and proper choosing. Whatever He wants for His servants is appropriate for this world and the Hereafter. And the servant must submit to God's Wisdom, Mercy and Will. This type of submission is the highest form of spiritual worship and stems from morality of the Prophets and the Saints, and the sign of love and understanding of God's lovers and mystics. All of the following cases are God's pure Mercy, Kindness and His burning Love for His servants: the barren parents, the ones with a daughter; the ones with a son and the mother who bears twins, one being a girl and one being a boy.

> *To God belongs the dominion of the heavens and the Earth.* **"He creates what He wills (and Plans). He bestows (children) male or female according to His Will (and Plan), or He bestows both males and females, and He leaves Barren whom He will."** *[Holy Qur'an: Shura: 42:49-50]*

Based on this noble verse, female offspring are an aspect of the kingship of God and the manifestation of His will in Creation and the light of His knowledge and power in regards to man. His knowledge and power, action and will, rule and ownership deemed a couple to have a daughter. Getting upset about having a daughter is a great sin, since it implies being upset with divine Ownership, Creation, Choice, Knowledge and Ability. This is stupid, illogical and unwise. As Imam Sadiq has said a baby who dies will be given to Sarah and Abraham in the Purgatory to be raised, and then be saved for the parents until the Hereafter. In the book Maskan al-Fowad, Shahid has narrated the sixth Imam as saying that having patience when a baby dies and not crying a lot has a reward that is greater than if the baby had not died, but grew up and fought as a soldier of Imam Mahdi and became a martyr in God's way.

Imam Husayn took his six-month-old baby to the tent, and gave him to his sister Zaynab. Then he sat on the ground and asked God to accept his six-month-old martyred baby as a credit for the Hereafter When a dead child is so important and valuable for us ,then can you estimate the worth of a child which we raise, educate and train expending a lot of our efforts? There is no difference between a boy and a girl, just a child. It is said in verse twenty-eight of the Chapter Anfal that children are God's test for man. If man is pleased with his child, then he has succeeded in this test. If he tries to educate him and teach him religion; provides the means for his marriage as much as he can; respects him; honors him and respect his rights, then he shall attain a great reward. The Holy Qur'an has said:

"Wealth and sons are allurements of the life of this world. But the things that endure, good deeds, are best in the sight of thy Lord, as rewards, and best as (the foundation for) hopes." [Holy Qur'an: Kahf: 18:46]

One who strives to raise his children and gets them acquainted with God, the Prophets, the leadership of the Imams and the Qur'an shall leave a highly valuable thing behind which cannot be matched. This is better for him in the presence of God and will be good for the Hereafter. Are not Mary, Khadijah, Asia and Fatimah the best patrimonies that their fathers left behind. Why should anyone get upset about having a daughter? Who knows what is in the womb? Does anyone's will but God's affect the gender of the baby in the womb? This is God's will and we should surrender to it. It is His Mercy, favor and kindness to grant us a daughter. we should thank him all our life for this blessed daughter. Remember that the Prophet (Pbuh) was granted a few sons named Qasem, Tayib, Tahir and Abraham, however, neither one survived. God never congratulated him for having a son, and no special verse of the Qur'an was revealed on these occasions. But when Khadijah became pregnant with Fatimah, the Chapter Kauthar of the Qur'an was revealed and he was informed of receiving a great deal of blessings, and eternal goodness.

Highly Important Traditions Regarding Raising a Daughter

It is recommended to pray to God to give you a daughter, if you do not have one. Prophet Abraham, who had Issac and Ismael prayed to God to have a daughter. His prayer has been quoted by Imam Sadiq as: He asked God to give him a daughter so there be at least someone to cry after his death and remember him. [Vasa'il al-Shiaa, v.21, p.361; Al-i-Bayt Press].What is important in this tradition is not the goal, rather it is the fact that a Prophet prays to have a daughter. It is an honor to be the father of a girl, as the Noble Prophet of Islam was. It is a real honor to have a girl and become similar to the Prophet (Pbuh) in this respect. Imam Sadiq said: The Prophet (Pbuh) was the father of all girls. [Ibid]

If someone does not have a daughter, but has a sister, he still has some leeway to receive God's Mercy. The Sixth Imam said: Whoever has three daughters or three sisters should go to Heaven. [Ibid]

The Prophet (Pbuh) said: Daughters are a blessing: they are kind, helpful, good companions, blessed, and like cleanliness.[Vasa'il, v.21, p.362] The Sixth Imam said: Whoever is the guardian of either two daughters, two aunts, or two maternal aunts shall be protected from the fire of Hell.[Ibid]

A man informed another man who was sitting by the Prophet (Pbuh) that he had become the father of a girl. The man turned pale. The Prophet (Pbuh) asked the reason. He said: I left the house when my wife had pains. Now this man informed me that I have a daughter. The Prophet (Pbuh) said: The earth shall support her, the sky will be a shadow over her head, and God will grant her sustenance. She is like a scented bunch of flowers you can smell. Then he turned to his companions and said: Whoever has just one daughter has problems of raising her, guarding her, preparing her dowry and providing for her marriage. Help whoever has two daughters. Whoever has three daughters seems to be engaged in holy war, and he is forgiven if he does any acts which he is admonished not to do. [Ibid]

And please help, lend money and have mercy upon whoever has four daughters. [Vasa'il, v.21, p.365]

How dear daughters are that the Prophet (Pbuh) has advised his companions to help those who have daughters and has established such help as a duty for the Muslim nation!

At the time of Imam Sadiq a man's wife delivered a girl. He came to Imam Sadiq and looked upset and angry. Imam Sadiq said: What would you say if God sent you a revelation and asked you if you will let Him choose the gender of your child? He said: Of course, I would ask God to choose for me. Then Imam Sadiq said: Well, now God has chosen a daughter for you. Remember the story of Moses and Khizr. When Khizr killed that child by God's command he told Moses: "I willed that God give to his parents a better and more merciful child instead of him."

So we desired that their Lord would give them in exchange (a son) better in purity (of conduct) and closer in affection. [Holy Qur'an: Kahf: 18:81] Instead of that child that was killed by Khizr (and Moses objected to this act). God granted his parents a daughter from whose generation came seventy Prophets. [Kafi, v.6, p.6; Vasa'il, v.21]

Imam Sadiq said: Daughters are good deeds and boys are God's blessings. Good deeds will be given a reward, but one will be questioned about blessings.

[Vasa'il, v.21, pp.365-366]

God told his Prophet on the night of Ascension to Heaven:

Tell the father of girls, do not be impatient with your daughters, since I shall provide for their sustenance just as I created them. [Ibid]

Imam Sadiq said: One who wished for the death of his daughter will be admitted to God's presence in the Hereafter as a rebellious person [Ibid]. The Prophet (Pbuh) said: God the Glorious, and the Almighty is kinder to girls than He is to boys. On the Day of Judgment God will please one who pleases his daughters. [Vasa'il, v.20, p.364]

The Prophet (Pbuh) has said the following regarding the value of having a daughter:

Your best children are your daughters. [Bihar al-Anwar, v.104, p.91]

The Prophet (Pbuh) said: One who is the guardian of three daughters or sisters shall certainly go to Heaven. They asked him what if one takes care of just two?

He replied yes. They asked him what if he takes care of just one daughter or one sister? Again he replied yes.[Vasa'il, v.21, p.368]

The Prophet (Pbuh) said: One who goes to the market and buys something and brings it home for his wife and children is similar to one who supports the needy.

It is better to give a priority to daughters in gifts. In fact, whoever pleases his daughter gets the reward of having freed one of the slaves from the line of Islamel.[Bihar al-Anwar, v.104, p.69]

What an amazing tradition? No other culture has supported having daughters this much in human history.

In many tribes and nations, girls and women were in a terrible state. It was due to the efforts of the Prophet (Pbuh) that a great spiritual revolution happened in regards to the life of girls and women, and how they are treated. It is even more amazing that the Prophet (Pbuh) has said: Do not hit your babies since their crying has a meaning. The first four months of crying is professing the unity of God, the second four months of crying is sending salutations to the Prophet (Pbuh) and his household, and the third four months of crying is praying for the parents. [Bihar al-Anwar, v.60, p.381] Therefore you should not beat one who is professing God's unity, or is sending salutations to the Prophet (Pbuh) and his household, or is praying for his/her parents. You should be considerate of such a person, and be kind to him/her.

Also consider the following important tradition: Sakuni, who is one of the companions of Imam Sadiq, said: I went to see Imam Sadiq when I was really sad. He asked me the reason why and I replied that my wife had delivered a girl. He said: The earth will support her, God will give her sustenance, she lives in a different time period than you and she will eat her own share of daily bread. Then by God I was relieved of the burden. Then the Imam asked me what name I had chosen for her. When I said Fatimah, he put his hand over his fore-head giving a sigh of relief said: Now that you have named her Fatimah, do not beat her, swear at her nor damn her. [Kafi, v.6, p.48; Makarim al-Akhlagh, p.220; Vasa'il, v.21, p.482]

The Prophet (Pbuh) said: One who has a daughter should not prefer his sons over her, or despise or scorn her. Then God will take him to heaven. [Marriage in Islam, p.136]

He also said: The reward of one who has one daughter is greater than the reward of one who goes on pilgrimage a thousand times, engages in holy war a thousand times, makes sacrifices a thousand times or gives a thousand dinner parties. [Ibid]

Twenty-Six

Part 23: The Role of the Mother in Child Rearing

The Prophet (Pbuh) said: Heaven is under the feet of mothers. [Mizan al-Hikmat, v.10, p.712]

A Child as the Result of a Mother's Efforts

The Arabic word "Um" which means mother and is extensively used in the Qur'an and the traditions essentially means root and source. This is because a child is in the womb for six to nine months and extracts his/ her physical and spiritual needs from the body of the mother. Also, the baby constantly extracts his/her needs from the mother's physical and nervous system. In fact a mother is the root or source of the existence of a child, and a child is the product of his/her mother and a reflection of the mother's physical and spiritual existence. The duration of stay of the child in the father's loins is very short, but the duration of his/her stay in the mother's womb is nearly 270 days. For this reason, the child is mostly affected by the mother, and Islam has paid especial consideration to the mother and no one else. The mother's physical and spiritual states appear in the child, and the child's substance will knowingly or unknowingly be based on his mother.

Before a girl marries she should either realize herself, or be told that she will become a mother later. She must then be careful about the feeding, training, educating, and socializing of her children, so that we can have a good future generation. I read this sentence quoted from the French Emperor Napoleon in a book about women. When asked which was the most valuable nation in his opinion he said: The one with the most mothers. The dignity of motherhood should always remain constant in the mind of women, else we will not have a good future generation. A mother should honor her motherhood to raise her children. She should mother her children so that they do not develop any spiritual or emotional deficiencies.

A woman who abandons the attributes of a mother, lets herself on the loose as a Western woman does, flirts and associates with strange men, ignores herself, her husband and her children to derive material and physical pleasure, is no longer then a real mother. She is similar to a wild beast attacking her own family, or a dangerous wolf that will harm the nobility and honor of her family. To raise wise, strong, polite and good children, a mother must be pure with a healthy mind, and humane ethics.

The following is a part of Vareth's pilgrimage prayers addressing Imam Husayn, the Master of the Martyrs: I witness that, in fact, you were a light in lofty loins and pure wombs. A light which illuminated the world with knowledge, justice, wisdom and leadership during his life, and lit up the Hereafter after his martyrdom. In the same pilgrimage prayer, he is called as related to Fatimah and Khadijah: "Greetings and peace be upon you the son of Fatimah Zahra, Greetings to you the son of the great Khadijah".

The reason the Prophet of Islam (Pbuh) has recommended that young men who want to marry, should marry a girl from a noble, strong and religious family is to prevent corruption in the future generation. A girl who is flirtish, impolite, light-headed, untidy, lustful and a show-off with several boy friends is not suitable for marriage. She has lost her nobility, her qualifications to be a mother and her abilities to raise good children. Regarding such women, the Prophet (Pbuh) has said in a tradition: If they deliver snakes and scorpions it is better than babies, since they have corrupted their mind and soul seeking pleasure, and as such are unable to produce healthy children. Notice the following words of Noah:

And Noah said:

"O my Lord! Leave not of the unbelievers, a single one on Earth! For, if Thou dost leave (any of) them, they will but mislead Thy devotees, and they will breed none but wicked ungrateful ones."[Holy Qur'an: Nuh: 71:26-27]

If there were many mothers among the people of Noah, women who were faithful, grateful, polite and chaste, then God would not have said that none but unbelievers can be produced from them. As the Prophet (Pbuh) has said: If a woman is similar to vegetation grown on garbage, then you cannot expect her to produce humane, divine, and sweet products. A mother should not attend any parties, even if it be at the house of their relatives. Some of these parties are given for sinning. This will affect her spirit and she may even lose her identity as a mother. A mother should not eat whatever she pleases. She should only eat food that is obtained lawfully; which is harmless to herself and her children. She should be concerned about issues related to cleanliness, insist on the performance of religious duties and moral issues. Then she will be overcome with light and can become illuminating. We have been informed through the Immaculate Imams that they have used Hazrat Faimah Zahra as their model and followed her in all matters whether it be related to intellectual, spiritual, moral or belief ones. Fatimah is an exemplary model in all Creation. She is an example of a perfect mother. Our daughters and wives should use her as a model to follow, since a mother is the source of the creation of a child. Children will be influenced by their mother while they are in the womb. When they are born they will be solely looking at and listening to their mother. Thus, mothers who follow

Islamic ethics are polite, are centers of love and affection , and will positively affect their children. When Imam Husayn (Pbuh) put the head of Hur the son of Yazeed on his lap, he declared Hur's freedom from the rule of the Ummayad clan, and lust. This was a credit to his mother. He said: You are free, and you have earned this freedom from your mother. Also when Omr-i-Saed insisted that Imam Husayn (Pbuh) should swear allegiance to Yazeed, the Imam declared his and his followers unwillingness to swear such an allegiance to him because of their having pure and holy mothers.

The Fruit of the Garden of Purity

Abdullah Mubarak, who was a wise, mystic, scholarly man, was hired by a garden owner as a gardener. During the time when pomegranates ripen, the owner of the garden invited a few guests to the garden, and asked Mubarak to bring them some pomegranates. Mubarak brought a basket of pomegranates, but they were all sour. The garden owner asked again for sweet pomegranates. Mubarak brought some more, but they were all sour, too. Again he asked Mubarak: Didn't I ask you to bring sweet pomegranates? You have been working here for six months, but you do not know which tree has sweet pomegranates? Mubarak answered no. The owner asked why and Mubarak said we had signed a contract stating I would be a gardener, not someone to eat the fruits in the garden. Indeed a pure sperm, a pure womb and good training will raise a person who will protect people's property, not one who will devour the people's wealth.

My Mother Ruined My Life

It has been recorded that a young man was sentenced to death. They asked him to write out his will. He said he did not have a will, but he wished to see his mother before he died. They brought his mother to him. When saying good-bye he bit his mother's lips and tongue so hard that she fainted from the pain. They attacked him asking why he did that evil oppressive act. He said my mother was an oppressor. My mother ruined my life and caused me to be sentenced to death. I stole an egg from our neighbor when I was a child. She encouraged me so much so that I became a thief, so then I committed homicide. Indeed, Heaven is under the mother's feet, but she can also be the main cause of eternal torture in the Hereafter.

After Fatimah Zahra (Pbuh) passed away Imam Ali (Pbuh) told his brother Agheel who was familiar with Arab kinship: Choose me a wife who is born of one of the brave Arab mothers. After a while, Agheel told Imam Ali to marry Fatimah Kalabieh since there were no fathers among the Arabs who were braver than he was. Imam Ali (Pbuh) married her, and had four brave strong sons including Abulfazl al-Abbas.

After Malik Ashtar's martyrdom, the Commander of the Faithful went to the top of the minaret of Kufa's mosque. mosque and said: "I see no other mother who can deliver a child like Malik. What a man he was! He was like a lofty mountain and strong rock. He is in the same position in regards to me that I am in regards to the Prophet (Pbuh)."

Sometimes Worshipping Diminishes

A young fellow went to his mother and said sometimes the strength of his worshipping diminishes although he does not eat unlawfully earned food, does not associate with bad people, and avoids anything that might make him lazy about worshipping. He said at times he felt a strand of darkness shadowing his spiritual light. Then he said after having studied about this problem, he came to the conclusion that this must be a problem transferred from his mother to him. He asked for the truth to try to solve this problem. The mother told him that his father was on a trip when she was pregnant with the boy and she said: There were lots of plums on the market, but I could not leave the house and could not buy any. Once when I went to the roof to spread the clothes on the line to dry, I saw the plums that the neighbors had spread out to dry. I ate just one plum to taste it, but then I became sorry and I was too shy to tell the neighbor to ask for their consent. The young man told his mother that he had found the problem. He asked for her permission to go to the neighbor's house and solve the issue, so that he could continue God's worship without any attacks from Satan.

A Bright Marriage

When I was young, I heard the following from one of the religious authorities in the main city mosque called Jameh. When the father of that great religious authority, Moqadas Ardebili, went to ask one of his fellow citizens if he could marry his daughter, he said: My daughter is blind, deaf, dumb and crippled. Marry her if you wish. The man said: How can I live with such woman? Then her father replied: When I say she is blind, I mean she cannot see whoever is not intimate; when I say she is deaf I mean she cannot hear the sound of whoever is not intimate; when I say she is crippled, I mean her hands have not touched anyone who is not intimate or gone to a forbidden party. Then the man married that lady, and the product of that marriage was a noble scholar.

Sheik Shooshtary's Mother

Sheik Jafar Shooshtary reached a high position in knowledge and practice. He had a great influence in guiding the people. they once asked his mother if she is pleased with having such a child. She replied no. They asked her why? She said: during the two years of breast feeding, once I did not do my ablution before breast feeding, and did not hug him. I wished him to grow up and become Imam Sadiq but he turned out to be Jafar Shooshtary.

The Effect of Physical and Spiritual Purity in Upbringing

Once I traveled to Boroojerd to preach for ten nights. I wished to get more informed about the great Muslim scholar Ayatullah Boroojerdy. A ninety-year old man explained to me that his mother really tried to always perform her ablutions before breast-feeding him. On a cold night when she wanted to cleanse her body but could not leave the house (to go to a public bath-house) she washed herself with cold water, then fed the baby. The mother's spiritual attention, and the father's sincere efforts yielded a man which brought about vast changes in the Shiite religious schools in scientific, practical and moral issues.

Young girls should prepare themselves to become mothers. Equip yourselves with the divine, human and moral necessities of motherhood. And noble mothers should maintain their motherhood identity. Only God knows how rewarding it is to bring up such good children. Among the people who can intercede on one's behalf in the Hereafter are believers, religious scholars and martyrs. There is no set limit on how many people they can intercede for. They can intercede on behalf of whoever deserves it. Of course, the first and foremost person who shall benefit from this intercession is their mother. The Prophet (Pbuh) said:

Three groups of people can intercede on one's behalf in God's presence, and their intercession shall be accepted by God. They are the Prophets, then the scholars, then the martyrs. [Bihar al-Anwar, v.8, p.34]

Imam Baqir said:

Indeed believers intercede like the two tribes of Rabiah and Mozaer. Believers intercede even on behalf of their servants.

Why should daughters and mothers be such as to benefit from your scholar, martyr or believing children's intercession in the Hereafter? Is it not bad to lose your motherhood identity for the few days of this temporal life? Is not too terrible for you to ruin the spiritual foundation of your children, who are entrusted to you by God. Is it not awful for you to raise them up like Eastern devils?

Twenty-Seven

Part 24: The Role of the Father in Child Rearing

"O sister of Aaron! Thy father was not a man of evil, nor thy mother a woman unchaste! "[Holy Qur'an: Maryam: 19:28]

Consider the Following Four Facts

It is understood from verses 33-37 of the Chapter Al-i-Imran and verse 28 of Chapter Maryam that man's development and perfection depend upon the following four factors.

1-A believing father
2-A believing mother
3-A good and sympathetic teacher

4-Lawfully obtained food

When the Jews saw Jesus in the hands of Mary who was a girl without a husband, they told her out of their surprise:

O sister of Aaron! Thy father was not a man of evil, nor thy mother a woman unchaste! [Holy Qur'an: Maryam: 19:28]

They were not aware of the truth that Jesus was God's word induced into the womb of the noble, chaste Mary. They thought she had done wrong. Knowing that her father was a noble, believing man who followed divine etiquette and her mother was a chaste, believing woman, they could not believe that such a child of such parents would commit such an act. The people knew that a child was a reflection of the spiritual, behavioral and physical realities of his or her parents. It was only when baby Jesus spoke in the cradle that it became clear that such a child as Mary, with such a high position as to become the mother of a Prophet, will result from such parents. You note that the people expected her chastity primarily due to her father's pure character. For this reason they told her: Your father was not bad.

> *"O sister of Aaron! Thy father was not a man of evil, nor thy mother a wo- man unchaste! " [Holy Qur'an: Maryam: 19:28]*

They also considered her mother's character, That is why they told her: We know your mother she is chaste.

> *"O sister of Aaron! Thy father was not a man of evil, nor thy mother a woman unchaste!" [Holy Qur'an: Maryam: 19:28]*

In the previous chapter, the role of the mother in child-rearing and a mother's duties were discussed, and there is no need to discuss it here any more. The importance of eating legally obtained food was already discussed, too. Also, no one is unaware of the importance of the role of teachers and their character and behavior of their students. In this chapter, the role of the father, and his character concerning the up-bringing, morality and actions

258

of the child is discussed. A father must at first pay close attention to the religious moral and scientific training of the child. Secondly, he should treat his wife in such a way that the children's life is not bitter. Thirdly, he should be careful not to feed his wife and children with any unlawfully obtained food. It is recorded in traditions from the Household of the Prophet (Pbuh) that several groups of people will be tortured in the Hereafter without any reckoning. One of these groups are fathers who do not attend to the religious and moral training of their children. God the Almighty has created all the people to say prayers so as to reach the position of God's Caliph on Earth, to attain guidance, knowledge, wisdom, and to finally enter Heaven. The people themselves prepare the grounds for their torture.

The Commander of the Faithful Cried

When the Command of the Faithful won the war of Jamal, and things cooled down, he went amongst the dead and cried. This was an unprecedented event in the history of man for a military man who has won the war. They asked him the reason. He said: These people had accepted Islam. They prayed, fasted and worshipped God. They should have gone to Heaven. I feel sad that they came to wrongfully fight with an Immaculate Imam. They followed their selfish desires and have to suffer eternal torture.

People of Torture

The people of torture shall ask God to be saved five times, but they are turned down five times. Then they shut their mouths up forever. The following verse is regarding one of these times.

Therein will they cry aloud (for assistance):

> *"Our Lord! Bring us out: We shall work righteousness, not the (deeds) we used to do! "-"Did We not give you long enough life so that he that would should receive admonition? And (moreover) the warner came to you. So taste ye (the fruits of your deeds): for*

the wrong-doers there is no helper." [Holy Qur'an: Fatir: 35:37]

Fathers should note to paying close attention to the growth, development and perfection of their children. Do not be indifferent to your children. Keep the house clean for them. Give them lawfully obtained food to eat. Be considerate with your wives. This way your good deeds and behavior will influence your children, and they too will learn to be good parents for their children in the future. Remember that all your actions and plans are being observed by God, the Prophet (Pbuh) and the noble Imams.

"Work (righteousness): Soon will God observe your work, and His Apostle, and the Believers." [Holy Qur'an: Tauba: 9:105]

So be careful about how you live, what you say, and how you behave, since all your actions affect your family members. The Prophet (Pbuh) has informed fathers of their important role. The noble Imams have made many recommendations for fathers. At home the father is like the ruler of a country. He is responsible for his wife and children and will be questioned about his deeds in the Hereafter. Adorn your children with pure intentions. Encourage them to do good deeds. Develop the love for knowledge and sciences in their hearts. Take them along to religious gatherings. Teach them their obligatory religious duties before they reach puberty. Be friends with them and treat them kindly. The Prophet (Pbuh) and the Commander of the Faithful are the best models for fathers to follow. Study their life, and adopt their ways and manners in your own life. Let your children adopt the Prophet and the Master of the Mystics (Ali) as their life model instead of adopting corrupt foreign or local people. Try to provide the means for your house to be filled with the scent of Prophethood and leadership of the Imams, then you shall prosper in this world and the Hereafter.

An Amazing Point Regarding the Mother of HajjSheik Fazlol-lah Noory

That noble man who was a fighter in God's way, a religious authority and sympathetic for the nation was born from a noble father and a pure mother who tried hard to educate him. His father devoted all his effects to his growth, development and education and when he noticed that he loved knowledge and religious practices, he sent him to Najaf. He had many great teachers there. He gained much benefit from the teachings of Haj-Mirza Husayn Noory, Mirza Shirazi, Sheik Ansari and the enlightment of the Immaculate Imam. He returned to Tehran with a strong background in knowledge, wisdom, religious practices, ethics and piety and became the leader of the great scholars. He initiated the struggle against oppression through the Mashrootheh, a revolution which had succeeded. However, some selfish polluted folks got into the government and changed the direction of this revolution in such a way as to receive orders from London. Amongst the religious scholars, he was the one who objected to this the most, yelled, immigrated, made public announcements, etc. However, he couldn't succeed. Then he was arrested and condemned. He was condemned to death because he wanted the Mashrootheh Government and an Islamic Parliament, one which relies on the Qur'an the traditions, Nahj ul-Balaghah and Shiite jurisprudence. He had good and divine intentions. He was wise and sympathetic. He had learned all this from his father and his teachers and had acquired his perseverance from his mother and had mingled it all together with the lawfully obtained daily bread he had eaten. He was executed on the thirteenth of Rajab, the birthday of the Commander of the Faithful. He was killed for his rightful desires by the freemasons who thought his intentions were also executed, but they were unaware of the following Holy verse: Their intention is to extinguish God's Light (by blowing) with their mouths:

'But God will complete (the revelation of) His Light, even though

the Un- believers may detest (it)." [Holy Qur'an: Saff: 61:8]

Nearly eighty years later on the thirteenth of Rajab at 10 AM near the same place that he was killed the Islamic parliament was opened up as a result of the revolution of the Iranian nation under the leadership of Imam Khomeini. Thus, Sheik Fazlollah's intentions were realized. On that day I was one of the invitees to the parliament. I wasn't surprised at all since I knew God is the helper to the believers and has realized his care intentions although he was martyred. Prosperous be his father who will be honored in the Hereafter and win the presents of God, the Prophets and the Imams for having such a child.

Youth Beware

O' dear youth, Muslim children, and followers of the Prophet (Pbuh): I have an important recommendation for you. Attain the qualities of a good father before you get married. It is too late to do so when you get married. Try to cleanse yourselves of evil traits, try to improve your behavior and your associations and food, since genes transfer your traits to your next generation. This is not just one of the research findings of Western scientists which some might ignore or even consider to be invalidated in the future. It is a natural phenomenon which has been outlined by Islam from the very beginning. Note the following important tradition in this regard: A young man rushed in to see the Prophet (Pbuh) and told him worriedly that both his wife and he himself had white skin but their baby was dark-colored. The Prophet (Pbuh) said: Indeed genes transfer traits. Thus, he relieved the young man from his burden. The fact that father's traits transfer to their children as stated by the Prophet (Pbuh) is also proven by scientists today.

Therefore, try to attain the qualities that Islam requires of a father before you get married. Do not get married just for lust and material life. Then your children will not be useful for you and the society. The Prophet (Pbuh) and the noble Imams were pleased of being from the line of Abraham, the idol breaker, whose traits were transferred to his future generations. In the authentic Vareth supplication, we read that Husayn is the inheritor of Adam, Noah, Abraham, Moses, Jesus, Muhammad and the Commander of the Faithful. This inheritance is not material wealth; rather it is the spiritual states, religious knowledge, good behavior, honor and nobility. Why should we not benefit from all these spiritual assets, so that children too can inherit them?

Deviated Fathers and the Children's Duties

In some families, it may be the case that the father does not abide by the religion and does not perform his religious duties. He may not be interested in or accept divine facts. The children who have matured should politely invite him to accept God's way, and tell him about the losses he shall suffer in this world and the Hereafter. If he does not accept this, they should try to guard themselves from corruption while living with him. Take Musab ibn Amir as a model. He was a believing, faithful warrior in God's way who fought along with the Prophet (Pbuh) in the Battle of Uhad and was martyred. His parents were atheists, and they really loved him. He accepted the Prophethood due to his pure nature, and went to Medina to preach the people before the Prophet's immigration to Medina. He prepared the means for many of the people of Medina to accept Islam and thus Medina became prepared for the immigration of the Prophet. When the Prophet (Pbuh) saw him once in Medina wearing a shirt made of unprepared sheep skin, he showed him to his companions and said: Look at a man whose heart has been enlightened by God, I saw him in Mecca with his parents. They provided the best food and clothes for him, but the love for God and His Prophet has driven him to live as you see. [Mizan al-Hikmat, v10, p232]

O young fellows whose fathers live a life void of spirituality, and do not want you to be adorned with ethics, religion and spirituality: Their main effort is for you to either reach a position in material sciences, or attain wealth. Be kind with them. Do not quarrel with them, since this is against the orders of God and his Prophet. Do not follow them, and do not give up God, the Imams and the Hereafter for the sake of accepting their vain invitations. Follow Muhammad, the son of Abu Bakr, who was a pious, religious, noble and worshipping man in this regard. Live like him who lived with love of Ali, following the Qur'an, and the Prophets way of life, and was finally martyred in God's way and in order to help establish God's religion. Also coordinate your activities with morality and your behavior with divine order.

A Noble Father

I heard the following from the nephew of the late Ayatullah Hajj Sheik Abdulkarim Haeri, who was the founder of the great seminary in Qum, when I went to preach in Mehrgerd for a few nights. The Sheik's father could not have a child for fifteen years. He was sad. He was a butcher, which is a boring job. His wife thought that she may have a problem getting pregnant, so she told him that she would find him a good second wife so he may have a child. After a while she found a widow a few miles away and proposed his husband to marry her. They were married as usual, and on the wedding night the three-year-old daughter of the widow. would not leave her mother. The child's aunt picked her up, but she cried. The noble man was moved and told her that he could not bear to hear an orphan cry. Additionally he said their marriage and having a child might harm the orphan even more.

So he gave the nuptial gift to her and returned to Mehrgerd to be with his first wife. For this reason, on the same night his wife got pregnant with Hajj Sheik Abdulkarim, who later founded the seminary in Qum and taught nearly a thousand scholars and future religious authorities. One of the men he trained was Imam Khomeini, the reader of the Islamic revolution, who influenced both the East and the West and also saved Islam. So Khomeini was the product of Hajj Sheik Abdulkarim Haeri who himself was the son of a noble, divine and sincere butcher. Only God knows the reward of this butcher in the Hereafter next to his son, and his son's students and the Islamic Revolution of Iran.

Bad Fathers and Good Children

Hajaj, the son of Yusef Saqafi, was an evil, wicked, oppressor and criminal man with bad children. However, a noble, wise, poetic, knowledgeable, mystic, lover of the Household of the Prophet, and a singer of songs for the Immaculate Imams, specifically the Commander of the Faithful and the Master of Martyrs (Imam Husayn) was born in Hajaj's line during the time that Seyed Morteza was the religious authority. His name was Abu Abdullah Katib. He was totally different from his forefathers. He did not have their traits, and accepted God using the power of the intellect and his nature. He became divinely oriented and was especially paid attention to by the Household of the Prophet.

It has been said that Mirza Abdullah Afandi stated the following in Riaz al-Ulama: For some reason, Seyed Morteza spoke harsh words with Abu Abdullah Katib. Then he dreamt the same night and saw the Prophet (Pbuh) and the noble Imams. The Prophet (Pbuh) gave him a cold shoulder. He asked the Prophet (Pbuh) what he had done wrong? The Prophet (Pbuh) told him that he must apologize to the Shiite poet since he had not treated him well. When the sun rose, the noble Seyed walked all the way to Abu Abdullah Katib's house, apologized and asked for forgiveness. Then our noble young folks should realize that God has given them power to maintain their independence and not follow the impious ones, even if they be their own fathers. Therefore you should not be influenced by such fathers, but remain on the straight path, steadfastly.

A Distinguished Father

Sadr Al-Muteahalin Shirazi was an unprecedented philosopher, a wise scholar and a pious mystic. He brought about a major change in philosophy and wrote many scientific books in this field. He was the son of a rich and famous man in Shiraz. His father had a high government position, and was also a pearl and antiques dealers. His father was really interested in his son following the same job and working with him. So he stayed with his father for some time, and he stayed in Bushehr and Basra with the same job. He returned to Shiraz after a couple of years. He politely asked his father for permission to quit this job and go to study in the religious schools in Shiraz. The lofty father replied positively. Then he quit the business, and deprived himself of the comfort of the house, happiness and material pleasures. Shortly after he became a renown scientist when he was still young. This he owed to the sacrifice and love of his father. Then he found no one who could teach him anything else. Thus he asked for permission to go to Isfahan. This request too was instantly accepted. He then went to Isfahan and continued his studies under the guidance of Sheik Bahayee, Mirdamad and Mirfindereski, and he reached the position of Sadr al-Muteahelin after a while. Indeed a father's good character turned a shopkeeper into a professor of philosophy. Therefore it is true that a noble, wise, knowledgeable and sympathetic father can raise good offspring for humanity and science.

Ali Akbar Will Not be Raised With Forbidden Food

When I was a child, there used to live a noble old man who was pious and disciplined in our neighborhood. He was a dealer in the Bazaar in Tehran. Since he was polite, religious and trustworthy, he was respected by the business men. He used to attend the congregational prayers three times a day. He was very attractive to young kids. I was one who attended even the morning prayers at the mosque. He used to tell us various amazing stories. Once he said: A young religious fellow lived with his parents in the Naser Khosrow region. His father did not follow religious decrees. Since he was familiar with religious issues through his associations, he would advise his father, but it was of no use. Then he left his father and went to sell things on the streets in the city of Ray next to the shrine of Hazrat Abdul Azim Hassany, and instructed the people on religious issues.

On the dawn of Ashura, he came to Tehran to visit his parents. They had gone to attend the religious ceremonies. He too went there. By chance, the man who was supposed to enact the role of Shimr had become sick. They did not know him, so they asked him to perform the ceremonies. He accepted the role, and entered the theater and successfully played the role. His father recognized him, and became upset. When they all returned home after the ceremonies, his father asked him if he had had anything to eat. He answered no. His father told him there was jam and yogurt in the house, he could go and have some. When he went to the jam jar, there he saw a dead rat in the jar. He brought some yogurt to eat. His father asked him why he did not bring the jam. He responded that there was a dead rat in the jar and it was forbidden to eat the jam. His father yelled at him and asked why he had not quit being religious after one year. Then he asked why he enacted the role of the Shimr and not the role of Ali Akbar? The son replied that a father who eats some jam in a jar with a dead rat in it, which is forbidden to eat, should not expect to have a child who will become Ali Akbar; since the result of eating forbidden food is Shimr. O' young fellows. Try to become good fathers and have good children. O' fathers. If you have any problems which may harm your children's spirit, then try to remove that flaw. Indeed the Hereafter is a strange day for all.

Twenty-Eight

Part 25: The Rights of the Children

Imam Ali said: *A child's right over his/her parents is to choose him a good name, to give him the proper upbringing and to teach him the Qur'an. [Nahj ul-Balaghah, Hikmat, p399]*

The Path to Prosperity

At first we will mention the following words from the Commander of the Faithful about prosperity. These divine and wise words have risen out of his heavenly heart to guide man towards prosperity. In response to one who asked what prosperity is he said: Prosperity does not depend on having more wealth, children, but it depends on having more knowledge, patience and perseverance; and on being proud of your worshipping of God. Thank God if you have good behavior. Ask God for forgiveness, if you do bad deeds. There is no property in this world for anyone except those who have committed sins and repented; and those who have striven to do good deeds.

Deeds which are done with piety are not trivial. How can such deeds be so small if they are accepted? [Nahj ulBalaghah, Commented on by Ibn Abel Hadid, v.18, p.250]

In these divine sayings three facts have been pointed out: being knowledge; perseverance; and the application of both which is God's worship. It is also mentioned that knowledge, perseverance and their application should be void of sin to be accepted by God. Knowledge of an impious one, perseverance mixed with sin, and worship without piety are all sources of harm or a waste of time. Those who achieved something in this world achieved it through knowledge and wisdom, worship and repentance, and piety and abstinence. The uninformed and the unwise; the weak and the impatient; the slaves of lust and carnal desires; the ones who delve in sin; and the refugees from good deeds are all useless folks who are a source of harm.

We can conclude from these divine words that parents must first realize their Islamic duties towards their children, and then patiently perform their duties. They should be happy and proud of doing these duties, and thank God for enabling them to attend to the needs of their children, and respect their rights. If they have had some shortcomings in performing their duties, they should ask God to forgive them. They should be pious in all aspects so that their efforts are not wasted. There is no doubt that attending to the needs of the children, and striving to provide for them is a great form of worship and a good deed which will be rewarded both here and in the Hereafter.

Children's Rights

The Prophet (Pbuh) said:

The rights of the child over the father consist of teaching him/her writing, swimming and shooting, and should only feed him/her clean and lawfully-earned food.

Of course, one need not directly perform these duties. If the father just sends his child to school, and swimming and shooting classes, he has done his job. The duty of feeding them only lawfully earned food is really important, and one must be very careful about this so that no problems arise here or in the Hereafter. How good it would be if there were sports clubs and mosques next to all our schools so that our children could go to learn how to swim or shoot after their studies, or could go to the mosque to learn religious matters. Thus, in addition to physical and mental development, they would receive spiritual training too. Literacy, swimming, shooting and eating lawfully earned food are four sources of power for the children. Once they are equipped with these, they will be safe from many dangers. Pursuit of such activities shall fill the free time of the youth, and is very effective in balancing out their instincts and sexual energy. In the book entitled "Mukhlat", Sheik Bahayee has narrated that a man called Hassan said:

Should I find a bit of lawfully earned bread, I will dry it; grind it firmly until it turns into powder, and keep it. Then whenever someone comes to me with an illness being difficult to cure, I will feed him with a bit of it so that he gets cured.

Twenty-Nine

Part 26: The Rights of the Parents

"Thy Lord hath decreed that ye worship none but Him, And that ye be kind to parents." [Holy Qur'an: BaniIsrail: 17:23, p.700.]

A Heavy Burden

Honoring the rights of the parents is a really heavy burden which only those who truly believe in God and the Hereafter can bear. The Holy Qur'an h²€tated the characters of a believer in:

*The answer of the Believers, when summoned to God and His Apostle, in order that He may judge between them, is no other than this: They say, "**We hear and we obey**": It is such as these that will attain felicity. [Holy Qur'an: Nur: 24:51-52]*

Note the following verse regarding the rights of the parents: Thy Lord hath decreed that ye worship none but Him, And that ye be kind to parents. Whether one or both of them attain old age in thy life, say not to them a word of contempt, nor repel them, But address them in terms of honor. And, out of kindness, lower to them the wing of humility, and say:

"My Lord! bestow on them thy Mercy even as they cherished me in childhood." [Holy Qur'an: BaniIsrail: 17:23-24]

The fact that the rights of the parents are placed right after the rights of God shows the importance of these rights. This has been discussed in detail in the highly valuable book "Kafi, v.2, p.157. A tradition from Imam Sadiq has been written there. Usul al-Kafi is an authentic book due to the author being the noble, late Kolayni who lived during the period of the short absence of the twelfth Imam, its contents, and their narrators being close to the times of the Immaculate Imams. Its order and the attention it has received make it one of the most important sources of religious principles. Then no one's excuse shall be accepted after the interpretation of this important verse narrated from Imam Sadiq regarding the rights of parents. When Imam Sadiq was asked about the meaning of this verse, he said: When it is said treat your parents kindly it is meant that you should associate with them patiently and treat them kindly; do not encounter them with a bad attitude; provide for them whatever they may need without their having to ask for it, even if they are rich; and take them something whenever you go to visit them. Has not God said:

"By no means shall ye attain righteousness unless ye give (freely) of that which ye love." [Holy Qur'an: Al-i-Imran: 3:92] Imam Sadiq said:

If one of your parents or both of them were old, impatient and weak so much so that it bothers you, do not say the least thing to them. Do not raise your voice even if they hit you. Speak with them kindly, using only noble words. If they try to hit you again, just tell them may God forgive both of you.

These are noble words. Then Imam Sadiq instructs us to be most humble with them; to look at them with passion; to always honor them and to never walk in advance. He says you must pray for them to receive God's Mercy since they raised you from childhood till now. In another verse God said:

> *And We have enjoined on man (to be good) to his parents: in travail upon travail did his mother bear him, and in years twain was his weaning: (hear the command), "Show gratitude to Me and to thy parents: to Me is (thy final) Goal. But if they strive to make thee join in worship with Me things of which thou hast no knowledge, obey them not; yet bear their company in this life with justice (and consideration), and follow the way of those who turn to Me (in love): in the End the return of you all is to Me, and I will tell you the truth (and meaning) of all that ye did." [Holy Qur'an: Luqman: 31:14-15]*

An Amazing Point

Once he was appointed to the Prophethood, Moses was ordered to use gentle speech when dealing with the Pharaoh. He asked the reason why and was told that Pharaoh had spent fifteen years of his life to raise him, and had suffered much hardship to raise him from when he was a baby until he matured. Then he had the rights of parents and Moses should not talk in harsh words with him.

A Delicate Issue

In the Qur'anic interpretation called Menhaj, we read the following regarding the verse.

> *"Did He not find thee an orphan and give thee shelter (and care)?"*

273

[Holy Qur'an: Dhuha: 93:6]

God the Almighty told the Prophet (Pbuh) that He took away his father before his birth, and took away his mother when he was still a child. This was done because the Prophet (Pbuh) would have had a great difficulty in honoring the rights of his parents, given his especial circumstances as a Prophet of God.

Traditions Regarding Parent's Rights

A narrator asked Imam Sadiq: Which of our deeds are the best? He replied: Being punctual about praying, being kind to parents, and fighting in the way of God. [Kafi, v.2, p.158]

Imam Sadiq said:

What prevents you from treating your parents kindly whether they are living or have passed away. One asked the Imam what he should do for his parents who have passed away. He replied: Pray, give charity, go on the Hajj pilgrimage and fast on their behalf.[Kafi; v.2, p.159]

Zacharias Serves His Parents

Zacharias, the son of Abraham, said he was a strict Christian, and then became a Muslim. He said he was happy and went to Mecca to see Imam Sadiq. Imam Sadiq told him to ask any questions he wished to ask. Then he told Imam Sadiq that his family members were all Christian. His mother was blind, and he had to live with them since his father had no one else to rely on. He said his parents liked him to eat and drink from the same set of dishes. Imam Sadiq asked him if his parents ate any pork. He replied no. Then he asked if they touched any pigs? He answered no. Then Imam Sadiq ordered him not to leave their house; not to separate from his mother; to take care of her; to bathe her; to change her clothes; and to feed her.

He said he followed all these instructions upon his return to Kufa. Then his mother told him to tell her the truth about having become a Muslim.

Then he told her yes, and said he had been ordered by his living leader, Imam Sadiq who was a descendant of the Prophet (Pbuh), to perform all these services. His mother asked him if he was the Prophet. He replied no. He is the sixth Imam and is the descendant of the Prophet. The mother replied no: The things you do for me are the decrees of the Prophets of God. I am blind, but I realize that your religion is better than mine. I want you to guide me towards your religion. Then he guided his mother to become a Muslim, and she performed her noon prayers with him. At eve, she asked to say his evening prayers and let her say her prayers with him. She did so, and passed away after she had finished her prayers.

Then he remembered that Imam Sadiq had instructed him to bury his mother by himself if she passed away. He invited the Shiites early the next morning. Then they told him to call in her priest. He told them that she was a Muslim, and they helped him to bury her. [Vasa'il, v.21, p.491]. Jaber Jafi said the following: I was in the presence of Imam Sadiq. A man came and said: My parents are Sunni and very strict in their ways so how should I treat them? Imam asked him how he treats real Shiites. He replied with love, and assist them in solving their problems. Imam said: Treat your parents likewise. [Ibid, p.490]

Imam Baqir said:

A young fellow served his parents well during their lifetime. However, his parents willed that he should repay a loan they could not. He refused to do so, and did not even ask God to forgive them. For this reason, God ordered that he be registered as one who is damned by his parents.

Another child who was damned by his parents during his lifetime, paid back their debts after they passed away, and sought God's forgiveness for them, and was registered amongst those who treat their parents well. [Bihar al-Anwar, v.74, p.59].

Imam Sadiq has been narrated as saying the following in the book called Amali:

Moses saw a beautiful face in the shade of heaven. He asked whose shadow was over him? He was told he was one who has really treated his parents well and had never gossiped or caused disunion.

The sixth Imam said:

If you desire death to be easy for you, visit your relatives and be kind to your parents. Then the angel of death will be told to take it easy on you, and you will not become poor during your lifetime.

Next to the Ka'aba a man asked Abuzar why he looked at Ali's face a lot. He replied that when he was next to the Prophet (Pbuh) and there was not any distance between him and the Imam, the Prophet, told him: Looking at Ali's face and kindly looking at one's parents is considered to be worship. [Bihar al-Anwar, v.38, p.196]

Imam Ali said:

Accept all your parents orders, except for sinning. The seventh Imam said:

A man asked the Prophet (Pbuh) to explain the rights of the father. He said: Do not call him by his name. Do not walk ahead of him. Do not sit down before he does, and do not swear at him. [Bihar al-Anwar, v.74, p.45]

Imam Sadiq said:

Three things are obligatory for children regarding their parents. They should always be grateful to them; they should accept their advice on all matters except sinning, and they should always wish them well. [Tuhaf ul-Uqool, v.47, p.238].

The Prophet (Pbuh) said that the following statement implies parents' damnation:

Do whatever you wish, I will not forgive you. [Bihar al-Anwar, v.74, pp.61-74]

He also said:

Two things are quickly penalized in this world. They are being damned by one's parents and committing fornication. [Ibid]

He also said:

Anyone who makes his/her parents really sad, is damned by them. [Ibid]

The sixth Imam said:

Looking meanly at parents causes damnation.

A man told the Prophet: There is no evil deed which I have not done. Is there any way for me to repent? The Prophet (Pbuh) asked him if his parents were alive. He replied that his mother had passed away, but his father was alive. He told him to go and treat his father kindly so that his sins be forgiven. When the man left the mosque, the Prophet (Pbuh) said: He would have been closer to forgiveness by God, if his mother was still alive. Moses asked God for some recommendations three times. Then he was twice recommended to treat his mother well, and once to treat his father well. [Bihar al-Anwar, v.13, p.330]

Imam Baqir said:

One is not free in the following three cases: He is not free to do as he pleases in regards to what he is entrusted with, his promise, and being kind to his parents. [Vasa'il, v.21, p.490].

Sheik Ansari and His Mother

The great jurisprudent, and noble scholar called Sheik Ansari used to carry his mother on his back to the public bath house, and would then take her back home after her bath was finished. He used to come to kiss her hands at night, and would not leave the house without her permission. After she died, he cried a lot saying that he cries because he is now deprived of the great blessing of serving her. He compensated for all of her missed prayers by praying even though he was really busy teaching and had many who came to visit him. Although his mother was one of the most religious women at that time, he performed all those duties.

Mother's Damnation

A young man was about to die. The Prophet (Pbuh) came to visit him, and told him to profess to God's unity and his Prophethood. He turned away his face and refused to profess. The Prophet (Pbuh) asked if he had a mother. He replied positively. He called her in and asked if she was not pleased with him. She replied positively. The Prophet (Pbuh) asked her to forgive him since he could not profess to God's unity. She said he had hurt her and she was upset with him. The Prophet (Pbuh) asked her to forgive him for the sake of the Prophet. She agreed and forgave her son. Then the Prophet (Pbuh) asked the young man to profess to God's unity and his Prophethood. The man uttered the words. Then the Prophet (Pbuh) asked him why he had not uttered it the first time. The man said a scary dragon would attack him and he could not talk. He added that now it had left and he could talk.[Manazel al-Akherat, Mohades Qumi]. Imam Sajjad said:

Note the following regarding your mother. She carried you for nearly nine months in her womb, no one else could do so. She dedicated her love to you, no one else would do so; she protected you with all her existence, fed you and was hungry herself; gave you things to drink; and she remained thirsty herself; she clothed you, and did not care for her own clothing; she felt hot, but protected you from heat; she stayed up to care for you at night; and protected you in all circumstances so that she may have a child like you. You cannot be grateful enough for all she did unless God helps you. [Bihar al-Anwar, v.14, p.6]

Hakam Nami said that he told the sixth Imam: My father had donated a house to me, and he now plans to move back into it. The Imam said: Your father's deed is not good, but do not fight back if he fights with you; and talk calmly with him, if he yells at you. [Vasa'il, v.18, p.224]

Thirty

Part 27: A Couple's Duties to Their Relatives

~⦿⦿⦿~

"Say: Whatever ye spend that is good, is for parents and kindred..." [Holy Qur'an: Baqara: 2:215]

Relatives

Each husband and wife has some relatives. Neither one is allowed to force the other to stop seeing them. Each one has parents, brothers and sisters, uncles, aunts, nieces and nephews, grandparents, etc. Visiting them is considered worship, and associating with them is an excellent deed and can help resolve many difficulties. A wife should not be so unreasonable not to let her husband's relatives come to visit them, or be rude with them when they come for a visit. She should not stop her husband from associating with his relatives. The house is the husband's property, and God has granted him authority over the wealth and property. A woman is religiously required to obey her husband. Bothering him is also religiously forbidden. Preventing him from associating with his parents, brothers and sisters, or other relatives is totally immoral, inhumane and against man's nature. A man should not prevent his wife from associating with her parents and relatives either. This too is against human passion and love. The wife and children who prevent one from performing good deeds, worshipping, and associating with relatives are considered man's enemies by the Qur'an. They are not enemies whose hearts are filled with hatred. Rather they are enemies who want to prevent us from attaining prosperity in this world and the Hereafter.

A man should not give in to his wife or children in his attempts to do good deeds, solving the problems of the people, associating with relatives, aiding his parents, brothers or sisters. Of course, believing women who accept the Hereafter; feel responsible; want to prosper in the Hereafter; recognize that they must respect their husband's rights; adhere to divine etiquette and are in total agreement with their husbands. They even encourage their husbands to associate with and help his relatives, whenever they feel that their husbands are not serious enough in this regard. But women who oppose God, or children who demand things opposed to God's religion, are considered to be man's enemy by the Qur'an. Man is instructed to do the following in these situations:

> *"O ye who believe! Truly, among your wives and your children are (some that are) enemies to yourselves: so beware of them! But if ye forgive and overlook, and cover up (their faults), verily God is Oft-forgiving, Most Merciful." [Holy Qur'an: Tagabun: 64:14, p.1558.]*

You should not fight, separate, or get angry in this case. Just let them insist on their views, and you yourself stay steadfast in obeying God and spending in his way. Some women are really unreasonable. They are deprived of God's Mercy, and wish to deprive others of God's Mercy too.

Some men are also too strict, and do this unreasonably and without any gain but deprivation from God's Mercy and favor. Why do some women refuse to let their husband's relatives come to their house, and not let their husband assist his relatives financially, while all their own relatives can come to their house and use the husband's property to serve them as they please. In these cases, many months or years go by and the husband aspires to see his relatives and visit him, but the wife's relatives are continually coming and going. Is this not a form of oppression against the husband and his relatives?

Is this not the same dangerous mental state which is damned by God and deprived of His Mercy. Such a woman will not have a good Hereafter. And why do some men prevent their wives from visiting their relatives. This is not liked by God, is a Satanic act and is certainly going to cause one to be deprived of God's Mercy. In addition to the verses on visiting the next of kin, the Holy Qur'an has mentioned relatives twentythree times, and has issued some very important decrees in this regard. A believing man is supposed to use the Prophet (Pbuh) as his model and abide by his decrees in all issues. One duty is to guide his relatives, since man always needs guidance.

"And admonish thy nearest kinsmen" [Holy Qur'an: Shu'araa: 26:214]

How good is it for a man to gather his relatives and those of his wife in his house every once in a while; and advise them about the religiously forbidden and allowed things; and admonish them about the consequences of evil acts and bad behavior; and introduce jurisprudence and religious issues to them. Guiding the people towards divine issues is similar to the act of the Prophets of God and the Imams, and has an astonishing reward. It is said that Allameh Majlesi carried out this program for his wife, child and relatives every Thursday night; and he considered it a duty since scientific charity is similar to financial charity, and is liked by God. The Qur'an considers being kind to one's relatives similar to being kind to one's parents, thus showing the importance of having good family ties.

And remember We took a covenant from the Children of Israel (to this effect): "Worship none but God; treat with kindness your parents and kindred; and orphans and those in need; speak fair to the people; be steadfast in prayer; and practise regular charity. Then did ye turn back, except a few among you, and ye backslide (even now)." [Holy Qur'an: Baqara 2:83]

Love for wealth and property is a part of human nature. Was it not for this love, no one would be motivated to go to work in industry, arts, business or agriculture. Man loves what he earns by hard work. The Glorious Qur'an asks man to use what he loves so much for solving the problems of his relatives. Doing so is one of the signs of the believers.

"To spend of your substance, out of love for Him, for your kin, for orphans." [Holy Qur'an: Baqara: 2:177]

Relatives are so important in relation to one that they inherit one's property after his/her death. Note the following verse in this regard.

"But if at the time of division other relatives..." [Holy Qur'an: Nisaa: 4:8]

The respect for relatives is very important. They are so honorable that God's book orders us to be just even when we talk to our relatives.

"Whenever ye speak, speak justly, even if a near relative is concerned." [Holy Qur'an: An'am: 6:152]

Belittling, making fun of or vain talk about relatives are all against the religion and are immoral acts. God has ordered everyone to be kind and just, and has specifically mentioned relatives in this regard.

"God commands justice, the doing of good, and liberality to kith

and kin." [Holy Qur'an: Nahl: 16:90]

God does not like one who is rich to ignore those who need his charity. This is also unaccepted from the viewpoint of the intellect, logic, man's nature, ethics and the religion.

"Let not those among you who are endued with grace and am-
plitude of means resolve by oath against helping their kinsmen."
[Holy Qur'an: Nur: 24:22]

We are strictly ordered to be just when we witness in a court, and also avoid hiding what we know and can witness to even if it is against our interest and that of our parents and relatives.

"O ye who believe! Stand out firmly for justice, as witnesses to God,
even as against yourselves, or your parents, or your kin." [Holy
Qur'an: Nisaa: 4:135]

Also we are instructed not to seek forgiveness for our relatives as long as they are polytheists.

"It is not fitting, for the Prophet and those who believe, that they
should pray for forgiveness for Pagans, even though they be of
kin." [Holy Qur'an: Tauba: 9:113]

We are also instructed not to be friends with our parents, children or relatives if they are enemies of God and his Prophet.

"Thou wilt not find any people who believe in God and the Last
Day, loving those who resist God and His Apostle, even though
they were their fathers or their sons, or their brothers, or their
kindred. For such He has written Faith in their hearts, and
strengthened them with a spirit from Himself. And He will admit

them to Gardens beneath which Rivers flow, to dwell therein (forever). God will be well pleased with them, and they with Him. They are the Party of God. Truly it is the Party of God that will achieve Felicity." [Holy Qur'an Mujadila 58:22]

Except for these especial cases, relatives are considered as a unit. The husband or the wife do not have the right to forbid the other one from associating with his/her relatives. Women, especially, are not allowed to forbid their husbands from such highly rewarding acts. I recommend to couples to honor the twenty-three verses of the Qur'an about relatives, and respect their relatives, invite them over, and help them financially if they need so. As can be understood from the traditions, the woman should be careful not to make her husband angry, since his anger and unhappiness is similar to God's anger and unhappiness. None of the deeds of a woman whose husband is not pleased with her is accepted by God. [Bihar al-Anwar, v.100, p.244].

Imam Sadiq said: Damned is a woman who bothers her husband and makes him sad. [Ibid, p.253].

This can be partly related to the husband's relatives. She may be unreasonable without any logical or religious reasons, and in this way she deprives herself of God's Mercy.

Thirty-One

Part 28: Observing the Relations of the Womb

◈

"Those who join together those things which God hath commanded to be joined." [Holy Qur'an: Ra'd: 13:21]

The Qur'an and Visiting Relatives

Visiting relatives is one of the very good deeds that the Prophet, and the Imams have much insisted on. Mulla Husayn Fayz, who was a great philosopher, mystic and scholar spent his life with the Glorious Qur'an and Prophetic traditions. He considered visiting the relatives to include going to see them, and helping the relatives with their finances or business, or

285

helping young couples to marry. This meaning can be understood from the Qur'anic verses and traditions, too. The Prophet and the Imams did exactly these things when they visited their relatives, too. This act is greatly stressed in the Qur'an. It is done by the wise, and cutting off relations with the relatives is considered to be an act of corruption. The Qur'an has instructed us to fear God when interacting with our relatives, and God has mentioned relatives just after Himself Reverence God,

> *"through Whom ye demand your mutual (rights), and (reverence) the wombs (that bore you)"* [Holy Qur'an: Nisaa: 4:1]

The wise are considered to have some traits as mentioned in the Holy Chapter Ra'd. The benefits gained in the Hereafter are being greeted and welcomed by angels.

> *"Those who join together those things which God hath commanded to be joined."* [Holy Qur'an: Ra'd: 13:21]

We read in the Chapter Baqara the following regarding cutting off of relations:

> *"And who sunder what God has ordered to be joined, and do mischief on earth: These cause loss (only) to themselves."* [Holy Qur'an: Baqara: 2:27]

Yes, cutting off relations is a cause for a great loss. There is another alarming verse in the chapter Ra'd regarding this issue:

> *"And cut asunder those things which God has commanded to be joined, and work mischief in the land;— on them is the Curse; for them is the terrible Home!"* [Holy Qur'an: Ra'd: 13:25]

We read in chapter Muhammad:

"Then, is it to be expected of you, if ye were put in authority, that ye will do mischief in the land, and break your ties of kith and kin?" [Holy Qur'an: Muhammad: 47:22]

So we see that visiting relatives is so important that it yields prosperity and the greeting and welcoming of man by angels in the Hereafter. And the cutting off of relations with relatives will result in damnation, a bad ending and not being saved. Respectfully helping the relatives with their financial problems is highly rewarding.

And the likeness of those who spend their substance, seeking to please God and to strengthen their souls, is as a garden, high and fertile: ***"Heavy rain falls on it but makes it yield a double increase of harvest, and if it receives not heavy rain, light moisture sufficeth it. God seeth well whatever ye do. [Holy Qur'an: Baqara: 2:265]***

"If ye disclose (acts of) charity, even so it is well, but if ye conceal them, and make them reach those (really) in need, that is best for you: It will remove from you some of your (stains of) evil. And God is well acquainted with what ye do." [Holy Qur'an: Baqara: 2:271]

"Those who (in charity) spend of their goods by night and by day, in secret and in public, have their reward with their Lord: on them shall be no fear, nor shall they grieve."[Holy Qur'an: Baqara: 2:274]

A Good Plan

Let's invite all our relatives, and recite to the rich ones the verses and traditions on visiting and helping relatives and ask each one of them to donate some money regularly. Then we can open an account or give the money to a trustworthy member of the family. If a problem arises for a poor relative, we can respectfully give him a loan or a donation. Then he can use the money to buy a house, some needed furniture, a trousseau for his daughter or pay for marrying off his son. This is a very good act, it helps a lot of people and is highly rewarding as stated before. Let's try to describe this plan to others and encourage them to implement it. If this is widely implemented in the country, then a heavy burden is lifted off of the government's budget, and the assisting relatives get a great reward. In the Qur'anic verses on charity, helping the relatives has the highest priority. Then the orphans, the disabled, the poor, and the bankrupt are mentioned.

"To spend of your substance, out of love for Him, for your kin, for orphans." [Holy Qur'an: Baqara: 2:177]

An Amazing Story

Saduq has narrated Imam Sadiq as having said the following based on an authentic document:

Jonah was supplicating and praying inside the stomach of a fish. His voice was delivered to Korah's soul which was undergoing God's Punishment at the time of an eclipse. He asked whose voice it was. The Angel of Punishment said that it was the voice of one of the Israelite Prophets. He requested permission to have a brief talk with him. Permission was granted. He asked about Aaron and Moses. Then Jonah replied that they had both perished and he was living at a different time. Then Korah cried. God said His Punishment should be reduced due to feeling sorry for his relatives.

Traditions About Visiting Relatives

The Prophet (Pbuh) said:

Help your relatives, even if you give them a drink of water. The best form of helping relatives is not to bother them. [Bihar al-Anwar, v.74, p.103].

The relatives' feelings get injured when they are ignored or belittled. That is why the best form of helping relatives is not to injure their feelings. He also said: Visit your relatives in this world even if you just say hello. [Bihar al-Anwar, v.74, p.104]

288

The Prophet (Pbuh) has been narrated as saying: Walk one year to visit your relatives. He also has said the following in an important tradition: To the society at this time and the times to come, and those who are in their father's loin or their mother's womb, I advise you all to visit your relatives even if it takes a whole year. Indeed visiting your relatives is a part of your religion. [Ibid].

There are many important traditions which outline the benefits of visiting relatives. [Bihar al-Anwar, v.74, pp.111-126]. We will cite a few of these traditions here. Imam Baqir said:

Visiting relatives will purify your deeds, increase your wealth, remove any catastrophes, and delay the time of your death.

Imam Sadiq said:

Visiting relatives and doing good deeds will ease the accounting for our deeds in the Hereafter, and will protect us from committing sins. Then visit your relatives and be kind with your brethren, even if it is just limited to warm greetings.

The Prophet (Pbuh) said: Visiting relatives will prolong your life and eliminate poverty. Visiting relatives will expand towns, and prolong the lives, even if those you visit are not good people. God shall grant the reward of one hundred martyrs to the one who visits his relatives and helps them with his life and property. For each step that you take to visit your relatives, God will record four thousand good deeds, and remove four thousand evil deeds, and provide four thousand raises in your status. It is just as if you have sincerely worshipped God for one-hundred years.

The Prophet (Pbuh) said:

There is a heavenly status that only those who are just leaders, visit their relatives, or patiently take care of their wife and children shall attain. He told Abuzar to go to visit his relatives, even if they go mad when seeing him. He said if they did not accept you, go again. Finally you will succeed. If they do not follow God's orders, don't follow suit.

A man told the Prophet (Pbuh) that he visited his relatives, but some of them bothered him, and he wanted to cut off his relations with them. The Prophet (Pbuh) told him that if he did that, God would abandon all of them.

289

He asked what he should do. The Prophet (Pbuh) told him to visit those who cut off their relations, and forgive those who mistreated him. Then God will raise him higher in status over them.

Traditions About Cutting Off Relations

Abu Basir has narrated that when he asked Imam Sadiq about someone who wished to cut off his relations from those who oppose the Imam, the Imam replied this was not right. [Bihar al-Anwar, v.75, p.185].

Jahm, the son of Hamid said that he told Imam Sadiq the following: I have relatives who follow other religions. Do they have any rights over me? The Imam replied: Nothing can nullify the rights of relatives. If they were Muslim, then they had two rights: First being a relative and the second being a Muslim. [Bihar al-Anwar, v.74, p.131].

Imam Baqir said:

I found the following in the Prophet's book (the Qur'an): When the people cut off their ties from their relatives, the wicked people get a hold of their property.[Bihar al-Anwr, v.73, p.369.]

The Prophet (Pbuh) said:

Three groups of people will not enter Heaven: alcoholics, those who believe in magic, and those who cut off their ties from their relatives. [Bihar al-Anwar, v.74, p.90]

The Commander of the Faithful said:

I seek refuge with God from sins which hasten death.

He was asked whether there existed sins that bring on death faster. He replied:

Yes. Woe to you! It is the sin of cutting off relations from your relatives. [Bihar al-Anwar, v.74, p.137]

He also said:

The worst of all sins are the cutting off of relations with relatives and being damned by parents. [Mizan al-Hikmat, v.4, p.89].

The Prophet (Pbuh) said:

God's Mercy shall not be bestowed upon a nation in which these are some who cut off relations with their relatives. [Ibid]

The Prophet (Pbuh) said:

The angels will not descend upon those people among whom these are ones who cut off relations with their relatives. [Mizan al-Hikmat, v.4, p.89].

Mutevakel's son. told Imam Hadi that his father deserved to be killed and asked for permission to do so. He was asked not to do so since he was his son. He was also warned that should he do so, he will not stay alive for more than six months.

Thirty-Two

Part 29: Prosperity or Ruin of a Family

~⟋⟍⟋⟍⟋⟍~

"So fear God as much as ye can; listen and obey; and spend in charity for the benefit of your own souls. And those saved from the covetousness of their own souls, — they are the ones that achieve prosperity." [Holy Qur'an: Tagabun: 64:16]

Prosperity or Ruin

Attaining prosperity or ruin is the result of one's acts, morals and beliefs. Good morals, righteous beliefs and good deeds will result in prosperity, while wrong belief, bad character and wicked deeds will result in one's life getting ruined. Prosperity implies happiness in this world and the Hereafter, while getting ruined implies a disastrous life here and loss in the Hereafter. The result of prosperity is God's Pleasure and Eternal Residence in Heaven, while the result of getting ruined is God's animosity and eternal torture. The

292

Muslim families should remember these facts. A couple should try to gain what causes prosperity and avoid what causes their ruin by helping each other when they marry. Thus, they will have a healthy home environment for their children.

Profiting from faith, good deeds and good morality, the family should establish the basis of attaining God's Pleasure and an entrance ticket to God's Heaven. The subjects of prosperity and getting ruined, and the underlying causes have been extensively discussed in the Qur'an and Prophetic traditions. All people have been warned not to deprive themselves of their prosperity and ruin their lives. The families need to consider morality and watch out for bad deeds to gain prosperity. We shall leave the subjects of faith and actions to more detailed books.

Most families, especially the Iranian ones have faith in God and the Hereafter, Prophethood and Leadership of the Immaculate Imams, and perform their obligatory deeds such as prayer, fasting, pilgrimage, and charity. They also avoid what has been forbidden, such as having forbidden foods or drinks, and committing immoral lustful acts, etc. Most problems that the families have to be more concerned with are abiding by moral issues, and avoiding wicked desires. We shall suffice to describe just two issues here.

Justice

Justice implies being just, serving others, wanting for others what we want for ourselves, and not wanting for others what we do not wish for ourselves. This issue must be considered by both the husband, the wife and the children in regards to each other. Based on Islam, each person is bound to be just to others, and consider the rights of the people in all cases. Imam Sadiq has narrated the Prophet (Pbuh) as saying:

The most just person is one who wants for others what he wants for himself, and dislikes for others what he dislikes for himself. [Bihar al-Anwar, v.72, p.25].

The Prophet (Pbuh) said:

Whoever aids the poor, and is just to others is a true believer. [Bihar alAnwar v.72, p.25-28].

The Prophet (Pbuh) told the Commander of the Faithful that three things constitute faith:

Charity in times of poverty, being just to others, and bestowing knowledge to whoever needs it. [Ibid].

A man asked the Prophet:

Please teach me something to ease attaining Heaven for me. The Prophet (Pbuh) replied:

Do not get angry, do not beg, and want for others whatever you want for yourself. [Ibid].

The Commander of the Faithful said:

Beware that God will increase the grandeur and majesty of those who are just to people. [Bihar al-Anwar, v.72, p.33].

How sweet will be the life of a family whose members are all concerned about each other and are just to one another. They do not wish for others what they do not like for themselves in all that they do. It should not be the case that the husband and the children do all the resting, and the wife does all the work, or the parents work hard, but the kids eat, drink and expect more. They should all be just to each other, and help in all the affairs of the house. This way they will become prosperous, and not get ruined.

Being Kind

It is important in Islam for the members of the family to be kind to each other, and treat each other with passion. This is a form of worship which is highly rewarding. The Prophet (Pbuh) said:

Being kind to each other is good and blessed while non-compliance and improper deeds are wicked. [Bihar al-Anwar, v.72, p.51-2]

He also said:

Should I inform you about people who will be safe from the fire of Hell? They answered yes. He said:

Whoever takes it easy in life, and is kind and complaisant in one's life.

[Ibid]

Moses told God:

What is the reward of one who does not bother others, and treats everybody kindly?

God said:

O' Moses,The Fire of Hell shall tell him/her that you cannot enter. [Ibid] The Prophet (Pbuh) was asked:

What is the best thing for one. He replied:

If all Muslims are safe from one's tongue and hands. [Bihar al-Anwar, v.72, p.53-54]

The Prophet (Pbuh) said:

No deed is better than faith, and kindness to others in the sight of God and his Prophet, and no deed is worse than atheism and treating others harshly. [Ibid]

Advice

Giving advice and wishing the best for people has a reward in this world and the Hereafter. Accepting advice is a cause of enlightenment of the heart, and awareness, too. Everyone should advise others as much as he/she can and wish them the best. The listener should take the advice and use it, too. One must not be too shy to advise, and not too haughty to accept advice. The Prophet (Pbuh) has considered shyness to be silly and haughtiness to be a satanic trait which prevent us from accepting advice. The head of the household should give advice to his wife and children every once in a while. He should remind them of their duties. Sometimes the wife should advise her husband, and at times the children should advise their parents. Each one is required to put haughtiness aside and accept the advice given. Imam Sadiq said:

Whoever notes that his brother is facing a lossand can help him out but does not do so by warning himhas been disloyal to his friend. [Bihar alAnwar, v.72, p.65]

Politeness

Being polite implies being respectful, talking properly, being a gentleman and respecting others. A husband, a wife, and the children should all be polite to each other. Being polite is a human value which is a source of one's respect; it improves one's social status; increases the number of our friends. In addition, it causes one to obtain God's Mercy and it is also a form of worship. The Commander of the Faithful said: There is nothing better than politeness. [Bihar al-Anwar, v.72, p.67]

In some wise words he said:

As a sign of being polite, it is enough to dislike for others what you dislike for yourself. [Ibid]

In other saying he said:

The good thing about being polite is that it is like being a gentleman.

Protection of the Family from Accusations

As viewed by Islam, all the members of the family should behave and associate with others in such a way that the family does not get accused. Any accusation may destroy the foundations of the family, and make it hard to live. One may feel that it is proper to meet someone, but others may think different and misjudge. This may be gradually misinterpreted, and then the people will think different about one and his/her honor will be endangered in the society. Then the family will be harmed. One may then try to engage in a business deal, or a social affair like getting a wife for his son, or marrying off his daughter, and this undue accusation may hinder him. Imam Sadiq said:

My father admonished me by saying the following: O' my son. Anyone who associates with bad people will not remain healthy. Whoever engages in a bad affair, will be accused and whoever does not watch what he says will be sorry. [Bihar al-Anwar, v.72, p.90].

The Prophet (Pbuh) said:

Those who associate with the accused will be the most proper candidates for accusation. [Ibid].

The Commander of the Faithful said:

Whoever gets in a situation whereby he/she may be accused, should not blame those who make accusations against him/her.[Ibid]

Imam Sadiq has been narrated as saying the following:

Avoid going to places where you may get accused. And do not stand in public places with your mother, since not all people know that the person you are with is your mother.[Bihar al-Anwar, v.72, p.91].

Indeed someone who does not know, or is ignorant spreads the word around that you are flirting with a strange woman. He may warn people against associating with you to protect the honor of his family. The man of the house, the woman and the children should seriously avoid going to places where they may get accused. This may harm the honor of the family, and Islam is really strict in this regard.

Honoring One's Oath

Religiously speaking it is obligatory to honor one's oath. The wedding contract between a couple is a divine contract to which both the husband and wife must remain loyal. This is an oath between the husband and wife, and to each other's families. Any kind of oath that the parents give to their children, is to be honored, too. The Qur'an states:

> *"And fulfill (every) engagement, for (every) engagement will be inquired into (on the Day of Reckoning)." [Holy Qur'an: Bani Isra'il: 17:34]*

Honoring one's oath is a sure sign of a believer.

> *"Those who faithfully observe their trusts and their covenants."[Holy Qur'an: Mu-minun: 23:8]*

Imam Sajjad has considered all religious decrees to be summarized in the following three things: Righteous words, acting justly, and honoring one's oath. [Bihar al-Anwar, v.72, p.92].

Imam Sadiq said:

No one's excuse shall be accepted in this world and the Hereafter regarding the following issues: Safeguarding what one has been entrusted with, whether it is from a good person or a bad one; honoring one's oath to a believer or a corrupt person; and treating one's parents; kindly whether they are good or bad. [Ibid].

The Prophet (Pbuh) said:

One who does not respect his own oath and does not do what he has promised to do is irreligious.

Imam Reza said: We are members of a Household who consider our oath as a debt just as the Prophet (Pbuh) said. [Bihar al-Anwar, v.7, p.97]

Consultation

A house should not be ruled by one who imposes whatever he/she wishes upon the family. There are many benefits in consultation, and the husband and wife will benefit if they consult with their elders who are more experienced, or consult with their grown-up children. Insist on consultation and respect the views of others. Do not think that you are the know it all. Allow everyone to participate in consultations, as this will help you a lot, and may at times help you out of disasters. The Qur'an has placed especial emphasis on consultation in verse 159 of Al-i-Imran, and verses 36-38 of Shura. Thus, consulting with others is a way of following the Qur'an, a way to solve one's problems and a guard against dangers. Imam Sadiq has said:

Consult with those who fear God about your life affairs. [Bihar al-Anwar, v.72, p.98].

He also said:

Three things are burdensome: Overestimating your deeds, forgetting your sins, and being stubborn.[Ibid]

The Commander of the Faithful said: Whoever is self-centered will be endangered [Bihar al-Anwar, v.72, pp.98-99].

One who is being consulted with should be considerate and provide the best possible guidance. Giving wrong advice on purpose is considered to be a great sin. Imam Ali said: I hate whoever is not sincere when he/she is being consulted by the Muslims.[Ibid].

Humbleness

Humbleness which is the sweet by-product of self-recognition and an individual's mysticismis an Islamic, humans and moral state. A person who considers himself to be a servant of God, and recognizes that God is the source of all the blessings he has; considers others to be superior to him, considers the people to be God's servants and knows that he is nothing in this vast universe, is deeply involved in humbleness.

A man who considers his wife to be God's servant, and considers God to be the owner of his children, considers himself to be their servants. He who considers his wife and children to be what God has entrusted him with will be humble towards them. When a woman is not haughty, does not overestimate her family's status when she faces her husband, and does not overestimate her knowledge or degree, will then be humble towards her husband and children. Also, wise children are humble towards their parents. Humbleness will result in nobility and honor, and will maintain a home sweet. It will bring love and strengthen the family bonds. A haughty person should know that no one, even his wife and children like him or respect him. Imam Hassan Askari said:

Anyone who is humble towards his religious brethren in this world will be considered righteous by God, and is a true follower of Imam Ali. [Bihar al-Anwar, v.72, p.117].

Imam Sadiq has narrated his grandfathers as saying:

Signs of humbleness are to sit wherever there is room when you enter a family or public meeting, to greet anyone you visit, to avoid quarreling even if you are right, not to like to be admired for piety and righteousness. [Bihar al-Anwar, v.72, pp.118-119]

When the Commander of the Faithful was about to pass away, he said: I advise you to be humble as this is the best form of worship.[Ibid]

Kindness to Younger Ones and Respecting the Elders

Islam has instructed all men and women to be kind with the younger ones and respect the elders. The house must be a place to act upon the instructions of God, the Prophet and the Imams. Then you can prosper. It is a sin to get angry with, ignore, not kiss or not honor a promise given to a younger one. It is also a sin to disrespect the elders, give them a mean look, not fulfill their needs, or express that you get bored with them. We have brought the younger ones into this world, and we are responsible for them until they settle down. We should take care of them kindly. We have been raised by the elders, so we should respect them since we owe them a lot. When the Commander of the Faithful was about to pass away, he said:

Be kind with the young members of the family, and honor and respect the elders. [Bihar al-Anwar, v.72, p.136] The Prophet (Pbuh) said:

Respect the elders as this is equal to respecting God. [Ibid]. The Prophet (Pbuh) said:

Whoever is not kind to the younger ones, or does not respect the elders is not from my nation. [Bihar al-Anwar, v.72, p.137]

Hospitality

Some families are really strict about accepting guests. This is either a sign of laziness or a sign of jealousy. Hospitality has been a way of the Prophets and the Imams, and is an example of divine and righteous men. Jealousy or laziness are not proper, in whatever form. The husband, the wife, and the children should all treat their guests warmly. This action which is according to the ethics of God's saints will please God and ease our affairs, bring God's Mercy and Favor, and cast away any catastrophes from the members of the family. Hospitality is so encouraged in Islam that we believe the guest brings in his daily bread, and the host is the guest of his guests. It is highly praised to encourage hospitality. This will improve our morality, and the opposite is inhumane and despised by God. The sixth Imam said: There are ten characters that make up nobility. Try to attain them all. One is hospitality. [Bihar al-Anwar, v.72, p.458]

Imam Sadiq has said: Whenever guests enter your house, they bring

God's forgiveness for you and your household, and when they leave, they take away your sins and those of your wife. [Bihar al-Anwar, v.72, pp.459-460].

Imam Baqir said: Feeding four Muslims is equivalent to freeing a slave from the descendants of Ismael. [Ibid].

Therefore being just, kind, wishing the best, politeness, staying away from accusations, honoring one's oath, humbleness, being kind to younger ones, and respecting the elders, and hospitality are all the basis of nobility and cause prosperity in this world and the Hereafter.

Cause of Getting Ruined

Families should avoid the following issues, each of which is described in many traditions and the Qur'anic verses: Not talking, separating, accusing the innocent, quarreling, finding faults, and gossiping, causing quarrels, deceit, wastefulness, haughtiness, jealousy, following sinners, being a burden and hostility. Families should avoid the above, since they are sins, some of which are great sins and will ruin the family and cause misfortune. In addition to the Qur'an, you can find a discussion of these issues in books like Kafi, v.2, Vasa'il, v.11, Shafi Fayz,Muhjat ul-Biyza, Jami al-Saadat Naraqi, and other moral or traditions books. These are beyond our scope.

Thirty-Three

Part 30: Divorce and Inheritance

One of the things which angers God, the Almighty is divorce, [Vasa'il, v.22, p.7]

Divorce is Despised

Divorce is not good. It is despised by God, the Prophet, and the Imams unless it is for a religiously acceptable reason. Divorcing based on the man or the woman's lust is immoral, inhumane, irreligious, and disrespectful to the other party. Here I shall discuss the most important tradition on divorce first, and then discuss the relevant Qur'anic verses and the conditions for divorce. In his book "Sharh i-Mathnavi, the great scholar Hajji Sabzevari has narrated the Immaculate Imams as saying the following: Nothing is more loved by God than freeing slaves, and nothing is more despised by God then separation and divorce. [Sharh-i-Mathnavi, p.142]. The Prophet

(Pbuh) said:

From among what is allowed by God, nothing is worse than divorce. [Vasa'il, v.15, p.280]

The Prophet (Pbuh) said:

God does not like men and women who treat their spouses as toys and want to divorce. [Mizan al-Hikmat, v.5, p.546]

Imam Baqir said:

Indeed God, the Almighty is angry with at whoever repeatedly divorces. [Vasa'il, Al-i-Bayt Press, v.22, p.8]

Imam Sadiq said: God likes a house in which there is a marriage, and despises one in which there is a divorce. [Vasa'il, v.22, p.7]

The Prophet (Pbuh) asked someone what he had done to his wife. He said he divorced her. Then the Prophet asked him why? He asked if there were any flaws in her, or if she was ugly? The man answered yes. The man married again. The same sequence repeated over and over. Then the Prophet (Pbuh) said: God, the Almighty hates or damns any man, or woman, who repeatedly marries and gets divorced. [Vasa'il, v.22, p.7]

Causes for Divorce

Divorce is allowed in cases when there exist conditions in the woman or the man which cannot be corrected for and make the continuation of the marriage difficult. In such cases, the couple and their relatives should not worsen the conditions, and not say any improper things. The problems that the couple have should not become a reason for them or others to commit other sins such as gossiping, accusing, belittling, etc. Such acts will only increase the hatred of the couple and their families, and will cause torture in the Hereafter.

It is unfortunate to say that whenever the issue of divorce comes up, the families start to gossip, make accusations, or express hatred, and many commit these sins. It may be that the woman is too difficult to live with because she does not attend to the needs of the family, or the man does not abide by the conditions which he has accepted at the time of the wedding, in which case the woman can ask for a divorce. If these conditions exist, the couple should respectfully get divorced without committing any sins. The families should not get involved, or commit any sins. I must mention two great sins which the families may commit early after divorce. Hopefully, by paying close attention to divine issues, sins will be avoided.

Gossip

The Qur'an states:

> *"Nor speak ill of each other behind their backs. Would any of you like to eat the flesh of his dead brother? Nay, ye would abhor it... " [Holy Qur'an: Hujurat: 49:12]*

The Prophet (Pbuh) said:

Gossip will ruin a Muslim's religion faster than food gets digested in his stomach [Vasa'il, v.72, p.152]

He also said:

I admonish you against gossiping as it is worse than fornication [Bihar al-Anwar, V.75, p.222]

The Prophet (Pbuh) said:

On the Night of Ascension, I saw some people who were peeling off their skin of their face with their nails, I asked Gabriel who they were. He said they are the ones who gossiped. [Mizan al-Hikmat, v.7, pp.332-333].

The Prophet (Pbuh) said:

God has forbidden gossiping, as he has forbidden harming a Muslim's property or life. [Ibid]. The Commander of the Faithful said:

Gossiping is a sign of hypocrisy.[Ibid] He also said:

Gossiping about the good people is one of the most wicked acts.[Ibid] The seventh Imam said:

One who gossips about his believing brothers is deprived of God's Mercy [Bihar al-Anwar, V.77, p.117]

The Master of the Martyrs (Imam Husayn) told a man who was gossiping:

Protect yourself from gossip as it is the food for the dogs in the Hell [Bihar al-Anwar, v.78, p.117].

In fact, there is no reason to gossip about a lustful, oppressive ruler or one who is already an evil-doer. [Bihar al-Anwar, V.75, p.253]

The Commander of the Faithful has said:

One who listens to another who gossips is similar to one who gossips [Mizan al-Hikmat, V.7, p.352].

There is also a tradition from the Prophet (Pbuh) related to not listening to gossip:

God will protect whoever defends the honor of his Muslim brothers in front of one who gossips, from the Fire of Hell. [Mizan al-Hikmat, v.7, p.353].

Therefore the only thing that must be discussed in a divorce is divorce and nothing else. There should be no unjust talk since this will only cause you to go to Hell.

Accusations

There are times when the husband or the wife accuses the other one to justify the divorce. This may also be done by either family. This is a very wicked deed with a serious misfortune in the Hereafter. Imam Sadiq narrated a wise man as saying:

Accusing an innocent person is even heavier than tall mountains.[Vasa'il, V.12, P.288] Imam Reza has narrated his grandfathers as having quoted the Prophet (Pbuh) saying:

God will throw the one who accuses some innocent person, or ascribes something to someone without a justification into a fire in Hell until he proves what he has claimed.[Vasa'il al-Shiaa, V.12, P.288]

A Lesson

They asked a man who wanted to divorce his wife for the reason. He said it is forbidden to gossip about my wife. Then they got divorced, and the woman got married to someone else. Again they asked that man why he had divorced his wife. He replied it is forbidden to gossip about someone else's wife.

Divorce as Viewed by Qur'an

It is better if the couple can resolve their problems themselves. If not, they should each chose a religious, wise, patient and smart representative to discuss their problems. Perhaps this way they can avoid a divorce.

> *"If ye fear a breach between them twain, appoint (two) arbiters, one from his family, and the other from hers; If they wish for peace, God will cause their reconciliation: for God hath full knowledge, and is acquainted with all things."[Holy Qur'an: Nisaa: 4:35]*

A divorce is only permissible twice: after that, the parties should either hold together on equitable terms, or separate with kindness. It is not lawful for you, (men), to take back any of your gifts (from your wives), except when both parties fear that they would be unable to keep the limits ordained by God.

> *"If ye (judges) do indeed fear that they would be unable to keep the limits ordained by God, there is no blame on either of them if she give something for her freedom. These are the limits ordained by God: So do not transgress them. If any do transgress the limits ordained by God, such persons wrong (themselves as well as others)."[Holy Qur'an: Baqara 2: 229]*
>
> *"When ye divorce women, and they fulfill the term of their*

('Iddat), either take them back on equitable terms or set them free on equitable terms; but do not take them back to injure them, (or) to take undue advantage; if anyone does that, he wrongs his own soul. Do not treat God's Signs as a jest, but solemnly rehearse God's favors on you, and the fact that he sent down to you the Book and Wisdom, for your instruction. And fear God, and know that God is well acquainted with all things." [Holy Qur'an: Baqara 2:231]

Note that the Qur'an reminds us of the blessings, the Qur'an, God's Infinite Knowledge and Wisdom when discussing divorce. This is so that justice is fully honored. It is obvious that divorce will not be mentioned in families which are religious and believe in God and the Hereafter, and are adorned with good morals and deeds. They will live together in peace forever and will raise their children with love and affection. The laziness, depressions, addiction, quitting education, and corruption of many of our children are rooted in the differences between their parents or their divorce. If we want this horrible dragon called divorce to disappear, then the man should not be oppressive, he must respect the rights of his wife and honor his obligations, and use humane and Islamic principles in treating his wife and children. The woman should perform her duties as a mother and wife, too. God dislikes divorce, and whoever is responsible for it will be questioned in the Hereafter.

We should try to reduce the statistics of divorce. We should stop sinning, flirting, and oppressing others so that there be no more divorce. The judicial system of the country should publish a leaflet outlining moral issues and stating the evil aspects of divorce. This should be handed out to those who wish to get divorced. Reading it may change their mind, and they may not return to separation. Their life may be re-established. It is better that widows as widowers not enter the society, since they may be corrupted by those whose faith is weak.

Termination of Life

Life is the place for action to achieve our aspirations. It is terminated by death which will transfer us to the Hereafter where we shall face the results of our deeds, beliefs, and ethics. The Qur'an asks both men and women to strive to put something aside for the Hereafter while they live.

> *"And let every soul look to what (provision) he has sent forth for the morrow."[Holy Qur'an: Hashr 59:18]*

A very important issue to consider is a good will and testament as to how to best spend one third of one's property. Each person can explicitly will what to be done with this portion of his property, and should choose a good person to carry out his will. All the Prophets, the Imams and the saints paid close attention to this issue and none passed away without a will. We have been instructed to leave a will by the Prophet (Pbuh) and the Immaculate Imams and by verse 180 by Baqara.

> *"It is prescribed, when death approaches any of you, if he leave any goods, that he make a bequest to parents and next of kin, according to reasonable usage; this is due from the God-fearing."* *[Holy Qur'an: Baqara 2:180]*

The Prophet (Pbuh) said:

Every Muslim has the right to a will [Mizan al-Hikmat, V.10, pp.494-495]. He also said:

A Muslim should not sleep without a will [Ibid]. He also said:

Whoever passes away and has a will has died according to the traditions of God and His Prophet, and his death is based on virtue and martyrdom, and God's Forgiveness. [Ibid]

It is much better today for one to act upon his will before he dies since the laws are cumbersome and really bother the inheritors. One can do whatever he wants done after he died when he is still alive. He can spend his wealth and property in a good way , like providing for the means of marriage of his sons and daughters, paying for the expenses of the orphans, building schools, mosques, and housing for the poor, and he can get rewarded after he dies. Imam Ali has recommended this: O' son of Adam act upon your will regarding your own wealth and property, and do what you want done after you die now that you are alive. Anyway, try to leave lawfully earned property behind, since what is unlawfully earned cannot be inherited.

Do not will that more than one third of it to be spent as you wish, since this will not be effective. Divide the other two-thirds according to the Qur'an. This way none of the inheritors will be hurt. It is obligatory for the inheritors to act according to a will that is prepared according to the Holy Qur'an. Such an act is worship, and is rewarding for the one who has passed away, and the inheritors who act accordingly. The inheritors should pay off any business debts, alms, the nuptial gift of the wife, and personal debts or required pilgrimage expenses first. They cannot divide and use money which belongs to others, since this will result in God's Punishment. The share for the wife, the parents and the sons and daughters should strictly be considered according to the divine book. Otherwise, a breach of God's Limits has occurred which will deserve Divine Retribution.

Please consult the practical treatise of Muslim scholars regarding the division of inheritance, or go to visit an expert in Islamic jurisprudence. This way the soul of the one who has passed away will be pleased. The inheritors should remember that the person who has passed away has spent all his life working hard to run your lives, and he suffered much. He may have even made some fiscal sins, so do not forget him. Pray for him, fast for him, give charity, and do good deeds. Try to remember him and please his soul any time you can especially on the eve of Thursdays, the month of Ramazan and Rajab. This way your children too will learn to remember you after you die.

Go to visit their graves every once in a while since God will then grant their soul to become accustomed to you, then they may pray for you from Purgatory. I have a friend who said whenever he had a problem, he immediately went to Qum to visit the graves of his parents. He read the Fatihah chapter of the Qur'an, prayed and paid charity for them. Then he asked them to pray for him and he returns to Tehran. He has experienced that his parents' prayers for him follow him and his problem gets resolved before sunset. It is not right to forget one's parents who spent all their life and energy to raise their children. Something should be done to help them be forgiven.'

www.ingramcontent.com/pod-product-compliance
Lightning Source LLC
Chambersburg PA
CBHW030400130626
46549CB00004B/1573